OF
HUMAN
BONDAGE
I

W. Somerset Maugham

CONTENTS

Chapter 1   001

Chapter 2   004

Chapter 3   008

Chapter 4   014

Chapter 5   020

Chapter 6   025

Chapter 7   032

Chapter 8   036

Chapter 9   043

Chapter 10   051

Chapter 11   057

Chapter 12   064

Chapter 13   069

Chapter 14   073

Chapter 15   081

Chapter 16   090

Chapter 17   099

Chapter 18   107

Chapter 19 113

Chapter 20 120

Chapter 21 126

Chapter 22 140

Chapter 23 145

Chapter 24 152

Chapter 25 155

Chapter 26 159

Chapter 27 169

Chapter 28 177

Chapter 29 185

Chapter 30 189

Chapter 31 199

Chapter 32 203

Chapter 33 214

Chapter 34 227

Chapter 35 234

Chapter 36 246

Chapter 37 253

Chapter 38 261

Chapter 39 270

Chapter 40   277

Chapter 41   287

Chapter 42   298

Chapter 43   306

Chapter 44   317

Chapter 45   326

Chapter 46   338

Chapter 47   346

Chapter 48   359

Chapter 49   370

Chapter 50   379

Chapter 51   389

Chapter 52   395

Chapter 53   405

Chapter 54   412

Chapter 55   420

Chapter 56   428

Chapter 57   435

Chapter 58   442

Chapter 59   452

Chapter 60   462

Chapter 61 467

Chapter 62 475

Chapter 63 483

Chapter 64 489

Chapter 65 496

Chapter 66 501

Chapter 67 510

Chapter 68 518

Chapter 69 525

Chapter 70 536

Chapter 71 546

Chapter 72 554

Chapter 73 562

Chapter 74 573

Chapter 75 582

Chapter 76 591

Chapter 77 602

Chapter 78 608

Chapter 79 617

Chapter 80 627

Chapter 81 633

Chapter 82   645

Chapter 83   651

Chapter 84   658

Chapter 85   666

Chapter 86   674

Chapter 87   681

Chapter 88   692

Chapter 89   702

Chapter 90   707

Chapter 91   715

Chapter 92   721

Chapter 93   731

Chapter 94   738

Chapter 95   750

Chapter 96   759

Chapter 97   770

Chapter 98   777

Chapter 99   786

Chapter 100   790

Chapter 101   801

Chapter 102   807

Chapter 103   812

Chapter 104   819

Chapter 105   825

Chapter 106   833

Chapter 107   844

Chapter 108   851

Chapter 109   862

Chapter 110   872

Chapter 111   879

Chapter 112   888

Chapter 113   896

Chapter 114   905

Chapter 115   913

Chapter 116   920

Chapter 117   930

Chapter 118   938

Chapter 119   947

Chapter 120   955

Chapter 121   962

Chapter 122   971

Chapter 1

The day broke grey and dull. The clouds hung heavily, and there was a rawness in the air that suggested snow. A woman servant came into a room in which a child was sleeping and drew the curtains. She glanced mechanically at the house opposite, a stucco house with a portico, and went to the child's bed.

"Wake up, Philip," she said.

She pulled down the bedclothes, took him in her arms, and carried him downstairs. He was only half awake.

"Your mother wants you," she said.

She opened the door of a room on the floor below and took the child over to a bed in which a woman was lying. It was his mother. She stretched out her arms, and the child nestled by her side. He did not ask why he had been awakened. The woman kissed his eyes, and with thin, small hands felt the warm body through his white flannel nightgown. She pressed him closer to herself.

"Are you sleepy, darling?" she said.

Her voice was so weak that it seemed to come already from a

great distance. The child did not answer, but smiled comfortably. He was very happy in the large, warm bed, with those soft arms about him. He tried to make himself smaller still as he cuddled against his mother, and he kissed her sleepily. In a moment he closed his eyes and was fast asleep. The doctor came forwards and stood by the bedside.

"Oh, don't take him away yet," she moaned.

The doctor, without answering, looked at her gravely. Knowing she would not be allowed to keep the child much longer, the woman kissed him again; and she passed her hand down his body till she came to his feet; she held the right foot in her hand and felt the five small toes; and then slowly passed her hand over the left one. She gave a sob.

"What's the matter?" said the doctor. "You're tired."

She shook her head, unable to speak, and the tears rolled down her cheeks. The doctor bent down.

"Let me take him."

She was too weak to resist his wish, and she gave the child up. The doctor handed him back to his nurse.

"You'd better put him back in his own bed."

"Very well, sir."

The little boy, still sleeping, was taken away. His mother sobbed now broken-heartedly.

"What will happen to him, poor child?"

The monthly nurse tried to quiet her, and presently, from exhaustion, the crying ceased. The doctor walked to a table on the other side of the room, upon which, under a towel, lay the body of a still-born child. He lifted the towel and looked. He was hidden from the bed by a screen, but the woman guessed what he was doing.

"Was it a girl or a boy?" she whispered to the nurse.

"Another boy."

The woman did not answer. In a moment the child's nurse came back. She approached the bed.

"Master Philip never woke up," she said.

There was a pause. Then the doctor felt his patient's pulse once more.

"I don't think there's anything I can do just now," he said. "I'll call again after breakfast."

"I'll show you out, sir," said the child's nurse.

They walked downstairs in silence. In the hall the doctor stopped.

"You've sent for Mrs. Carey's brother-in-law, haven't you?"

"Yes, sir."

"D'you know at what time he'll be here?"

"No, sir, I'm expecting a telegram."

"What about the little boy? I should think he'd be better out of the way."

"Miss Watkin said she'd take him, sir."

"Who's she?"

"She's his godmother, sir. D'you think Mrs. Carey will get over it, sir?"

The doctor shook his head.

Chapter 2

It was a week later. Philip was sitting on the floor in the drawing-room at Miss Watkin's house in Onslow Gardens. He was an only child and used to amusing himself. The room was filled with massive furniture, and on each of the sofas were three big cushions. There was a cushion too in each armchair. All these he had taken and, with the help of the gilt rout chairs, light and easy to move, had made an elaborate cave in which he could hide himself from the Red Indians who were lurking behind the curtains. He put his ear to the floor and listened to the herd of buffaloes that raced across the prairie. Presently, hearing the door open, he held his breath so that he might not be discovered; but a violent hand pulled away a chair and the cushions fell down.

"You naughty boy, Miss Watkin *will* be cross with you."

"Hulloa, Emma!" he said.

The nurse bent down and kissed him, then began to shake out the cushions, and put them back in their places.

"Am I to come home?" he asked.

"Yes, I've come to fetch you."

"You've got a new dress on."

It was in 1885, and she wore a bustle. Her gown was of black velvet, with tight sleeves and sloping shoulders, and the skirt had three large flounces. She wore a black bonnet with velvet strings. She hesitated. The question she had expected did not come, and so she could not give the answer she had prepared.

"Aren't you going to ask how your mamma is?" she said at length.

"Oh, I forgot. How is mamma?"

Now she was ready.

"Your mamma is quite well and happy."

"Oh, I am glad."

"Your mamma's gone away. You won't ever see her any more."

Philip did not know what she meant.

"Why not?"

"Your mamma's in heaven."

She began to cry, and Philip, though he did not quite understand, cried too. Emma was a tall, big-boned woman, with fair hair and large features. She came from Devonshire and, notwithstanding her many years of service in London, had never lost the breadth of her accent. Her tears increased her emotion, and she pressed the little boy to her heart. She felt vaguely the pity of that child deprived of the only love in the world that is quite unselfish. It seemed dreadful that he must be handed over to strangers. But in a little while she pulled herself together.

"Your Uncle William is waiting in to see you," she said. "Go and say good-bye to Miss Watkin, and we'll go home."

"I don't want to say good-bye," he answered, instinctively anxious to hide his tears.

"Very well, run upstairs and get your hat."

He fetched it, and when he came down Emma was waiting for him in the hall. He heard the sound of voices in the study behind the dining-room. He paused. He knew that Miss Watkin and her sister were talking to friends, and it seemed to him—he was nine years old—that if he went in they would be sorry for him.

"I think I'll go and say good-bye to Miss Watkin."

"I think you'd better," said Emma.

"Go in and tell them I'm coming," he said.

He wished to make the most of his opportunity. Emma knocked at the door and walked in. He heard her speak.

"Master Philip wants to say good-bye to you, miss."

There was a sudden hush of the conversation, and Philip limped in. Henrietta Watkin was a stout woman, with a red face and dyed hair. In those days to dye the hair excited comment, and Philip had heard much gossip at home when his godmother's changed colour. She lived with an elder sister, who had resigned herself contentedly to old age. Two ladies, whom Philip did not know, were calling, and they looked at him curiously.

"My poor child," said Miss Watkin, opening her arms.

She began to cry. Philip understood now why she had not been in to luncheon and why she wore a black dress. She could not speak.

"I've got to go home," said Philip, at last.

He disengaged himself from Miss Watkin's arms, and she

kissed him again. Then he went to her sister and bade her good-bye too. One of the strange ladies asked if she might kiss him, and he gravely gave her permission. Though crying, he keenly enjoyed the sensation he was causing; he would have been glad to stay a little longer to be made much of, but felt they expected him to go, so he said that Emma was waiting for him. He went out of the room. Emma had gone downstairs to speak with a friend in the basement, and he waited for her on the landing. He heard Henrietta Watkin's voice.

"His mother was my greatest friend. I can't bear to think that she's dead."

"You oughtn't to have gone to the funeral, Henrietta," said her sister. "I knew it would upset you."

Then one of the strangers spoke.

"Poor little boy, it's dreadful to think of him quite alone in the world. I see he limps."

"Yes, he's got a club-foot. It was such a grief to his mother."

Then Emma came back. They called a hansom, and she told the driver where to go.

Chapter 3

When they reached the house Mrs. Carey had died in—it was in a dreary, respectable street between Notting Hill Gate and High Street, Kensington—Emma led Philip into the drawing-room. His uncle was writing letters of thanks for the wreaths which had been sent. One of them, which had arrived too late for the funeral, lay in its cardboard box on the hall-table.

"Here's Master Philip," said Emma.

Mr. Carey stood up slowly and shook hands with the little boy. Then on second thoughts he bent down and kissed his forehead. He was a man of somewhat less than average height, inclined to corpulence, with his hair, worn long, arranged over the scalp so as to conceal his baldness. He was clean-shaven. His features were regular, and it was possible to imagine that in his youth he had been good-looking. On his watch-chain he wore a gold cross.

"You're going to live with me now, Philip," said Mr. Carey. "Shall you like that?"

Two years before Philip had been sent down to stay at the

vicarage after an attack of chicken-pox; but there remained with him a recollection of an attic and a large garden rather than of his uncle and aunt.

"Yes."

"You must look upon me and your Aunt Louisa as your father and mother."

The child's mouth trembled a little, he reddened, but did not answer.

"Your dear mother left you in my charge."

Mr. Carey had no great ease in expressing himself. When the news came that his sister-in-law was dying, he set off at once for London, but on the way thought of nothing but the disturbance in his life that would be caused if her death forced him to undertake the care of her son. He was well over fifty, and his wife, to whom he had been married for thirty years, was childless; he did not look forward with any pleasure to the presence of a small boy who might be noisy and rough. He had never much liked his sister-in-law.

"I'm going to take you down to Blackstable tomorrow," he said.

"With Emma?"

The child put his hand in hers, and she pressed it.

"I'm afraid Emma must go away," said Mr. Carey.

"But I want Emma to come with me."

Philip began to cry, and the nurse could not help crying too. Mr. Carey looked at them helplessly.

"I think you'd better leave me alone with Master Philip for a moment."

"Very good, sir."

Though Philip clung to her, she released herself gently. Mr. Carey took the boy on his knee and put his arm round him.

"You mustn't cry," he said. "You're too old to have a nurse now. We must see about sending you to school."

"I want Emma to come with me," the child repeated.

"It costs too much money, Philip. Your father didn't leave very much, and I don't know what's become of it. You must look at every penny you spend."

Mr. Carey had called the day before on the family solicitor. Philip's father was a surgeon in good practice, and his hospital appointments suggested an established position; so that it was a surprise on his sudden death from blood-poisoning to find that he had left his widow little more than his life insurance and what could be got from the lease of their house in Bruton Street. This was six months ago; and Mrs. Carey, already in delicate health, finding herself with child, had lost her head and accepted for the lease the first offer that was made. She stored her furniture, and, at a rent which the parson thought outrageous, took a furnished house for a year, so that she might suffer from no inconvenience till her child was born. But she had never been used to the management of money, and was unable to adapt her expenditure to her altered circumstances. The little she had slipped through her fingers in one way and another, so that now, when all expenses were paid, not much more than two thousand pounds remained to support the boy till he was able to earn his own living. It was impossible to explain all this to Philip and he was sobbing still.

"You'd better go to Emma," Mr. Carey said, feeling that she

could console the child better than anyone.

Without a word Philip slipped off his uncle's knee, but Mr. Carey stopped him.

"We must go tomorrow, because on Saturday I've got to prepare my sermon, and you must tell Emma to get your things ready today. You can bring all your toys. And if you want anything to remember your father and mother by you can take one thing for each of them. Everything else is going to be sold."

The boy slipped out of the room. Mr. Carey was unused to work, and he turned to his correspondence with resentment. On one side of the desk was a bundle of bills, and these filled him with irritation. One especially seemed preposterous. Immediately after Mrs. Carey's death Emma had ordered from the florist masses of white flowers for the room in which the dead woman lay. It was sheer waste of money. Emma took far too much upon herself. Even if there had been no financial necessity, he would have dismissed her.

But Philip went to her, and hid his face in her bosom, and wept as though his heart would break. And she, feeling that he was almost her own son—she had taken him when he was a month old—consoled him with soft words. She promised that she would come and see him sometimes, and that she would never forget him; and she told him about the country he was going to and about her own home in Devonshire—her father kept a turnpike on the high-road that led to Exeter, and there were pigs in the sty, and there was a cow, and the cow had just had a calf— till Philip forgot his tears and grew excited at the thought of his approaching journey. Presently she put him down, for there was much to be done, and he helped her to lay out his clothes on the bed. She sent him into the nursery to gather up his toys, and in a little while he was playing happily.

But at last he grew tired of being alone and went back to the bed-room, in which Emma was now putting his things into a big tin box; he remembered then that his uncle had said he might take something to remember his father and mother by. He told Emma and asked her what he should take.

"You'd better go into the drawing-room and see what you fancy."

"Uncle William's there."

"Never mind that. They're your own things now."

Philip went downstairs slowly and found the door open. Mr. Carey had left the room. Philip walked slowly round. They had been in the house so short a time that there was little in it that had a particular interest to him. It was a stranger's room, and Philip saw nothing that struck his fancy. But he knew which were his mother's things and which belonged to the landlord, and presently fixed on a little clock that he had once heard his mother say she liked. With this he walked again rather disconsolately upstairs. Outside the door of his mother's bedroom he stopped and listened. Though no one had told him not to go in, he had a feeling that it would be wrong to do so; he was a little frightened, and his heart beat uncomfortably; but at the same time something impelled him to turn the handle. He turned it very gently, as if to prevent anyone within from hearing, and then slowly pushed the door open. He stood on the threshold for a moment before he had the courage to enter. He was not frightened now, but it seemed strange. He closed the door behind him. The blinds were drawn, and the room, in the cold light of a January afternoon, was dark. On the dressing-table were Mrs. Carey's brushes and the hand mirror. In a little tray were hairpins. There was a photograph of himself on the chimney-piece and one of his father. He had often been in the room when his mother was not in it, but now it seemed different. There was something curious in the look of the chairs. The bed was made as though someone were going to sleep in it that night, and in a case on the pillow was a night-dress.

Philip opened a large cupboard filled with dresses and, stepping in, took as many of them as he could in his arms and buried his face in them. They smelt of the scent his mother used. Then he pulled open the drawers, filled with his mother's things, and looked at them: there were lavender bags among the linen, and their scent was fresh and pleasant. The strangeness of the room left it, and it seemed to him that his mother had just gone out for a walk. She would be in presently and would come upstairs to have nursery tea with him. And he seemed to feel her kiss on his lips.

It was not true that he would never see her again. It was not true simply because it was impossible. He climbed up on the bed and put his head on the pillow. He lay there quite still.

Chapter 4

Philip parted from Emma with tears, but the journey to Blackstable amused him, and, when they arrived, he was resigned and cheerful. Blackstable was sixty miles from London. Giving their luggage to a porter, Mr. Carey set out to walk with Philip to the vicarage; it took them little more than five minutes, and, when they reached it, Philip suddenly remembered the gate. It was red and five-barred; it swung both ways on easy hinges; and it was possible, though forbidden, to swing backwards and forwards on it. They walked through the garden to the front door. This was only used by visitors and on Sundays, and on special occasions, as when the Vicar went up to London or came back. The traffic of the house took place through a side door, and there was a back door as well for the gardener and for beggars and tramps. It was a fairly large house of yellow brick, with a red roof, built about five-and-twenty years before in an ecclesiastical style. The front door was like a church porch, and the drawing-room windows were Gothic.

Mrs. Carey, knowing by what train they were coming, waited

in the drawing-room and listened for the click of the gate. When she heard it she went to the door.

"There's Aunt Louisa," said Mr. Carey, when he saw her. "Run and give her a kiss."

Philip started to run, awkwardly, trailing his club-foot, and then stopped. Mrs. Carey was a little, shrivelled woman of the same age as her husband, with a face extraordinarily filled with deep wrinkles, and pale blue eyes. Her grey hair was arranged in ringlets according to the fashion of her youth. She wore a black dress, and her only ornament was a gold chain, from which hung a cross. She had a shy manner and a gentle voice.

"Did you walk, William?" she said, almost reproachfully, as she kissed her husband.

"I didn't think of it," he answered, with a glance at his nephew.

"It didn't hurt you to walk, Philip, did it?" she asked the child.

"No. I always walk."

He was a little surprised at their conversation. Aunt Louisa told him to come in, and they entered the hall. It was paved with red and yellow tiles, on which alternately were a Greek Cross and the Lamb of God. An imposing staircase led out of the hall. It was of polished pine, with a peculiar smell, and had been put in because fortunately, when the church was reseated, enough wood remained over. The balusters were decorated with emblems of the Four Evangelists.

"I've had the stove lighted as I thought you'd be cold after your journey," said Mrs. Carey.

It was a large black stove that stood in the hall and was only lighted if the weather was very bad and the Vicar had a cold. It was not lighted if Mrs. Carey had a cold. Coal was expensive. Besides, Mary Ann, the maid, didn't like fires all over the place. If they wanted all them fires they must keep a second girl. In the winter Mr. and Mrs. Carey lived in the dining-room so that one fire should do, and in the summer they could not get out of the habit, so the drawing-room was used only by Mr. Carey on Sunday afternoons for his nap. But every Saturday he had a fire in the study so that he could write his sermon.

Aunt Louisa took Philip upstairs and showed him into a tiny bed-room that looked out on the drive. Immediately in front of the window was a large tree, which Philip remembered now because the branches were so low that it was possible to climb quite high up it.

"A small room for a small boy," said Mrs. Carey. "You won't be frightened at sleeping alone?"

"Oh, no."

On his first visit to the vicarage he had come with his nurse, and Mrs. Carey had had little to do with him. She looked at him now with some uncertainty.

"Can you wash your own hands, or shall I wash them for you?"

"I can wash myself," he answered firmly.

"Well, I shall look at them when you come down to tea," said Mrs. Carey.

She knew nothing about children. After it was settled that Philip should come down to Blackstable, Mrs. Carey had thought much how she should treat him; she was anxious to do her duty; but now he was there she found herself just as shy of him as he was of her. She hoped he would not be noisy and rough, because her husband did not like rough and noisy boys. Mrs. Carey made an excuse to leave Philip alone, but in a moment came back and knocked at the door; she asked him, without coming in, if he could pour out the water himself. Then she went downstairs and rang the bell for tea.

The dining-room, large and well proportioned, had windows on two sides of it, with heavy curtains of red rep; there was a big table in the middle; and at one end an imposing mahogany sideboard with a looking-glass in it. In one corner stood a harmonium. On each side of the fireplace were chairs covered in stamped leather, each with an antimacassar; one had arms and was called the husband, and the other had none and was called the wife. Mrs. Carey never sat in the armchair; she said she preferred a chair that was not too comfortable; there was always a lot to do, and if her chair had had arms she might not be so ready to leave it.

Mr. Carey was making up the fire when Philip came in, and he pointed out to his nephew that there were two pokers. One was large and bright and polished and unused, and was called the Vicar; and the other, which was much smaller and had evidently passed through many fires, was called the Curate.

"What are we waiting for?" said Mr. Carey.

"I told Mary Ann to make you an egg. I thought you'd be hungry after your journey."

Mrs. Carey thought the journey from London to Blackstable

very tiring. She seldom travelled herself, for the living was only three hundred a year, and, when her husband wanted a holiday, since there was not money for two, he went by himself. He was very fond of Church Congresses and usually managed to go up to London once a year; and once he had been to Paris for the exhibition, and two or three times to Switzerland. Mary Ann brought in the egg, and they sat down. The chair was much too low for Philip, and for a moment neither Mr. Carey nor his wife knew what to do.

"I'll put some books under him," said Mary Ann.

She took from the top of the harmonium the large Bible and the prayer-book from which the Vicar was accustomed to read prayers, and put them on Philip's chair.

"Oh, William, he can't sit on the Bible," said Mrs. Carey, in a shocked tone. "Couldn't you get him some books out of the study?"

Mr. Carey considered the question for an instant.

"I don't think it matters this once if you put the prayer-book on the top, Mary Ann," he said. "The book of Common Prayer is the composition of men like ourselves. It has no claim to divine authorship."

"I hadn't thought of that, William," said Aunt Louisa.

Philip perched himself on the books, and the Vicar, having said grace, cut the top off his egg.

"There," he said, handing it to Philip, "you can eat my top if you like."

Philip would have liked an egg to himself, but he was not offered one, so took what he could.

"How have the chickens been laying since I went away?" asked the Vicar.

"Oh, they've been dreadful, only one or two a day."

"How did you like that top, Philip?" asked his uncle.

"Very much, thank you."

"You shall have another one on Sunday afternoon."

Mr. Carey always had a boiled egg at tea on Sunday, so that he might be fortified for the evening service.

Chapter 5

Philip came gradually to know the people he was to live with, and by fragments of conversation, some of it not meant for his ears, learned a good deal both about himself and about his dead parents. Philip's father had been much younger than the Vicar of Blackstable. After a brilliant career at St. Luke's Hospital he was put on the staff, and presently began to earn money in considerable sums. He spent it freely. When the parson set about restoring his church and asked his brother for a subscription, he was surprised by receiving a couple of hundred pounds: Mr. Carey, thrifty by inclination and economical by necessity, accepted it with mingled feelings; he was envious of his brother because he could afford to give so much, pleased for the sake of his church, and vaguely irritated by a generosity which seemed almost ostentatious. Then Henry Carey married a patient, a beautiful girl but penniless, an orphan with no near relations, but of good family; and there was an array of fine friends at the wedding. The parson, on his visits to her when he came to London, held himself with reserve. He felt shy with her and in his heart he resented her great beauty: she dressed more magnificently than became the wife of a hardworking surgeon; and the charming furniture of her house, the flowers among which she lived even in winter, suggested an extravagance which he deplored. He heard her talk of entertainments she was going to; and, as he told his wife on getting home again, it was impossible to accept hospitality without making some return. He had seen grapes in the dining-room that must have cost at least eight shillings a pound; and at luncheon he had been given asparagus two months before it was ready in the vicarage garden. Now all he had anticipated was come to pass; the Vicar felt the satisfaction of the prophet who saw fire and brimstone consume the city which would not mend its way to his warning. Poor Philip was practically penniless, and what was the good of his mother's fine friends now? He heard that his father's extravagance was really criminal, and it was a mercy that Providence had seen fit to take his dear mother to itself: she had no more idea of money than a child.

When Philip had been a week at Blackstable an incident happened which seemed to irritate his uncle very much. One morning he found on the breakfast table a small packet which had been sent on by post from the late Mrs. Carey's house in London. It was addressed to her. When the parson opened it he found a dozen photographs of Mrs. Carey. They showed the head and shoulders only, and her hair was more plainly done than usual, low on the forehead, which gave her an unusual look; the face was thin and worn, but no illness could impair the beauty of her features. There was in the large dark eyes a sadness which Philip did not remember. The first sight of the dead woman gave Mr.

Carey a little shock, but this was quickly followed by perplexity. The photographs seemed quite recent, and he could not imagine who had ordered them.

"D'you know anything about these, Philip?" he asked.

"I remember mamma said she'd been taken," he answered. "Miss Watkin scolded her.... She said: I wanted the boy to have something to remember me by when he grows up."

Mr. Carey looked at Philip for an instant. The child spoke in a clear treble. He recalled the words, but they meant nothing to him.

"You'd better take one of the photographs and keep it in your room," said Mr. Carey. "I'll put the others away."

He sent one to Miss Watkin, and she wrote and explained how they came to be taken.

One day Mrs. Carey was lying in bed, but she was feeling a little better than usual, and the doctor in the morning had seemed hopeful; Emma had taken the child out, and the maids were downstairs in the basement; suddenly Mrs. Carey felt desperately alone in the world. A great fear seized her that she would not recover from the confinement which she was expecting in a fortnight. Her son was nine years old. How could he be expected to remember her? She could not bear to think that he would grow up and forget, forget her utterly; and she had loved him so passionately, because he was weakly and deformed, and because he was her child. She had no photographs of herself taken since her marriage, and that was ten years before. She wanted her son to know what she looked like at the end. He could not forget her then, not forget utterly. She knew that if she called her maid and told her she wanted to get up, the maid would prevent her, and perhaps send for the doctor, and she had not the strength now to struggle or argue. She got out of bed and began to dress herself. She had been on her back so long that her legs gave way beneath her, and then the soles of her feet tingled so that she could hardly bear to put them to the ground. But she went on. She was unused to doing her own hair and, when she raised her arms and began to brush it, she felt faint. She could never do it as her maid did. It was beautiful hair, very fine, and of a deep rich gold. Her eyebrows were straight and dark. She put on a black skirt, but chose the bodice of the evening dress which she liked best: it was of white damask which was fashionable in those days. She looked at herself in the glass. Her face was very pale, but her skin was clear: she had never had much colour, and this had always made the redness of her beautiful mouth emphatic. She could not restrain a sob. But she could not afford to be sorry for herself; she was feeling already desperately tired; and she put on the furs which Henry had given her the Christmas before— she had been so proud of them and so happy then—and slipped downstairs with beating heart. She got safely out of the house and drove to a photographer. She paid for a dozen photographs. She was obliged to ask for a glass of water in the middle of the sitting; and the assistant, seeing she was ill, suggested that she should come another day, but she insisted on staying till the end. At last it was finished, and she drove back again to the dingy little house in Kensington which she hated with all her heart. It was a horrible house to die in.

She found the front door open, and when she drove up

the maid and Emma ran down the steps to help her. They had been frightened when they found her room empty. At first they thought she must have gone to Miss Watkin, and the cook was sent round. Miss Watkin came back with her and was waiting anxiously in the drawing-room. She came downstairs now full of anxiety and reproaches; but the exertion had been more than Mrs. Carey was fit for, and when the occasion for firmness no longer existed she gave way. She fell heavily into Emma's arms and was carried upstairs. She remained unconscious for a time that seemed incredibly long to those that watched her, and the doctor, hurriedly sent for, did not come. It was next day, when she was a little better, that Miss Watkin got some explanation out of her. Philip was playing on the floor of his mother's bed-room, and neither of the ladies paid attention to him. He only understood vaguely what they were talking about, and he could not have said why those words remained in his memory.

"I wanted the boy to have something to remember me by when he grows up."

"I can't make out why she ordered a dozen," said Mr. Carey. "Two would have done."

Chapter 6

One day was very like another at the vicarage.

Soon after breakfast Mary Ann brought in *The Times*. Mr. Carey shared it with two neighbours. He had it from ten till one, when the gardener took it over to Mr. Ellis at the Limes, with whom it remained till seven; then it was taken to Miss Brooks at the Manor House, who, since she got it late, had the advantage of keeping it. In summer Mrs. Carey, when she was making jam, often asked her for a copy to cover the pots with. When the Vicar settled down to his paper his wife put on her bonnet and went out to do the shopping. Philip accompanied her. Blackstable was a fishing village. It consisted of a high street in which were the shops, the bank, the doctor's house, and the houses of two or three coalship owners; round the little harbor were shabby streets in which lived fishermen and poor people; but since they went to chapel they were of no account. When Mrs. Carey passed the dissenting ministers in the street she stepped over to the other side to avoid meeting them, but if there was not time for this fixed her eyes on the pavement. It was a scandal to which the

Vicar had never resigned himself that there were three chapels in the High Street: he could not help feeling that the law should have stepped in to prevent their erection. Shopping in Blackstable was not a simple matter; for dissent, helped by the fact that the parish church was two miles from the town, was very common; and it was necessary to deal only with churchgoers; Mrs. Carey knew perfectly that the vicarage custom might make all the difference to a tradesman's faith. There were two butchers who went to church, and they would not understand that the Vicar could not deal with both of them at once; nor were they satisfied with his simple plan of going for six months to one and for six months to the other. The butcher who was not sending meat to the vicarage constantly threatened not to come to church, and the Vicar was sometimes obliged to make a threat: it was very wrong of him not to come to church, but if he carried iniquity further and actually went to chapel, then of course, excellent as his meat was, Mr. Carey would be forced to leave him for ever. Mrs. Carey often stopped at the bank to deliver a message to Josiah Graves, the manager, who was choir-master, treasurer, and churchwarden. He was a tall, thin man with a sallow face and a long nose; his hair was very white, and to Philip he seemed extremely old. He kept the parish accounts, arranged the treats for the choir and the schools; though there was no organ in the parish church, it was generally considered (in Blackstable) that the choir he led was the best in Kent; and when there was any ceremony, such as a visit from the Bishop for confirmation or from the Rural Dean to preach at the Harvest Thanksgiving, he made the necessary preparations. But he had no hesitation in doing all manner of things without more than a perfunctory consultation with the Vicar, and the Vicar, though always ready to be saved trouble, much resented the churchwarden's managing ways. He really seemed to look upon himself as the most important person in the parish. Mr. Carey constantly told his wife that if Josiah Graves did not take care he would give him a good rap over the knuckles one day; but Mrs. Carey advised him to bear with Josiah Graves: he meant well, and it was not his fault if he was not quite a gentleman. The Vicar, finding his comfort in the practice of a Christian virtue, exercised forbearance; but he revenged himself by calling the churchwarden Bismarck behind his back.

Once there had been a serious quarrel between the pair, and Mrs. Carey still thought of that anxious time with dismay. The Conservative candidate had announced his intention of addressing a meeting at Blackstable; and Josiah Graves, having arranged that it should take place in the Mission Hall, went to Mr. Carey and told him that he hoped he would say a few words. It appeared that the candidate had asked Josiah Graves to take the chair. This was more than Mr. Carey could put up with. He had firm views upon the respect which was due to the cloth, and it was ridiculous for a churchwarden to take the chair at a meeting when the Vicar was there. He reminded Josiah Graves that parson meant person, that is, the vicar was the person of the parish. Josiah Graves answered that he was the first to recognize the dignity of the church, but this was a matter of politics, and in his turn he reminded the Vicar that their Blessed Saviour had enjoined upon them to render unto Caesar the things that were Caesar's. To this Mr. Carey replied that the devil could quote scripture to his purpose, himself had sole authority over the Mission Hall, and if he were not asked to be chairman he would refuse the use of it for a political meeting. Josiah Graves told Mr. Carey that he might do as he chose, and for his part he thought the Wesleyan Chapel would be an equally suitable place. Then Mr. Carey said that if Josiah Graves set foot in what was little better than a heathen temple he was not fit to be churchwarden in a Christian parish. Josiah Graves thereupon resigned all his offices, and that very evening sent to the church for his cassock and surplice. His sister, Miss Graves, who kept house for him, gave up her secretaryship of the Maternity Club, which provided the pregnant poor with flannel, baby linen, coals, and five shillings. Mr. Carey said he was at last master in his own house. But soon he found that he was obliged to see to all sorts of things that he knew nothing about; and Josiah Graves, after the first moment of irritation, discovered that he had lost his chief interest in life. Mrs. Carey and Miss Graves were much distressed by the quarrel; they met after a discreet exchange of letters, and made up their minds to put the matter right: they talked, one to her husband, the other to her brother, from morning till night; and since they were persuading these gentlemen to do what in their hearts they wanted, after three weeks of anxiety a reconciliation was effected. It was to both their interests, but they ascribed it to a common love for their Redeemer. The meeting was held at the Mission Hall, and the doctor was asked to be chairman. Mr. Carey and Josiah Graves both made speeches.

When Mrs. Carey had finished her business with the banker, she generally went upstairs to have a little chat with his sister; and while the ladies talked of parish matters, the curate, or the new bonnet of Mrs. Wilson—Mr. Wilson was the richest man in

Blackstable, he was thought to have at least five hundred a year, and he had married his cook—Philip sat demurely in the stiff parlour, used only to receive visitors, and busied himself with the restless movements of goldfish in a bowl. The windows were never opened except to air the room for a few minutes in the morning, and it had a stuffy smell which seemed to Philip to have a mysterious connection with banking.

Then Mrs. Carey remembered that she had to go to the grocer, and they continued on their way. When the shopping was done they often went down a side street of little houses, mostly of wood, in which fishermen dwelt (and here and there a fisherman sat on his doorstep mending his nets, and nets hung to dry upon the doors), till they came to a small beach, shut in on each side by warehouses, but with a view of the sea. Mrs. Carey stood for a few minutes and looked at it, it was turbid and yellow (and who knows what thoughts passed through her mind?) while Philip searched for flat stones to play ducks and drakes. Then they walked slowly back. They looked into the post office to get the right time, nodded to Mrs. Wigram the doctor's wife, who sat at her window sewing, and so got home.

Dinner was at one o'clock; and on Monday, Tuesday, and Wednesday it consisted of beef, roast, hashed, and minced, and on Thursday, Friday, and Saturday of mutton. On Sunday they ate one of their own chickens. In the afternoon Philip did his lessons. He was taught Latin and mathematics by his uncle who knew neither, and French and the piano by his aunt. Of French she was ignorant, but she knew the piano well enough to accompany the old-fashioned songs she had sung for thirty years. Uncle William used to tell Philip that when he was a curate his wife had known twelve songs by heart, which she could sing at a moment's notice whenever she was asked. She often sang still when there was a tea-party at the vicarage. There were few people whom the Careys cared to ask there, and their parties consisted always of the curate, Josiah Graves with his sister, Dr. Wigram and his wife. After tea Miss Graves played one or two of Mendelssohn's *Songs without Words*, and Mrs. Carey sang *When the Swallows Homeward Fly*, or *Trot, Trot, My Pony*.

But the Careys did not give tea-parties often; the preparations upset them, and when their guests were gone they felt themselves exhausted. They preferred to have tea by themselves, and after tea they played backgammon. Mrs. Carey arranged that her husband should win, because he did not like losing. They had cold supper at eight. It was a scrappy meal because Mary Ann resented getting anything ready after tea, and Mrs. Carey helped to clear away. Mrs. Carey seldom ate more than bread and butter, with a little stewed fruit to follow, but the Vicar had a slice of cold meat. Immediately after supper Mrs. Carey rang the bell for prayers, and then Philip went to bed. He rebelled against being undressed by Mary Ann and after a while succeeded in establishing his right to dress and undress himself. At nine o'clock Mary Ann brought in the eggs and the plate. Mrs. Carey wrote the date on each egg and put the number down in a book. She then took the plate-basket on her arm and went upstairs. Mr. Carey continued to read one of his old books, but as the clock struck ten he got up, put out the lamps, and followed his wife to bed.

When Philip arrived there was some difficulty in deciding on which evening he should have his bath. It was never easy to get plenty of hot water, since the kitchen boiler did not work, and it was impossible for two persons to have a bath on the same day. The only man who had a bathroom in Blackstable was Mr. Wilson, and it was thought ostentatious of him. Mary Ann had her bath in the kitchen on Monday night, because she liked to begin the week clean. Uncle William could not have his on Saturday, because he had a heavy day before him and he was always a little tired after a bath, so he had it on Friday. Mrs. Carey had hers on Thursday for the same reason. It looked as though Saturday were naturally indicated for Philip, but Mary Ann said she couldn't keep the fire up on Saturday night: what with all the cooking on Sunday, having to make pastry and she didn't know what all, she did not feel up to giving the boy his bath on Saturday night; and it was quite clear that he could not bath himself. Mrs. Carey was shy about bathing a boy, and of course the Vicar had his sermon. But the Vicar insisted that Philip should be clean and sweet for the Lord's Day. Mary Ann said she would rather go than be put upon—and after eighteen years she didn't expect to have more work given her, and they might show some consideration—and Philip said he didn't want anyone to bath him, but could very well bath himself. This settled it. Mary Ann said she was quite sure he wouldn't bath himself properly, and rather than he should go dirty—and not because he was going into the presence of the Lord, but because she couldn't abide a boy who wasn't properly washed—she'd work herself to the bone even if it was Saturday night.

Chapter 7

Sunday was a day crowded with incident. Mr. Carey was accustomed to say that he was the only man in his parish who worked seven days a week.

The household got up half an hour earlier than usual. No lying abed for a poor parson on the day of rest, Mr. Carey remarked as Mary Ann knocked at the door punctually at eight. It took Mrs. Carey longer to dress, and she got down to breakfast at nine, a little breathless, only just before her husband. Mr. Carey's boots stood in front of the fire to warm. Prayers were longer than usual, and the breakfast more substantial. After breakfast the Vicar cut thin slices of bread for the communion, and Philip was privileged to cut off the crust. He was sent to the study to fetch a marble paperweight, with which Mr. Carey pressed the bread till it was thin and pulpy, and then it was cut into small squares. The amount was regulated by the weather. On a very bad day few people came to church, and on a very fine one, though many came, few stayed for communion. There were most when it was dry enough to make the walk to church pleasant, but not so fine that people wanted to hurry away.

Then Mrs. Carey brought the communion plate out of the safe, which stood in the pantry, and the Vicar polished it with a chamois leather. At ten the fly drove up, and Mr. Carey got into his boots. Mrs. Carey took several minutes to put on her bonnet, during which the Vicar, in a voluminous cloak, stood in the hall with just such an expression on his face as would have become an early Christian about to be led into the arena. It was extraordinary that after thirty years of marriage his wife could not be ready in time on Sunday morning. At last she came, in black satin; the Vicar did not like colours in a clergyman's wife at any time, but on Sundays he was determined that she should wear black; now and then, in conspiracy with Miss Graves, she ventured a white feather or a pink rose in her bonnet, but the Vicar insisted that it should disappear; he said he would not go to church with the scarlet woman: Mrs. Carey sighed as a woman but obeyed as a wife. They were about to step into the carriage when the Vicar remembered that no one had given him his egg. They knew that he must have an egg for his voice, there were two women in the house, and no one had the least regard for his comfort. Mrs. Carey scolded Mary Ann, and Mary Ann answered that she could not think of everything. She hurried away to fetch an egg, and Mrs. Carey beat it up in a glass of sherry. The Vicar swallowed it at a gulp. The communion plate was stowed in the carriage, and they set off.

The fly came from *The Red Lion* and had a peculiar smell of stale straw. They drove with both windows closed so that the Vicar should not catch cold. The sexton was waiting at the porch to take the communion plate, and while the Vicar went to the vestry Mrs. Carey and Philip settled themselves in the vicarage pew. Mrs. Carey placed in front of her the sixpenny bit she was accustomed to put in the plate, and gave Philip threepence for the same purpose. The church filled up gradually and the service began.

Philip grew bored during the sermon, but if he fidgeted Mrs. Carey put a gentle hand on his arm and looked at him reproachfully. He regained interest when the final hymn was sung and Mr. Graves passed round with the plate.

When everyone had gone Mrs. Carey went into Miss Graves' pew to have a few words with her while they were waiting for the gentlemen, and Philip went to the vestry. His uncle, the curate, and Mr. Graves were still in their surplices. Mr. Carey gave him the remains of the consecrated bread and told him he might eat it. He had been accustomed to eat it himself, as it seemed blasphemous to throw it away, but Philip's keen appetite relieved him from the duty. Then they counted the money. It consisted of pennies, sixpences, and threepenny bits. There were always two single shillings, one put in the plate by the Vicar and the other by Mr. Graves; and sometimes there was a florin. Mr. Graves told the Vicar who had given this. It was always a stranger to Blackstable, and Mr. Carey wondered who he was. But Miss Graves had observed the rash act and was able to tell Mrs. Carey that the stranger came from London, was married, and had children. During the drive home Mrs. Carey passed the information on, and the Vicar made up his mind to call on him and ask for a subscription to the Additional Curates Society. Mr. Carey asked if Philip had behaved properly; and Mrs. Carey remarked that

Mrs. Wigram had a new mantle, Mr. Cox was not in church, and somebody thought that Miss Phillips was engaged. When they reached the vicarage they all felt that they deserved a substantial dinner.

When this was over Mrs. Carey went to her room to rest, and Mr. Carey lay down on the sofa in the drawing-room for forty winks.

They had tea at five, and the Vicar ate an egg to support himself for evensong. Mrs. Carey did not go to this so that Mary Ann might, but she read the service through and the hymns. Mr. Carey walked to church in the evening, and Philip limped along by his side. The walk through the darkness along the country road strangely impressed him, and the church with all its lights in the distance, coming gradually nearer, seemed very friendly. At first he was shy with his uncle, but little by little grew used to him, and he would slip his hand in his uncle's and walk more easily for the feeling of protection.

They had supper when they got home. Mr. Carey's slippers were waiting for him on a footstool in front of the fire, and by their side Philip's, one the shoe of a small boy, the other misshapen and odd. He was dreadfully tired when he went up to bed, and he did not resist when Mary Ann undressed him. She kissed him after she tucked him up, and he began to love her.

Chapter 8

Philip had led always the solitary life of an only child, and his loneliness at the vicarage was no greater than it had been when his mother lived. He made friends with Mary Ann. She was a chubby little person of thirty-five, the daughter of a fisherman, and had come to the vicarage at eighteen; it was her first place and she had no intention of leaving it; but she held a possible marriage as a rod over the timid heads of her master and mistress. Her father and mother lived in a little house off Harbour Street, and she went to see them on her evenings out. Her stories of the sea touched Philip's imagination, and the narrow alleys round the harbour grew rich with the romance which his young fancy lent them. One evening he asked whether he might go home with her; but his aunt was afraid that he might catch something, and his uncle said that evil communications corrupted good manners. He disliked the fisher folk, who were rough, uncouth, and went to chapel. But Philip was more comfortable in the kitchen than in the dining-room, and, whenever he could, he took his toys and played there. His aunt was not sorry. She did not like disorder, and though she recognized that boys must be expected to be untidy she preferred that he should make a mess in the kitchen. If he fidgeted his uncle was apt to grow restless and say it was high time he went to school. Mrs. Carey thought Philip very young for this, and her heart went out to the motherless child; but her attempts to gain his affection were awkward, and the boy, feeling shy, received her demonstrations with so much sullenness that she was mortified. Sometimes she heard his shrill voice raised in laughter in the kitchen, but when she went in, he grew suddenly silent, and he flushed darkly when Mary Ann explained the joke. Mrs. Carey could not see anything amusing in what she heard, and she smiled with constraint.

"He seems happier with Mary Ann than with us, William," she said, when she returned to her sewing.

"One can see he's been very badly brought up. He wants licking into shape."

On the second Sunday after Philip arrived an unlucky incident occurred. Mr. Carey had retired as usual after dinner for a little snooze in the drawing-room, but he was in an irritable mood and could not sleep. Josiah Graves that morning had objected strongly to some candlesticks with which the Vicar had adorned the altar. He had bought them second-hand in Tercanbury, and he thought they looked very well. But Josiah Graves said they were popish. This was a taunt that always aroused the Vicar. He had been at Oxford during the movement which ended in the secession from the Established Church of Edward Manning, and he felt a certain sympathy for the Church of Rome. He would willingly have made the service more ornate than had been usual in the low-church parish of Blackstable, and in his secret soul he yearned for processions and lighted candles. He drew the line at incense. He hated the word protestant. He called himself a Catholic. He was accustomed to say that Papists required an epithet, they were Roman Catholic; but the Church of England was Catholic in the best, the fullest, and the noblest sense of the term. He was pleased to think that his shaven face gave him the look of a priest, and in his youth he had possessed an ascetic air which added to the impression. He often related that on one of his holidays in Boulogne, one of those holidays upon which his wife for economy's sake did not accompany him, when he was sitting in a church, the *curé* had come up to him and invited him to preach a sermon. He dismissed his curates when they married, having decided views on the celibacy of the unbeneficed clergy. But when at an election the Liberals had written on his garden fence in large blue letters: *This way to Rome*, he had been very angry, and threatened to prosecute the leaders of the Liberal party in Blackstable. He made up his mind now that nothing Josiah Graves said would induce him to remove the candlesticks from the altar, and he muttered Bismarck to himself once or twice irritably.

Suddenly he heard an unexpected noise. He pulled the handkerchief off his face, got up from the sofa on which he was lying, and went into the dining-room. Philip was seated on the table with all his bricks around him. He had built a monstrous castle, and some defect in the foundation had just brought the structure down in noisy ruin.

"What are you doing with those bricks, Philip? You know you're not allowed to play games on Sunday."

Philip stared at him for a moment with frightened eyes, and, as his habit was, flushed deeply.

"I always used to play at home," he answered.

"I'm sure your dear mamma never allowed you to do such a wicked thing as that."

Philip did not know it was wicked; but if it was, he did not wish it to be supposed that his mother had consented to it. He hung his head and did not answer.

"Don't you know it's very, very wicked to play on Sunday? What d'you suppose it's called the day of rest for? You're going to church tonight, and how can you face your Maker when you've been breaking one of His laws in the afternoon?"

Mr. Carey told him to put the bricks away at once, and stood over him while Philip did so.

"You're a very naughty boy," he repeated. "Think of the grief you're causing your poor mother in heaven."

Philip felt inclined to cry, but he had an instinctive disinclination to letting other people see his tears, and he clenched his teeth to prevent the sobs from escaping. Mr. Carey sat down in his armchair and began to turn over the pages of a book. Philip stood at the window. The vicarage was set back from the high road to Tercanbury, and from the dining-room one saw a semicircular strip of lawn and then as far as the horizon green fields. Sheep were grazing in them. The sky was forlorn and grey. Philip felt infinitely unhappy.

Presently Mary Ann came in to lay the tea, and Aunt Louisa descended the stairs.

"Have you had a nice little nap, William?" she asked.

"No," he answered. "Philip made so much noise that I couldn't sleep a wink."

This was not quite accurate, for he had been kept awake by his own thoughts; and Philip, listening sullenly, reflected that he had only made a noise once, and there was no reason why his uncle should not have slept before or after. When Mrs. Carey asked for an explanation the Vicar narrated the facts.

"He hasn't even said he was sorry," he finished.

"Oh, Philip, I'm sure you're sorry," said Mrs. Carey, anxious that the child should not seem wickeder to his uncle than need be.

Philip did not reply. He went on munching his bread and butter. He did not know what power it was in him that prevented him from making any expression of regret. He felt his ears tingling, he was a little inclined to cry, but no word would issue from his lips.

"You needn't make it worse by sulking," said Mr. Carey.

Tea was finished in silence. Mrs. Carey looked at Philip surreptitiously now and then, but the Vicar elaborately ignored him. When Philip saw his uncle go upstairs to get ready for church he went into the hall and got his hat and coat, but when the Vicar came downstairs and saw him, he said:

"I don't wish you to go to church tonight, Philip. I don't think you're in a proper frame of mind to enter the House of God."

Philip did not say a word. He felt it was a deep humiliation that was placed upon him, and his cheeks reddened. He stood silently watching his uncle put on his broad hat and his voluminous cloak. Mrs. Carey as usual went to the door to see him off. Then she turned to Philip.

"Never mind, Philip, you won't be a naughty boy next Sunday, will you, and then your uncle will take you to church with him in the evening."

She took off his hat and coat, and led him into the dining-room.

"Shall you and I read the service together, Philip, and we'll sing the hymns at the harmonium. Would you like that?"

Philip shook his head decidedly. Mrs. Carey was taken aback. If he would not read the evening service with her, she did not know what to do with him.

"Then what would you like to do until your uncle comes back?" she asked helplessly.

Philip broke his silence at last.

"I want to be left alone," he said.

"Philip, how can you say anything so unkind? Don't you know that your uncle and I only want your good? Don't you love me at all?"

"I hate you. I wish you was dead."

Mrs. Carey gasped. He said the words so savagely that it gave her quite a start. She had nothing to say. She sat down in her husband's chair; and as she thought of her desire to love the friendless, crippled boy and her eager wish that he should love her—she was a barren woman and, even though it was clearly God's will that she should be childless, she could scarcely bear to look at little children sometimes, her heart ached so—the tears rose to her eyes and one by one, slowly, rolled down her cheeks. Philip watched her in amazement. She took out her handkerchief, and now she cried without restraint. Suddenly Philip realized that she was crying because of what he had said, and he was sorry. He went up to her silently and kissed her. It was the first kiss he had ever given her without being asked. And the poor lady, so small in her black satin, shrivelled up and sallow, with her funny corkscrew curls, took the little boy on her lap and put her arms around him and wept as though her heart would break. But her tears were partly tears of happiness, for she felt that the strangeness between them was gone. She loved him now with a new love because he had made her suffer.

Chapter 9

On the following Sunday, when the Vicar was making his preparations to go into the drawing-room for his nap—all the actions of his life were conducted with ceremony—and Mrs. Carey was about to go upstairs, Philip asked:

"What shall I do if I'm not allowed to play?"

"Can't you sit still for once and be quiet?"

"I can't sit still till tea-time."

Mr. Carey looked out of the window, but it was cold and raw, and he could not suggest that Philip should go into the garden.

"I know what you can do. You can learn by heart the collect for the day."

He took the prayer-book which was used for prayers from the harmonium, and turned the pages till he came to the place he wanted.

"It's not a long one. If you can say it without a mistake when I come in to tea you shall have the top of my egg."

Mrs. Carey drew up Philip's chair to the dining-room table—they had bought him a high chair by now—and placed the book in front of him.

"The devil finds work for idle hands to do," said Mr. Carey.

He put some more coals on the fire so that there should be a cheerful blaze when he came in to tea, and went into the drawing-room. He loosened his collar, arranged the cushions, and settled himself comfortably on the sofa. But thinking the drawing-room a little chilly, Mrs. Carey brought him a rug from the hall; she put it over his legs and tucked it round his feet. She drew the blinds so that the light should not offend his eyes, and since he had closed them already went out of the room on tiptoe. The Vicar was at peace with himself today, and in ten minutes he was asleep. He snored softly.

It was the Sixth Sunday after Epiphany, and the collect began with the words: *O God, whose blessed Son was manifested that he might destroy the works of the devil, and make us the sons of God, and heirs of Eternal life*. Philip read it through. He could make no sense of it. He began saying the words aloud to himself, but many of them were unknown to him, and the construction of the sentence was strange. He could not get more than two lines in his head. And his attention was constantly wandering: there were fruit trees trained on the walls of the vicarage, and a long twig beat now and then against the windowpane; sheep grazed stolidly in the field beyond the garden. It seemed as though there were knots inside his brain. Then panic seized him that he would not know the words by tea-time, and he kept on whispering them to himself quickly; he did not try to understand, but merely to get them parrot-like into his memory.

Mrs. Carey could not sleep that afternoon, and by four o'clock she was so wide awake that she came downstairs. She thought she would hear Philip say his collect so that he should make no mistakes when he said it to his uncle. His uncle then would be pleased; he would see that the boy's heart was in the right place. But when Mrs. Carey came to the dining-room and was about to go in, she heard a sound that made her stop suddenly. Her heart gave a little jump. She turned away and quietly slipped out of the front door. She walked round the house till she came to the dining-room window and then cautiously looked in. Philip was still sitting on the chair she had put him in, but his head was on the table buried in his arms, and he was sobbing desperately. She saw the convulsive movement of his shoulders. Mrs. Carey was frightened. A thing that had always struck her about the child was that he seemed so collected. She had never seen him cry. And now she realized that his calmness was some instinctive shame of showing his feelings: he hid himself to weep.

Without thinking that her husband disliked being wakened suddenly, she burst into the drawing-room.

"William, William," she said. "The boy's crying as though his heart would break."

Mr. Carey sat up and disentangled himself from the rug about his legs.

"What's he got to cry about?"

"I don't know…. Oh, William, we can't let the boy be unhappy. D'you think it's our fault? If we'd had children we'd have known what to do."

Mr. Carey looked at her in perplexity. He felt extraordinarily helpless.

"He can't be crying because I gave him the collect to learn. It's not more than ten lines."

"Don't you think I might take him some picture books to look at, William? There are some of the Holy Land. There couldn't be anything wrong in that."

"Very well, I don't mind."

Mrs. Carey went into the study. To collect books was Mr. Carey's only passion, and he never went into Tercanbury without spending an hour or two in the second-hand shop; he always brought back four or five musty volumes. He never read them, for he had long lost the habit of reading, but he liked to turn the pages, look at the illustrations if they were illustrated, and mend the bindings. He welcomed wet days because on them he could stay at home without pangs of conscience and spend the afternoon with white of egg and a glue-pot, patching up the Russia leather of some battered quarto. He had many volumes of old travels, with steel- engravings, and Mrs. Carey quickly found two which described Palestine. She coughed elaborately at the door so that Philip should have time to compose himself, she felt that he would be humiliated if she came upon him in the midst of his tears; then she rattled the door handle. When she went in Philip was poring over the prayer-book, hiding his eyes with his hands so that she might not see he had been crying.

"Do you know the collect yet?" she said.

He did not answer for a moment, and she felt that he did not trust his voice. She was oddly embarrassed.

"I can't learn it by heart," he said at last, with a gasp.

"Oh, well, never mind," she said. "You needn't. I've got

some picture books for you to look at. Come and sit on my lap, and we'll look at them together."

Philip slipped off his chair and limped over to her. He looked down so that she should not see his eyes. She put her arms round him.

"Look," she said, "that's the place where our Blessed Lord was born."

She showed him an Eastern town with flat roofs and cupolas and minarets. In the foreground was a group of palm-trees, and under them were resting two Arabs and some camels. Philip passed his hand over the picture as if he wanted to feel the houses and the loose habiliments of the nomads.

"Read what it says," he asked.

Mrs. Carey in her even voice read the opposite page. It was a romantic narrative of some Eastern traveller of the thirties, pompous maybe, but fragrant with the emotion with which the East came to the generation that followed Byron and Chateaubriand. In a moment or two Philip interrupted her.

"I want to see another picture."

When Mary Ann came in and Mrs. Carey rose to help her lay the cloth. Philip took the book in his hands and hurried through the illustrations. It was with difficulty that his aunt induced him to put the book down for tea. He had forgotten his horrible struggle to get the collect by heart; he had forgotten his tears. Next day it was raining, and he asked for the book again. Mrs. Carey gave it him joyfully. Talking over his future with her husband she had found that both desired him to take orders, and this eagerness for the book which described places hallowed by the presence of Jesus seemed a good sign. It looked as though the boy's mind addressed itself naturally to holy things. But in a day or two he asked for more books. Mr. Carey took him into his study, showed him the shelf in which he kept illustrated works, and chose for him one that dealt with Rome. Philip took it greedily. The pictures led him to a new amusement. He began to read the page before and the page after each engraving to find out what it was about, and soon he lost all interest in his toys.

Then, when no one was near, he took out books for himself; and perhaps because the first impression on his mind was made by an Eastern town, he found his chief amusement in those which described the Levant. His heart beat with excitement at the pictures of mosques and rich palaces; but there was one, in a book on Constantinople, which peculiarly stirred his imagination. It was called the Hall of the Thousand Columns. It was a Byzantine cistern, which the popular fancy had endowed with fantastic vastness; and the legend which he read told that a boat was always moored at the entrance to tempt the unwary, but no traveller venturing into the darkness had ever been seen again. And Philip wondered whether the boat went on for ever through one pillared alley after another or came at last to some strange mansion.

One day a good fortune befell him, for he hit upon Lane's translation of *The Thousand Nights and a Night*. He was captured first by the illustrations, and then he began to read, to start with, the stories that dealt with magic, and then the others; and those he liked he read again and again. He could think of nothing else. He forgot the life about him. He had to be called two or three times before he would come to his dinner. Insensibly he formed the most delightful habit in the world, the habit of reading: he did not know that thus he was providing himself with a refuge from all the distress of life; he did not know either that he was creating for himself an unreal world which would make the real world of every day a source of bitter disappointment. Presently he began to read other things. His brain was precocious. His uncle and aunt, seeing that he occupied himself and neither worried nor made a noise, ceased to trouble themselves about him. Mr. Carey had so many books that he did not know them, and as he read little he forgot the odd lots he had bought at one time and another because they were cheap. Haphazard among the sermons and homilies, the travels, the lives of the Saints, the Fathers, the histories of the church, were old-fashioned novels; and these Philip at last discovered. He chose them by their titles, and the first he read was *The Lancashire Witches*, and then he read *The Admirable Crichton*, and then many more. Whenever he started a book with two solitary travellers riding along the brink of a desperate ravine he knew he was safe.

The summer was come now, and the gardener, an old sailor, made him a hammock and fixed it up for him in the branches of a weeping willow. And here for long hours he lay, hidden from anyone who might come to the vicarage, reading, reading passionately. Time passed and it was July; August came: on Sundays the church was crowded with strangers, and the collection at the offertory often amounted to two pounds. Neither the Vicar nor Mrs. Carey went out of the garden much during this period; for they disliked strange faces, and they looked upon the visitors from London with aversion. The house opposite was taken for six weeks by a gentleman who had two little boys, and he sent in to ask if Philip would like to go and play with them; but Mrs. Carey returned a polite refusal. She was afraid that Philip would be corrupted by little boys from London. He was going to be a clergyman, and it was necessary that he should be preserved from contamination. She liked to see in him an infant Samuel.

Chapter 10

The Careys made up their minds to send Philip to King's School at Tercanbury. The neighbouring clergy sent their sons there. It was united by long tradition to the Cathedral: its headmaster was an honorary Canon, and a past headmaster was the Archdeacon. Boys were encouraged there to aspire to Holy Orders, and the education was such as might prepare an honest lad to spend his life in God's service. A preparatory school was attached to it, and to this it was arranged that Philip should go. Mr. Carey took him into Tercanbury one Thursday afternoon towards the end of September. All day Philip had been excited and rather frightened. He knew little of school life but what he had read in the stories of *The Boy's Own Paper*. He had also read *Eric, or Little by Little*.

When they got out of the train at Tercanbury, Philip felt sick with apprehension, and during the drive in to the town sat pale and silent. The high brick wall in front of the school gave it the look of a prison. There was a little door in it, which opened on their ringing; and a clumsy, untidy man came out and fetched

Philip's tin trunk and his play-box. They were shown into the drawing-room; it was filled with massive, ugly furniture, and the chairs of the suite were placed round the walls with a forbidding rigidity. They waited for the headmaster.

"What's Mr. Watson like?" asked Philip, after a while.

"You'll see for yourself."

There was another pause. Mr. Carey wondered why the headmaster did not come. Presently Philip made an effort and spoke again.

"Tell him I've got a club-foot," he said.

Before Mr. Carey could speak the door burst open and Mr. Watson swept into the room. To Philip he seemed gigantic. He was a man of over six feet high, and broad, with enormous hands and a great red beard; he talked loudly in a jovial manner; but his aggressive cheerfulness struck terror in Philip's heart. He shook hands with Mr. Carey, and then took Philip's small hand in his.

"Well, young fellow, are you glad to come to school?" he shouted.

Philip reddened and found no word to answer.

"How old are you?"

"Nine," said Philip.

"You must say sir," said his uncle.

"I expect you've got a good lot to learn," the headmaster bellowed cheerily.

To give the boy confidence he began to tickle him with rough fingers. Philip, feeling shy and uncomfortable, squirmed under his touch.

"I've put him in the small dormitory for the present...."

You'll like that, won't you?" he added to Philip. "Only eight of you in there. You won't feel so strange."

Then the door opened, and Mrs. Watson came in. She was a dark woman with black hair, neatly parted in the middle. She had curiously thick lips and a small round nose. Her eyes were large and black. There was a singular coldness in her appearance. She seldom spoke and smiled more seldom still. Her husband introduced Mr. Carey to her, and then gave Philip a friendly push towards her.

"This is a new boy, Helen. His name's Carey."

Without a word she shook hands with Philip and then sat down, not speaking, while the headmaster asked Mr. Carey how much Philip knew and what books he had been working with. The Vicar of Blackstable was a little embarrassed by Mr. Watson's boisterous heartiness, and in a moment or two got up.

"I think I'd better leave Philip with you now."

"That's all right," said Mr. Watson. "He'll be safe with me. He'll get on like a house on fire. Won't you, young fellow?"

Without waiting for an answer from Philip the big man burst into a great bellow of laughter. Mr. Carey kissed Philip on the forehead and went away.

"Come along, young fellow," shouted Mr. Watson. "I'll show you the schoolroom."

He swept out of the drawing-room with giant strides, and Philip hurriedly limped behind him. He was taken into a long, bare room with two tables that ran along its whole length; on each side of them were wooden forms.

"Nobody much here yet," said Mr. Watson. "I'll just show

you the playground, and then I'll leave you to shift for yourself."

Mr. Watson led the way. Philip found himself in a large playground with high brick walls on three sides of it. On the fourth side was an iron railing through which you saw a vast lawn and beyond this some of the buildings of King's School. One small boy was wandering disconsolately, kicking up the gravel as he walked.

"Hulloa, Venning," shouted Mr. Watson. "When did you turn up?"

The small boy came forward and shook hands.

"Here's a new boy. He's older and bigger than you, so don't you bully him."

The headmaster glared amicably at the two children, filling them with fear by the roar of his voice, and then with a guffaw left them.

"What's your name?"

"Carey."

"What's your father?"

"He's dead."

"Oh! Does your mother wash?"

"My mother's dead, too."

Philip thought this answer would cause the boy a certain awkwardness, but Venning was not to be turned from his facetiousness for so little.

"Well, did she wash?" he went on.

"Yes," said Philip indignantly.

"She was a washerwoman then?"

"No, she wasn't."

"Then she didn't wash."

The little boy crowed with delight at the success of his dialectic. Then he caught sight of Philip's feet.

"What's the matter with your foot?"

Philip instinctively tried to withdraw it from sight. He hid it behind the one which was whole.

"I've got a club-foot," he answered.

"How did you get it?"

"I've always had it."

"Let's have a look."

"No."

"Don't then."

The little boy accompanied the words with a sharp kick on Philip's shin, which Philip did not expect and thus could not guard against. The pain was so great that it made him gasp, but greater than the pain was the surprise. He did not know why Venning kicked him. He had not the presence of mind to give him a black eye. Besides, the boy was smaller than he, and he had read in *The Boy's Own Paper* that it was a mean thing to hit anyone smaller than yourself. While Philip was nursing his shin a third boy appeared, and his tormentor left him. In a little while he noticed that the pair were talking about him, and he felt they were looking at his feet. He grew hot and uncomfortable.

But others arrived, a dozen together, and then more, and they began to talk about their doings during the holidays, where they had been, and what wonderful cricket they had played. A few new boys appeared, and with these presently Philip found himself talking. He was shy and nervous. He was anxious to make himself pleasant, but he could not think of anything to say. He was asked a great many questions and answered them all quite willingly. One boy asked him whether he could play cricket.

"No," answered Philip. "I've got a club-foot."

The boy looked down quickly and reddened. Philip saw that he felt he had asked an unseemly question. He was too shy to apologize and looked at Philip awkwardly.

Chapter 11

Next morning when the clanging of a bell awoke Philip he looked round his cubicle in astonishment. Then a voice sang out, and he remembered where he was.

"Are you awake, Singer?"

The partitions of the cubicle were of polished pitch-pine, and there was a green curtain in front. In those days there was little thought of ventilation, and the windows were closed except when the dormitory was aired in the morning.

Philip got up and knelt down to say his prayers. It was a cold morning, and he shivered a little; but he had been taught by his uncle that his prayers were more acceptable to God if he said them in his nightshirt than if he waited till he was dressed. This did not surprise him, for he was beginning to realize that he was the creature of a God who appreciated the discomfort of his worshippers. Then he washed. There were two baths for the fifty boarders, and each boy had a bath once a week. The rest of his washing was done in a small basin on a washstand, which, with the bed and a chair, made up the furniture of each cubicle. The boys chatted gaily while they dressed. Philip was all ears. Then another bell sounded, and they ran downstairs. They took their seats on the forms on each side of the two long tables in the schoolroom; and Mr. Watson, followed by his wife and the servants, came in and sat down. Mr. Watson read prayers in an impressive manner, and the supplications thundered out in his loud voice as though they were threats personally addressed to each boy. Philip listened with anxiety. Then Mr. Watson read a chapter from the Bible, and the servants trooped out. In a moment the untidy youth brought in two large pots of tea and on a second journey immense dishes of bread and butter.

Philip had a squeamish appetite, and the thick slabs of poor butter on the bread turned his stomach, but he saw other boys scraping it off and followed their example. They all had potted meats and such like, which they had brought in their play-boxes; and some had "extras," eggs or bacon, upon which Mr. Watson made a profit. When he had asked Mr. Carey whether Philip was to have these, Mr. Carey replied that he did not think boys should be spoilt. Mr. Watson quite agreed with him—he considered nothing was better than bread and butter for growing lads—but some parents, unduly pampering their offspring, insisted on it.

Philip noticed that "extras" gave boys a certain consideration and made up his mind, when he wrote to Aunt Louisa, to ask for them.

After breakfast the boys wandered out into the playground. Here the day-boys were gradually assembling. They were sons of the local clergy, of the officers at the Depot, and of such manufacturers or men of business as the old town possessed.

Presently a bell rang, and they all trooped into school. This consisted of a large, long room at opposite ends of which two under-masters conducted the second and third forms, and of a smaller one, leading out of it, used by Mr. Watson, who taught the first form. To attach the preparatory to the senior school these three classes were known officially, on speech days and in reports, as upper, middle, and lower second. Philip was put in the last. The master, a red-faced man with a pleasant voice, was called Rice; he had a jolly manner with boys, and the time passed quickly. Philip was surprised when it was a quarter to eleven and they were let out for ten minutes' rest.

The whole school rushed noisily into the playground. The new boys were told to go into the middle, while the others stationed themselves along opposite walls. They began to play *Pig in the Middle*. The old boys ran from wall to wall while the new boys tried to catch them: when one was seized and the mystic words said—one, two, three, and a pig for me—he became a prisoner and, turning sides, helped to catch those who were still free. Philip saw a boy running past and tried to catch him, but his limp gave him no chance; and the runners, taking their opportunity, made straight for the ground he covered. Then one of them had the brilliant idea of imitating Philip's clumsy run. Other boys saw it and began to laugh; then they all copied the first; and they ran round Philip, limping grotesquely, screaming in their treble voices with shrill laughter. They lost their heads with the delight of their new amusement, and choked with helpless merriment. One of them tripped Philip up and he fell, heavily as he always fell, and cut his knee. They laughed all the louder when he got up. A boy pushed him from behind, and he would have fallen again if another had not caught him. The game was forgotten in the entertainment of Philip's deformity. One of them invented an odd, rolling limp that struck the rest as supremely ridiculous, and several of the boys lay down on the ground and rolled about in laughter: Philip was completely scared. He could not make out why they were laughing at him. His heart beat so that he could hardly breathe, and he was more frightened than he had ever been in his life. He stood still stupidly while the boys ran round him, mimicking and laughing; they shouted to him to try and catch them; but he did not move. He did not want them to see him run any more. He was using all his strength to prevent himself from crying.

Suddenly the bell rang, and they all trooped back to school. Philip's knee was bleeding, and he was dusty and dishevelled. For some minutes Mr. Rice could not control his form. They were excited still by the strange novelty, and Philip saw one or two of them furtively looking down at his feet. He tucked them under the bench.

In the afternoon they went up to play football, but Mr. Watson stopped Philip on the way out after dinner.

"I suppose you can't play football, Carey?" he asked him.

Philip blushed self-consciously.

"No, sir."

"Very well. You'd better go up to the field. You can walk as far as that, can't you?"

Philip had no idea where the field was, but he answered all the same.

"Yes, sir."

The boys went in charge of Mr. Rice, who glanced at Philip and seeing he had not changed, asked why he was not going to play.

"Mr. Watson said I needn't, sir," said Philip.

"Why?"

There were boys all round him, looking at him curiously, and a feeling of shame came over Philip. He looked down without answering. Others gave the reply.

"He's got a club-foot, sir."

"Oh, I see."

Mr. Rice was quite young; he had only taken his degree a year before; and he was suddenly embarrassed. His instinct was to beg the boy's pardon, but he was too shy to do so. He made his voice gruff and loud.

"Now then, you boys, what are you waiting about for? Get on with you."

Some of them had already started and those that were left now set off, in groups of two or three.

"You'd better come along with me, Carey," said the master. "You don't know the way, do you?"

Philip guessed the kindness, and a sob came to his throat.

"I can't go very fast, sir."

"Then I'll go very slow," said the master, with a smile.

Philip's heart went out to the red-faced, commonplace young man who said a gentle word to him. He suddenly felt less unhappy.

But at night when they went up to bed and were undressing,

the boy who was called Singer came out of his cubicle and put his head in Philip's.

"I say, let's look at your foot," he said.

"No," answered Philip.

He jumped into bed quickly.

"Don't say no to me," said Singer. "Come on, Mason."

The boy in the next cubicle was looking round the corner, and at the words he slipped in. They made for Philip and tried to tear the bedclothes off him, but he held them tightly.

"Why can't you leave me alone?" he cried.

Singer seized a brush and with the back of it beat Philip's hands clenched on the blanket. Philip cried out.

"Why don't you show us your foot quietly?"

"I won't."

In desperation Philip clenched his fist and hit the boy who tormented him, but he was at a disadvantage, and the boy seized his arm. He began to turn it.

"Oh, don't, don't," said Philip. "You'll break my arm."

"Stop still then and put out your foot."

Philip gave a sob and a gasp. The boy gave the arm another wrench. The pain was unendurable.

"All right. I'll do it," said Philip.

He put out his foot. Singer still kept his hand on Philip's wrist. He looked curiously at the deformity.

"Isn't it beastly?" said Mason.

Another came in and looked too.

"Ugh," he said, in disgust.

"My word, it is rum," said Singer, making a face. "Is it hard?"

He touched it with the tip of his forefinger, cautiously, as though it were something that had a life of its own. Suddenly they heard Mr. Watson's heavy tread on the stairs. They threw the clothes back on Philip and dashed like rabbits into their cubicles. Mr. Watson came into the dormitory. Raising himself on tiptoe he could see over the rod that bore the green curtain, and he looked into two or three of the cubicles. The little boys were safely in bed. He put out the light and went out.

Singer called out to Philip, but he did not answer. He had got his teeth in the pillow so that his sobbing should be inaudible. He was not crying for the pain they had caused him, nor for the humiliation he had suffered when they looked at his foot, but with rage at himself because, unable to stand the torture, he had put out his foot of his own accord.

And then he felt the misery of his life. It seemed to his childish mind that this unhappiness must go on for ever. For no particular reason he remembered that cold morning when Emma had taken him out of bed and put him beside his mother. He had not thought of it once since it happened, but now he seemed to feel the warmth of his mother's body against his and her arms around him. Suddenly, it seemed to him that his life was a dream, his mother's death, and the life at the vicarage, and these two wretched days at school, and he would awake in the morning and be back again at home. His tears dried as he thought of it. He was too unhappy, it must be nothing but a dream, and his mother was alive, and Emma would come up presently and go to bed. He fell asleep.

But when he awoke next morning it was to the clanging of a bell, and the first thing his eyes saw was the green curtain of his cubicle.

Chapter 12

As time went on Philip's deformity ceased to interest. It was accepted like one boy's red hair and another's unreasonable corpulence. But meanwhile he had grown horribly sensitive. He never ran if he could help it, because he knew it made his limp more conspicuous, and he adopted a peculiar walk. He stood still as much as he could, with his club-foot behind the other, so that it should not attract notice, and he was constantly on the look out for any reference to it. Because he could not join in the games which other boys played, their life remained strange to him; he only interested himself from the outside in their doings; and it seemed to him that there was a barrier between them and him. Sometimes they seemed to think that it was his fault if he could not play football, and he was unable to make them understand. He was left a good deal to himself. He had been inclined to talkativeness, but gradually he became silent. He began to think of the difference between himself and others.

The biggest boy in his dormitory, Singer, took a dislike to him, and Philip, small for his age, had to put up with a good deal of hard treatment. About half-way through the term a mania ran through the school for a game called Nibs. It was a game for two, played on a table or a form with steel pens. You had to push your nib with the finger-nail so as to get the point of it over your opponent's, while he manoeuvred to prevent this and to get the point of his nib over the back of yours; when this result was achieved you breathed on the ball of your thumb, pressed it hard on the two nibs, and if you were able then to lift them without dropping either, both nibs became yours. Soon nothing was seen but boys playing this game, and the more skilful acquired vast stores of nibs. But in a little while Mr. Watson made up his mind that it was a form of gambling, forbade the game, and confiscated all the nibs in the boys' possession. Philip had been very adroit, and it was with a heavy heart that he gave up his winning; but his fingers itched to play still, and a few days later, on his way to the football field, he went into a shop and bought a pennyworth of J pens. He carried them loose in his pocket and enjoyed feeling them. Presently Singer found out that he had them. Singer had given up his nibs too, but he had kept back a very large one, called a Jumbo, which was almost unconquerable, and he could not resist the opportunity of getting Philip's Js out of him. Though Philip knew that he was at a disadvantage with his small nibs, he had an adventurous disposition and was willing to take the risk; besides, he was aware that Singer would not allow him to refuse. He had not played for a week and sat down to the game now with a thrill of excitement. He lost two of his small nibs quickly, and Singer was jubilant, but the third time by some chance the Jumbo slipped round and Philip was able to push his J across it. He crowed with triumph. At that moment Mr. Watson came in.

"What are you doing?" he asked.

He looked from Singer to Philip, but neither answered.

"Don't you know that I've forbidden you to play that idiotic game?"

Philip's heart beat fast. He knew what was coming and was dreadfully frightened, but in his fright there was a certain exultation. He had never been swished. Of course it would hurt, but it was something to boast about afterwards.

"Come into my study."

The headmaster turned, and they followed him side by side. Singer whispered to Philip:

"We're in for it."

Mr. Watson pointed to Singer.

"Bend over," he said.

Philip, very white, saw the boy quiver at each stroke, and after the third he heard him cry out. Three more followed.

"That'll do. Get up."

Singer stood up. The tears were streaming down his face. Philip stepped forward. Mr. Watson looked at him for a moment.

"I'm not going to cane you. You're a new boy. And I can't hit a cripple. Go away, both of you, and don't be naughty again."

When they got back into the schoolroom a group of boys, who had learned in some mysterious way what was happening, were waiting for them. They set upon Singer at once with eager questions. Singer faced them, his face red with the pain and marks of tears still on his cheeks. He pointed with his head at Philip, who was standing a little behind him.

"He got off because he's a cripple," he said angrily.

Philip stood silent and flushed. He felt that they looked at him with contempt.

"How many did you get?" one boy asked Singer.

But he did not answer. He was angry because he had been hurt.

"Don't ask me to play Nibs with you again," he said to Philip. "It's jolly nice for you. You don't risk anything."

"I didn't ask you."

"Didn't you!"

He quickly put out his foot and tripped Philip up. Philip was always rather unsteady on his feet, and he fell heavily to the ground.

"Cripple," said Singer.

For the rest of the term he tormented Philip cruelly, and though Philip tried to keep out of his way, the school was so small that it was impossible; he tried being friendly and jolly with him; he abased himself so far as to buy him a knife; but though Singer took the knife he was not placated. Once or twice, driven beyond endurance, he hit and kicked the bigger boy, but Singer was so much stronger that Philip was helpless, and he was always forced after more or less torture to beg his pardon. It was that which rankled with Philip: he could not bear the humiliation of apologies, which were wrung from him by pain greater than he could bear. And what made it worse was that there seemed no end to his wretchedness; Singer was only eleven and would not go to the upper school till he was thirteen. Philip realized that he must live two years with a tormentor from whom there was no escape.

He was only happy while he was working and when he got into bed. And often there recurred to him then that queer feeling that his life with all its misery was nothing but a dream, and that he would awake in the morning in his own little bed in London.

Chapter 13

Two years passed, and Philip was nearly twelve. He was in the first form, within two or three places of the top, and after Christmas when several boys would be leaving for the senior school he would be head boy. He had already quite a collection of prizes, worthless books on bad paper, but in gorgeous bindings decorated with the arms of the school: his position had freed him from bullying, and he was not unhappy. His fellows forgave him his success because of his deformity.

"After all, it's jolly easy for him to get prizes," they said, "there's nothing he *can* do but swot."

He had lost his early terror of Mr. Watson. He had grown used to the loud voice, and when the headmaster's heavy hand was laid on his shoulder Philip discerned vaguely the intention of a caress. He had the good memory which is more useful for scholastic achievements than mental power, and he knew Mr. Watson expected him to leave the preparatory school with a scholarship.

But he had grown very self-conscious. The new-born child

does not realize that his body is more a part of himself than surrounding objects, and will play with his toes without any feeling that they belong to him more than the rattle by his side; and it is only by degrees, through pain, that he understands the fact of the body. And experiences of the same kind are necessary for the individual to become conscious of himself; but here there is the difference that, although everyone becomes equally conscious of his body as a separate and complete organism, everyone does not become equally conscious of himself as a complete and separate personality. The feeling of apartness from others comes to most with puberty, but it is not always developed to such a degree as to make the difference between the individual and his fellows noticeable to the individual. It is such as he, as little conscious of himself as the bee in a hive, who are the lucky in life, for they have the best chance of happiness: their activities are shared by all, and their pleasures are only pleasures because they are enjoyed in common; you will see them on Whit-Monday dancing on Hampstead Heath, shouting at a football match, or from club windows in Pall Mall cheering a royal procession. It is because of them that man has been called a social animal.

Philip passed from the innocence of childhood to bitter conscious-ness of himself by the ridicule which his club-foot had excited. The circumstances of his case were so peculiar that he could not apply to them the ready-made rules which acted well enough in ordinary affairs, and he was forced to think for himself. The many books he had read filled his mind with ideas which, because he only half understood them, gave more scope to his imagination. Beneath his painful shyness something was growing up within him, and obscurely he realized his personality. But at times it gave him odd surprises; he did things, he knew not why, and afterwards when he thought of them found himself all at sea.

There was a boy called Luard between whom and Philip a friendship had arisen, and one day, when they were playing together in the school-room, Luard began to perform some trick with an ebony penholder of Philip's.

"Don't play the giddy ox," said Philip. "You'll only break it."

"I shan't."

But no sooner were the words out of the boy's mouth than the pen-holder snapped in two. Luard looked at Philip with dismay.

"Oh, I say, I'm awfully sorry."

The tears rolled down Philip's cheeks, but he did not answer.

"I say, what's the matter?" said Luard, with surprise. "I'll get you another one exactly the same."

"It's not about the penholder I care," said Philip, in a trembling voice, "only it was given me by my mater just before she died."

"I say, I'm awfully sorry, Carey."

"It doesn't matter. It wasn't your fault."

Philip took the two pieces of the penholder and looked at them. He tried to restrain his sobs. He felt utterly miserable. And yet he could not tell why, for he knew quite well that he had bought the penholder during his last holidays at Blackstable for one and twopence. He did not know in the least what had made him invent that pathetic story, but he was quite as unhappy as though it had been true. The pious atmosphere of the vicarage and the religious tone of the school had made Philip's conscience very sensitive; he absorbed insensibly the feeling about him that the Tempter was ever on the watch to gain his immortal soul; and though he was not more truthful than most boys he never told a lie without suffering from remorse. When he thought over this incident he was very much distressed, and made up his mind that he must go to Luard and tell him that the story was an invention. Though he dreaded humiliation more than anything in the world, he hugged himself for two or three days at the thought of the agonizing joy of humiliating himself to the Glory of God. But he never got any further. He satisfied his conscience by the more comfortable method of expressing his repentance only to the Almighty. But he could not understand why he should have been so genuinely affected by the story he was making up. The tears that flowed down his grubby cheeks were real tears. Then by some accident of association there occurred to him that scene when Emma had told him of his mother's death, and, though he could not speak for crying, he had insisted on going in to say good-bye to the Misses Watkin so that they might see his grief and pity him.

Chapter 14

Then a wave of religiosity passed through the school. Bad language was no longer heard, and the little nastinesses of small boys were looked upon with hostility; the bigger boys, like the lords temporal of the Middle Ages, used the strength of their arms to persuade those weaker than themselves to virtuous courses.

Philip, his restless mind avid for new things, became very devout. He heard soon that it was possible to join a Bible League, and wrote to London for particulars. These consisted in a form to be filled up with the applicant's name, age, and school; a solemn declaration to be signed that he would read a set portion of Holy Scripture every night for a year; and a request for half a crown; this, it was explained, was demanded partly to prove the earnestness of the applicant's desire to become a member of the League, and partly to cover clerical expenses. Philip duly sent the papers and the money, and in return received a calendar worth about a penny, on which was set down the appointed passage to be read each day, and a sheet of paper on one side of which was a picture of the Good Shepherd and a lamb, and on the other, decoratively framed in red lines, a short prayer which had to be said before beginning to read.

Every evening he undressed as quickly as possible in order to have time for his task before the gas was put out. He read industriously, as he read always, without criticism, stories of cruelty, deceit, ingratitude, dishonesty, and low cunning. Actions which would have excited his horror in the life about him, in the reading passed through his mind without comment, because they were committed under the direct inspiration of God. The method of the League was to alternate a book of the Old Testament with a book of the New, and one night Philip came across these words of Jesus Christ:

> *If ye have faith, and doubt not, ye shall not only do this which is done to the fig-tree, but also if ye shall say unto this mountain, Be thou removed, and be thou cast into the sea: it shall be done.*
>
> *And all this, whatsoever ye shall ask in prayer, believing, ye shall receive.*

They made no particular impression on him, but it happened that two or three days later, being Sunday, the Canon in residence chose them for the text of his sermon. Even if Philip had wanted to hear this it would have been impossible, for the boys of King's School sit in the choir, and the pulpit stands at the corner of the transept so that the preacher's back is almost turned to them. The distance also is so great that it needs a man with a fine voice and a knowledge of elocution to make himself heard in the choir; and according to long usage the Canons of Tercanbury are chosen for their learning rather than for any qualities which might be of use in a cathedral church. But the words of the text, perhaps because he had read them so short a while before, came clearly enough to Philip's ears, and they seemed on a sudden to have a personal application. He thought about them through most of the sermon, and that night, on getting into bed, he turned over the pages of the gospel and found once more the passage. Though he believed implicitly everything he saw in print, he had learned already that in the Bible things that said one thing quite clearly often mysteriously meant another. There was no one he liked to ask at school, so he kept the question he had in mind till the Christmas holidays, and then one day he made an opportunity. It was after supper and prayers were just finished. Mrs. Carey was counting the eggs that Mary Ann had brought in as usual and writing on each one the date. Philip stood at the table and pretended to turn listlessly the pages of the Bible.

"I say, Uncle William, this passage here, does it really mean that?"

He put his finger against it as though he had come across it accidentally.

Mr. Carey looked up over his spectacles. He was holding *The Blackstable Times* in front of the fire. It had come in that evening damp from the press, and the Vicar always aired it for ten minutes before he began to read.

"What passage is that?" he asked.

"Why, this about if you have faith you can remove

mountains."

"If it says so in the Bible it is so, Philip," said Mrs. Carey gently, taking up the plate-basket.

Philip looked at his uncle for an answer.

"It's a matter of faith."

"D'you mean to say that if you really believed you could move mountains you could?"

"By the grace of God," said the Vicar.

"Now, say good night to your uncle, Philip," said Aunt Louisa. "You're not wanting to move a mountain tonight, are you?"

Philip allowed himself to be kissed on the forehead by his uncle and preceded Mrs. Carey upstairs. He had got the information he wanted. His little room was icy, and he shivered when he put on his nightgown. But he always felt that his prayers were more pleasing to God when he said them under conditions of discomfort. The coldness of his hands and feet were an offering to the Almighty. And tonight he sank on his knees, buried his face in his hands, and prayed to God with all his might that He would make his club-foot whole. It was a very small thing beside the moving of mountains. He knew that God could do it if He wished, and his own faith was complete. Next morning, finishing his prayers with the same request, he fixed a date for the miracle.

"Oh, God, in Thy loving mercy and goodness, if it be Thy will, please make my foot all right on the night before I go back to school."

He was glad to get his petition into a formula, and he repeated it later in the dining-room during the short pause which the Vicar always made after prayers, before he rose from his knees. He said it again in the evening and again, shivering in his nightshirt, before he got into bed. And he believed. For once he looked forward with eagerness to the end of the holidays. He laughed to himself as he thought of his uncle's astonishment when he ran down the stairs three at a time; and after breakfast he and Aunt Louisa would have to hurry out and buy a new pair of boots. At school they would be astounded.

"Hullo, Carey, what have you done with your foot?"

"Oh, it's all right now," he would answer casually, as though it were the most natural thing in the world.

He would be able to play football. His heart leaped as he saw himself running, running, faster than any of the other boys. At the end of the Easter term there were the sports, and he would be able to go in for the races; he rather fancied himself over the hurdles. It would be splendid to be like everyone else, not to be stared at curiously by new boys who did not know about his deformity, nor at the baths in summer to need incredible precautions, while he was undressing, before he could hide his foot in the water.

He prayed with all the power of his soul. No doubts assailed him. He was confident in the word of God. And the night before he was to go back to school he went up to bed tremulous with excitement. There was snow on the ground, and Aunt Louisa had allowed herself the unaccustomed luxury of a fire in her bedroom; but in Philip's little room it was so cold that his fingers were numb, and he had great difficulty in undoing his collar. His teeth chattered. The idea came to him that he must do something more than usual to attract the attention of God, and he turned back the rug which was in front of his bed so that he could kneel on the bare boards; and then it struck him that his nightshirt was a softness that might displease his Maker, so he took it off and said his prayers naked. When he got into bed he was so cold that for some time he could not sleep, but when he did, it was so soundly that Mary Ann had to shake him when she brought in his hot water next morning. She talked to him while she drew the curtains, but he did not answer; he had remembered at once that this was the morning for the miracle. His heart was filled with joy and gratitude. His first instinct was to put down his hand and feel the foot which was whole now, but to do this seemed to doubt the goodness of God. He knew that his foot was well. But at last he made up his mind, and with the toes of his right foot he just touched the ground. Then he passed his hand over it.

He limped downstairs just as Mary Ann was going into the dining-room for prayers, and then he sat down to breakfast.

"You're very quiet this morning, Philip," said Aunt Louisa presently.

"He's thinking of the good breakfast he'll have at school tomorrow," said the Vicar.

When Philip answered, it was in a way that always irritated his uncle, with something that had nothing to do with the matter in hand. He called it a bad habit of wool-gathering.

"Supposing you'd asked God to do something," said Philip, "and really believed it was going to happen, like moving a mountain, I mean, and you had faith, and it didn't happen, what would it mean?"

"What a funny boy you are!" said Aunt Louisa. "You asked about moving mountains two or three weeks ago."

"It would just mean that you hadn't got faith," answered Uncle William.

Philip accepted the explanation. If God had not cured him, it was because he did not really believe. And yet he did not see how he could believe more than he did. But perhaps he had not given God enough time. He had only asked Him for nineteen days. In a day or two he began his prayer again, and this time he fixed upon Easter. That was the day of His Son's glorious resurrection, and God in His happiness might be mercifully inclined. But now Philip added other means of attaining his desire: he began to wish, when he saw a new moon or a dappled horse, and he looked out for shooting stars; during exeat they had a chicken at the vicarage, and he broke the lucky bone with Aunt Louisa and wished again, each time that his foot might be made whole. He was appealing unconsciously to gods older to his race than the God of Israel. And he bombarded the Almighty with his prayer, at odd times of the day, whenever it occurred to him, in identical words always, for it seemed to him important to make his request in the same terms. But presently the feeling came to him that this time also his faith would not be great enough. He could not resist the doubt that assailed him. He made his own experience into a general rule.

"I suppose no one ever has faith enough," he said.

It was like the salt which his nurse used to tell him about: you could catch any bird by putting salt on his tail; and once he had taken a little bag of it into Kensington Gardens. But he could never get near enough to put the salt on a bird's tail. Before Easter he had given up the struggle. He felt a dull resentment against his uncle for taking him in. The text which spoke of the moving of mountains was just one of those that said one thing and meant another. He thought his uncle had been playing a practical joke on him.

Chapter 15

The King's School at Tercanbury, to which Philip went when he was thirteen, prided itself on its antiquity. It traced its origin to an abbey school, founded before the Conquest, where the rudiments of learning were taught by Augustine monks; and, like many another establishment of this sort, on the destruction of the monasteries it had been reorganized by the officers of King Henry VIII and thus acquired its name. Since then, pursuing its modest course, it had given to the sons of the local gentry and of the professional people of Kent an education sufficient to their needs. One or two men of letters, beginning with a poet, than whom only Shakespeare had a more splendid genius, and ending with a writer of prose whose view of life has affected profoundly the generation of which Philip was a member, had gone forth from its gates to achieve fame; it had produced one or two eminent lawyers, but eminent lawyers are common, and one or two soldiers of distinction; but during the three centuries since its separation from the monastic order it had trained especially men of the church, bishops, deans, canons, and above all country clergymen: there were boys in the school whose fathers, grandfathers, great-grandfathers, had been educated there and had all been rectors of parishes in the diocese of Tercanbury; and they came to it with their minds made up already to be ordained. But there were signs notwithstanding that even there changes were coming; for a few, repeating what they had heard at home, said that the Church was no longer what it used to be. It wasn't so much the money; but the class of people who went in for it weren't the same; and two or three boys knew curates whose fathers were tradesmen; they'd rather go out to the Colonies (in those days the Colonies were still the last hope of those who could get nothing to do in England) than be a curate under some chap who wasn't a gentleman. At King's School, as at Blackstable Vicarage, a tradesman was anyone who was not lucky enough to own land (and here a fine distinction was made between the gentleman farmer and the landowner), or did not follow one of the four professions to which it was possible for a gentleman to belong. Among the day-boys, of whom there were about a hundred and fifty, sons of the local gentry and of the men stationed at the depot, those whose fathers were engaged in business were made to feel the degradation of their state.

The masters had no patience with modern ideas of education, which they read of sometimes in *The Times* or *The Guardian*, and hoped fervently that King's School would remain true to its old traditions. The dead languages were taught with such thoroughness that an old boy seldom thought of Homer or Virgil in after life without a qualm of boredom; and though in the common room at dinner one or two bolder spirits suggested that mathematics were of increasing importance, the general feeling was that they were a less noble study than the classics. Neither German nor chemistry was taught, and French only by the form-masters; they could keep order better than a foreigner, and, since they knew the grammar as well as any Frenchman, it seemed unimportant that none of them could have got a cup of coffee in the restaurant at Boulogne unless the waiter had known a little English. Geography was taught chiefly by making boys draw maps, and this was a favourite occupation, especially when the country dealt with was mountainous: it was possible to waste a great deal of time in drawing the Andes or the Apennines. The masters, graduates of Oxford or Cambridge, were ordained and unmarried; if by chance they wished to marry they could only do so by accepting one of the smaller livings at the disposal of the Chapter; but for many years none of them had cared to leave the refined society of Tercanbury, which owing to the cavalry depot had a martial as well as an ecclesiastical tone, for the monotony of life in a country rectory; and they were now all men of middle age.

The headmaster, on the other hand, was obliged to be married, and he conducted the school till age began to tell upon him. When he retired he was rewarded with a much better living than any of the under-masters could hope for, and an honorary Canonry.

But a year before Philip entered the school a great change had come over it. It had been obvious for some time that Dr. Fleming, who had been headmaster for the quarter of a century, was become too deaf to continue his work to the greater glory of

God; and when one of the livings on the outskirts of the city fell vacant, with a stipend of six hundred a year, the Chapter offered it to him in such a manner as to imply that they thought it high time for him to retire. He could nurse his ailments comfortably on such an income. Two or three curates who had hoped for preferment told their wives it was scandalous to give a parish that needed a young, strong, and energetic man to an old fellow who knew nothing of parochial work, and had feathered his nest already; but the mutterings of the unbeneficed clergy do not reach the ears of a cathedral Chapter. And as for the parishioners, they had nothing to say in the matter, and therefore nobody asked for their opinion. The Wesleyans and the Baptists both had chapels in the village.

When Dr. Fleming was thus disposed of it became necessary to find a successor. It was contrary to the traditions of the school that one of the lower-masters should be chosen. The common-room was unanimous in desiring the election of Mr. Watson, headmaster of the preparatory school; he could hardly be described as already a master of King's School, they had all known him for twenty years, and there was no danger that he would make a nuisance of himself. But the Chapter sprang a surprise on them. It chose a man called Perkins. At first nobody knew who Perkins was, and the name favourably impressed no one; but before the shock of it had passed away, it was realized that Perkins was the son of Perkins the linen-draper. Dr. Fleming informed the masters just before dinner, and his manner showed his consternation. Such of them as were dining in, ate their meal almost in silence, and no reference was made to the matter till the servants had left the room. Then they set to. The names of those present on this occasion are unimportant, but they had been known to generations of schoolboys as Sighs, Tar, Winks, Squirts, and Pat.

They all knew Tom Perkins. The first thing about him was that he was not a gentleman. They remembered him quite well. He was a small, dark boy, with untidy black hair and large eyes. He looked like a gipsy. He had come to the school as a day-boy, with the best scholarship on their endowment, so that his education had cost him nothing. Of course he was brilliant. At every Speech-Day he was loaded with prizes. He was their show-boy, and they remembered now bitterly their fear that he would try to get some scholarship at one of the larger public schools and so pass out of their hands. Dr. Fleming had gone to the linen-draper his father—they all remembered the shop, Perkins and Cooper, in St. Catherine's Street—and said he hoped Tom would remain with them till he went to Oxford. The school was Perkins and Cooper's best customer, and Mr. Perkins was only too glad to give the required assurance. Tom Perkins continued to triumph, he was the finest classical scholar that Dr. Fleming remembered, and on leaving the school took with him the most valuable scholarship they had to offer. He got another at Magdalen and settled down to a brilliant career at the University. The school magazine recorded the distinctions he achieved year after year, and when he got his double first Dr. Fleming himself wrote a few words of eulogy on the front page. It was with greater satisfaction that they welcomed his success, since Perkins and Cooper had fallen upon evil days: Cooper drank like a fish, and just before Tom Perkins took his degree the linen-drapers filed their petition in bankruptcy.

In due course Tom Perkins took Holy Orders and entered upon the profession for which he was so admirably suited. He had been an assistant master at Wellington and then at Rugby.

But there was quite a difference between welcoming his success at other schools and serving under his leadership in their own. Tar had frequently given him lines, and Squirts had boxed his ears. They could not imagine how the Chapter had made such a mistake. No one could be expected to forget that he was the son of a bankrupt linen-draper, and the alcoholism of Cooper seemed to increase the disgrace. It was understood that the Dean had supported his candidature with zeal, so the Dean would probably ask him to dinner; but would the pleasant little dinners in the precincts ever be the same when Tom Perkins sat at the table? And what about the depot? He really could not expect officers and gentlemen to receive him as one of themselves. It would do the school incalculable harm. Parents would be dissatisfied, and no one could be surprised if there were wholesale withdrawals. And then the indignity of calling him Mr. Perkins! The masters thought by way of protest of sending in their resignations in a body, but the uneasy fear that they would be accepted with equanimity restrained them.

"The only thing is to prepare ourselves for changes," said Sighs, who had conducted the fifth form for five-and-twenty years with unparalleled incompetence.

And when they saw him they were not reassured. Dr. Fleming invited them to meet him at luncheon. He was now a man of thirty-two, tall and lean, but with the same wild and unkempt look they remembered on him as a boy. His clothes, ill-made and shabby, were put on untidily. His hair was as black and as long as ever, and he had plainly never learned to brush it; it fell over his forehead with every gesture, and he had a quick movement of the hand with which he pushed it back from his eyes. He had a black moustache and a beard which came high up on his face almost to the cheek-bones, He talked to the masters quite easily, as though he had parted from them a week or two before; he was evidently delighted to see them. He seemed unconscious of the strangeness of the position and appeared not to notice any oddness in being addressed as Mr. Perkins.

When he bade them good-bye, one of the masters, for something to say, remarked that he was allowing himself plenty of time to catch his train.

"I want to go round and have a look at the shop," he answered cheerfully.

There was a distinct embarrassment. They wondered that he could be so tactless, and to make it worse Dr. Fleming had not heard what he said. His wife shouted it in his ear.

"He wants to go round and look at his father's old shop."

Only Tom Perkins was unconscious of the humiliation which the whole party felt. He turned to Mrs. Fleming.

"Who's got it now, d'you know?"

She could hardly answer. She was very angry.

"It's still a linen-draper's," she said bitterly. "Grove is the name. We don't deal there any more."

"I wonder if he'd let me go over the house."

"I expect he would if you explain who you are."

It was not till the end of dinner that evening that any

reference was made in the common-room to the subject that was in all their minds. Then it was Sighs who asked:

"Well, what did you think of our new head?"

They thought of the conversation at luncheon. It was hardly a conversation; it was a monologue. Perkins had talked incessantly. He talked very quickly, with a flow of easy words and in a deep, resonant voice. He had a short, odd little laugh which showed his white teeth. They had followed him with difficulty, for his mind darted from subject to subject with a connection they did not always catch. He talked of pedagogics, and this was natural enough; but he had much to say of modern theories in Germany which they had never heard of and received with misgiving. He talked of the classics, but he had been to Greece, and he discoursed of archaeology; he had once spent a winter digging; they could not see how that helped a man to teach boys to pass examinations, He talked of politics. It sounded odd to them to hear him compare Lord Beaconsfield with Alcibiades. He talked of Mr. Gladstone and Home Rule. They realized that he was a Liberal. Their hearts sank. He talked of German philosophy and of French fiction. They could not think a man profound whose interests were so diverse.

It was Winks who summed up the general impression and put it into a form they all felt conclusively damning. Winks was the master of the upper third, a weak-kneed man with drooping eyelids, He was too tall for his strength, and his movements were slow and languid. He gave an impression of lassitude, and his nickname was eminently appropriate.

"He's very enthusiastic," said Winks.

Enthusiasm was ill-bred. Enthusiasm was ungentlemanly. They thought of the Salvation Army with its braying trumpets and its drums. Enthusiasm meant change. They had goose-flesh when they thought of all the pleasant old habits which stood in imminent danger. They hardly dared to look forward to the future.

"He looks more of a gipsy than ever," said one, after a pause.

"I wonder if the Dean and Chapter knew that he was a Radical when they elected him," another observed bitterly.

But conversation halted. They were too much disturbed for words.

When Tar and Sighs were walking together to the Chapter House on Speech-Day a week later, Tar, who had a bitter tongue, remarked to his colleague:

"Well, we've seen a good many Speech-Days here, haven't we? I wonder if we shall see another."

Sighs was more melancholy even than usual.

"If anything worth having comes along in the way of a living I don't mind when I retire."

Chapter 16

A year passed, and when Philip came to the school the old masters were all in their places; but a good many changes had taken place notwithstanding their stubborn resistance, none the less formidable because it was concealed under an apparent desire to fall in with the new head's ideas. Though the form-masters still taught French to the lower school, another master had come, with a degree of doctor of philology from the University of Heidelberg and a record of three years spent in a French *lycée*, to teach French to the upper forms and German to anyone who cared to take it up instead of Greek. Another master was engaged to teach mathematics more systematically than had been found necessary hitherto. Neither of these was ordained. This was a real revolution, and when the pair arrived the older masters received them with distrust. A laboratory had been fitted up, army classes were instituted; they all said the character of the school was changing. And heaven only knew what further projects Mr. Perkins turned in that untidy head of his. The school was small as public schools go, there were not more than two hundred boarders; and it was difficult for it to grow larger, for it was huddled up against the cathedral; the precincts, with the exception of a house in which some of the masters lodged, were occupied by the cathedral clergy; and there was no more room for building. But Mr. Perkins devised an elaborate scheme by which he might obtain sufficient space to make the school double its present size. He wanted to attract boys from London. He thought it would be good for them to be thrown in contact with the Kentish lads, and it would sharpen the country wits of these.

"It's against all our traditions," said Sighs, when Mr. Perkins made the suggestion to him. "We've rather gone out of our way to avoid the contamination of boys from London."

"Oh, what nonsense!" said Mr. Perkins.

No one had ever told the form-master before that he talked nonsense, and he was meditating an acid reply, in which perhaps he might insert a veiled reference to hosiery, when Mr. Perkins in his impetuous way attacked him outrageously.

"That house in the Precincts—if you'd only marry I'd get the Chapter to put another couple of storeys on, and we'd make dormitories and studies, and your wife could help you."

The elderly clergyman gasped. Why should he marry? He was fifty-seven, a man couldn't marry at fifty-seven. He couldn't start looking after a house at his time of life. He didn't want to marry. If the choice lay between that and the country living he would much sooner resign. All he wanted now was peace and quietness.

"I'm not thinking of marrying," he said.

Mr. Perkins looked at him with his dark, bright eyes, and if there was a twinkle in them poor Sighs never saw it.

"What a pity! Couldn't you marry to oblige me? It would help me a great deal with the Dean and Chapter when I suggest rebuilding your house."

But Mr. Perkins's most unpopular innovation was his system of taking occasionally another man's form. He asked it as a favour, but after all it was a favour which could not be refused, and as Tar, otherwise Mr. Turner, said, it was undignified for all parties. He gave no warning, but after morning prayers would say to one of the masters:

"I wonder if you'd mind taking the Sixth today at eleven. We'll change over, shall we?"

They did not know whether this was usual at other schools, but certainly it had never been done at Tercanbury. The results were curious. Mr. Turner, who was the first victim, broke the news to his form that the headmaster would take them for Latin that day, and on the pretence that they might like to ask him a question or two so that they should not make perfect fools of themselves, spent the last quarter of an hour of the history lesson in construing for them the passage of Livy which had been set for the day; but when he rejoined his class and looked at the paper on which Mr. Perkins had written the marks, a surprise awaited him; for the two boys at the top of the form seemed to have done very ill, while others who had never distinguished themselves before were given full marks. When he asked Eldridge, his cleverest boy, what was the meaning of this the answer came sullenly:

"Mr. Perkins never gave us any construing to do. He asked me what I knew about General Gordon."

Mr. Turner looked at him in astonishment. The boys evidently felt they had been hardly used, and he could not help agreeing with their silent dissatisfaction. He could not see either what General Gordon had to do with Livy. He hazarded an inquiry afterwards.

"Eldridge was dreadfully put out because you asked him what he knew about General Gordon," he said to the headmaster, with an attempt at a chuckle.

Mr. Perkins laughed.

"I saw they'd got to the agrarian laws of Caius Gracchus, and I wondered if they knew anything about the agrarian troubles in Ireland. But all they knew about Ireland was that Dublin was on the Liffey. So I wondered if they'd ever heard of General Gordon."

Then the horrid fact was disclosed that the new head had a mania for general information. He had doubts about the utility of examinations on subjects which had been crammed for the occasion. He wanted common sense.

Sighs grew more worried every month; he could not get the thought out of his head that Mr. Perkins would ask him to fix a day for his marriage; and he hated the attitude the head adopted towards classical literature. There was no doubt that he was a fine scholar, and he was engaged on a work which was quite in the right tradition: he was writing a treatise on the trees in Latin literature, but he talked of it flippantly, as though it were a pastime of no great importance, like billiards, which engaged his leisure but was not to be considered with seriousness. And Squirts, the master of the middle-third, grew more ill-tempered every day.

It was in his form that Philip was put on entering the school. The Rev. B. B. Gordon was a man by nature ill-suited to be a schoolmaster: he was impatient and choleric. With no one to call him to account, with only small boys to face him, he had long lost all power of self-control. He began his work in a rage and ended it in a passion. He was a man of middle height and of a corpulent figure; he had sandy hair, worn very short and now growing grey, and a small bristly moustache. His large face, with indistinct features and small blue eyes, was naturally red, but during his frequent attacks of anger it grew dark and purple. His nails were bitten to the quick, for while some trembling boy was construing he would sit at his desk shaking with the fury that consumed him, and gnaw his fingers. Stories, perhaps exaggerated, were told of his violence, and two years before there had been some excitement in the school when it was heard that one father was threatening a prosecution: he had boxed the ears of a boy named Walters with a book so violently that his hearing was affected and the boy had to be taken away from the school. The boy's father lived in Tercanbury, and there had been much indignation in the city, the local paper had referred to the matter; but Mr. Walters was only a brewer, so the sympathy was divided. The rest of the boys, for reasons best known to themselves, though they loathed the master, took his side in the affair, and, to show their indignation that the school's business had been dealt with outside, made things as uncomfortable as they could for Walters's younger brother, who still remained. But Mr. Gordon had only escaped the country living by the skin of his teeth, and he had never hit a boy since. The right the masters possessed to cane boys on the hand was taken away from them, and Squirts could no longer emphasize his anger by beating his desk with the cane. He never did more now than take a boy by the shoulders and shake him. He still made a naughty or refractory lad stand with one arm stretched out for anything from ten minutes to half an hour, and he was as violent as before with his tongue.

No master could have been more unfitted to teach things to so shy a boy as Philip. He had come to the school with fewer terrors than he had when he first went to Mr. Watson's. He knew a good many boys who had been with him at the preparatory school. He felt more grown-up, and instinctively realized that among the larger numbers his deformity would be less noticeable. But from the first day Mr. Gordon struck terror in his heart; and the master, quick to discern the boys who were frightened of him, seemed on that account to take a peculiar dislike to him. Philip had enjoyed his work, but now he began to look upon the hours passed in school with horror. Rather than risk an answer which might be wrong and excite a storm of abuse from the master, he would sit stupidly silent, and when it came towards his turn to stand up and construe he became sick with apprehension. His happy moments were those when Mr. Perkins took the form. He was able to gratify the passion for general knowledge which beset the headmaster; he had read all sorts of strange books beyond his years, and often Mr. Perkins, when a question was going round the room, would stop at Philip with a smile that filled the boy with rapture, and say:

"Now, Carey, you tell them."

The good marks he got on these occasions increased Mr.

Gordon's indignation. One day it came to Philip's turn to translate, and the master sat there glaring at him and furiously biting his thumb. He was in a ferocious mood. Philip began to speak in a low voice.

"Don't mumble," shouted the master.

Something seemed to stick in Philip's throat.

"Go on. Go on. Go on."

Each time the words were screamed more loudly. The effect was to drive all he knew out of Philip's head, and he looked at the printed page vacantly. Mr. Gordon began to breathe heavily.

"If you don't know why don't you say so? Do you know it or not? Did you hear all this construed last time or not? Why don't you speak? Speak, you blockhead, speak!"

The master seized the arms of his chair and grasped them as though to prevent himself from falling upon Philip. They knew that in past days he often used to seize boys by the throat till they almost choked. The veins in his forehead stood out and his face grew dark and threatening. He was a man insane.

Philip had known the passage perfectly the day before, but now he could remember nothing.

"I don't know it," he gasped.

"Why don't you know it? Let's take the words one by one. We'll soon see if you don't know it."

Philip stood silent, very white, trembling a little, with his head bent down on the book. The master's breathing grew almost stertorous.

"The headmaster says you're clever. I don't know how he sees it. General information." He laughed savagely. "I don't know what they put you in his form for. Blockhead."

He was pleased with the word and he repeated it at the top of his voice.

"Blockhead! Blockhead! Club-footed blockhead!"

That relieved him a little. He saw Philip redden suddenly. He told him to fetch the Black Book. Philip put down his Caesar and went silently out. The Black Book was a sombre volume in which the names of boys were written with their misdeeds, and when a name was down three times it meant a caning. Philip went to the headmaster's house and knocked at his study-door. Mr. Perkins was seated at his table.

"May I have the Black Book, please, sir."

"There it is," answered Mr. Perkins, indicating its place by a nod of his head. "What have you been doing that you shouldn't?"

"I don't know, sir."

Mr. Perkins gave him a quick look, but without answering went on with his work. Philip took the book and went out. When the hour was up, a few minutes later, he brought it back.

"Let me have a look at it," said the headmaster. "I see Mr. Gordon has black-booked you for 'gross impertinence.' What was it?"

"I don't know, sir. Mr. Gordon said I was a club-footed blockhead."

Mr. Perkins looked at him again. He wondered whether there was sarcasm behind the boy's reply, but he was still much too shaken. His face was white and his eyes had a look of terrified distress. Mr. Perkins got up and put the book down. As he did so he took up some photographs.

"A friend of mine sent me some pictures of Athens this morning," he said casually. "Look here, there's the Acropolis."

He began explaining to Philip what he saw. The ruin grew vivid with his words. He showed him the theatre of Dionysus and explained in what order the people sat, and how beyond they could see the blue Aegean. And then suddenly he said:

"I remember Mr. Gordon used to call me a gipsy counter-jumper when I was in his form."

And before Philip, his mind fixed on the photographs, had time to gather the meaning of the remark, Mr. Perkins was showing him a picture of Salamis, and with his finger, a finger of which the nail had a little black edge to it, was pointing out how the Greek ships were placed and how the Persian.

Chapter 17

Philip passed the next two years with comfortable monotony. He was not bullied more than other boys of his size; and his deformity, withdrawing him from games, acquired for him an insignificance for which he was grateful. He was not popular, and he was very lonely. He spent a couple of terms with Winks in the Upper Third. Winks, with his weary manner and his drooping eyelids, looked infinitely bored. He did his duty, but he did it with an abstracted mind. He was kind, gentle, and foolish. He had a great belief in the honour of boys; he felt that the first thing to make them truthful was not to let it enter your head for a moment that it was possible for them to lie. "Ask much," he quoted, "and much shall be given to you." Life was easy in the Upper Third. You knew exactly what lines would come to your turn to construe, and with the crib that passed from hand to hand you could find out all you wanted in two minutes; you could hold a Latin Grammar open on your knees while questions were passing round; and Winks never noticed anything odd in the fact that the same incredible mistake was to be found in a dozen different exercises. He had no great faith in examinations, for he noticed that boys never did so well in them as in form: it was disappointing, but not significant. In due course they were moved up, having learned little but a cheerful effrontery in the distortion of truth, which was possibly of greater service to them in after life than an ability to read Latin at sight.

Then they fell into the hands of Tar. His name was Turner; he was the most vivacious of the old masters, a short man with an immense belly, a black beard turning now to grey, and a swarthy skin. In his clerical dress there was indeed something in him to suggest the tar-barrel; and though on principle he gave five hundred lines to any boy on whose lips he overheard his nickname, at dinner parties in the precincts he often made little jokes about it. He was the most worldly of the masters; he dined out more frequently than any of the others, and the society he kept was not so exclusively clerical. The boys looked upon him as rather a dog. He left off his clerical attire during the holidays and had been seen in Switzerland in gay tweeds. He liked a bottle of wine and a good dinner, and having once been seen at the Café Royal with a lady who was very probably a near relation, was thenceforward supposed by generations of schoolboys to indulge in orgies the circumstantial details of which pointed to an unbounded belief in human depravity.

Mr. Turner reckoned that it took him a term to lick boys into shape after they had been in the Upper Third; and now and then he let fall a sly hint, which showed that he knew perfectly what went on in his colleague's form. He took it good-humouredly. He looked upon boys as young ruffians who were more apt to be truthful if it was quite certain a lie would be found out, whose sense of honour was peculiar to themselves and did not apply to dealings with masters, and who were least likely to be troublesome when they learned that it did not pay. He was proud of his form and as eager at fifty-five that it should do better in examinations than any of the others as he had been when he first came to the school. He had the choler of the obese, easily roused and as easily calmed, and his boys soon discovered that there was much kindliness beneath the invective with which he constantly assailed them. He had no patience with fools, but was willing to take much trouble with boys whom he suspected of concealing intelligence behind their wilfulness. He was fond of inviting them to tea; and, though vowing they never got a look in with him at the cakes and muffins, for it was the fashion to believe that his corpulence pointed to a voracious appetite, and his voracious appetite to tapeworms, they accepted his invitations with real pleasure.

Philip was now more comfortable, for space was so limited that there were only studies for boys in the upper school, and till then he had lived in the great hall in which they all ate and in which the lower forms did preparation in a promiscuity which was vaguely distasteful to him. Now and then it made him restless to be with people and he wanted urgently to be alone. He set out for solitary walks into the country. There was a little stream, with pollards on both sides of it, that ran through green fields, and it made him happy, he knew not why, to wander along its banks. When he was tired he lay face-downward on the grass and watched the eager scurrying of minnows and of tadpoles. It gave him a peculiar satisfaction to saunter round the precincts.

On the green in the middle they practised at nets in the summer, but during the rest of the year it was quiet: boys used to wander round sometimes arm in arm, or a studious fellow with abstracted gaze walked slowly, repeating to himself something he had to learn by heart. There was a colony of rooks in the great elms, and they filled the air with melancholy cries. Along one side lay the Cathedral with its great central tower, and Philip, who knew as yet nothing of beauty, felt when he looked at it a troubling delight which he could not understand. When he had a study (it was a little square room looking on a slum, and four boys shared it), he bought a photograph of that view of the Cathedral, and pinned it up over his desk. And he found himself taking a new interest in what he saw from the window of the Fourth Form room. It looked on to old lawns, carefully tended, and fine trees with foliage dense and rich. It gave him an odd feeling in his heart, and he did not know if it was pain or pleasure. It was the first dawn of the aesthetic emotion. It accompanied other changes. His voice broke. It was no longer quite under his control, and queer sounds issued from his throat.

Then he began to go to the classes which were held in the headmaster's study, immediately after tea, to prepare boys for confirmation. Philip's piety had not stood the test of time, and he had long since given up his nightly reading of the Bible; but now, under the influence of Mr. Perkins, with this new condition of the body which made him so restless, his old feelings revived, and he reproached himself bitterly for his backsliding. The fires of Hell burned fiercely before his mind's eye. If he had died during that time when he was little better than an infidel he would have been lost; he believed implicitly in pain everlasting, he believed in it much more than in eternal happiness; and he shuddered at the dangers he had run.

Since the day on which Mr. Perkins had spoken kindly to him, when he was smarting under the particular form of abuse which he could least bear, Philip had conceived for his headmaster a dog-like adoration. He racked his brains vainly for some way to please him. He treasured the smallest word of commendation which by chance fell from his lips. And when he came to the quiet little meetings in his house he was prepared to surrender himself entirely. He kept his eyes fixed on Mr. Perkins' shining eyes, and sat with mouth half open, his head a little thrown forward so as to miss no word. The ordinariness of the surroundings made the matters they dealt with extraordinarily moving. And often the master, seized himself by the wonder of his subject, would push back the book in front of him, and with his hands clasped together over his heart, as though to still the beating, would talk of the mysteries of their religion. Sometimes Philip did not understand, but he did not want to understand, he felt vaguely that it was enough to feel. It seemed to him then that the headmaster, with his black, straggling hair and his pale face, was like those prophets of Israel who feared not to take kings to task; and when he thought of the Redeemer he saw Him only with the same dark eyes and those wan cheeks.

Mr. Perkins took this part of his work with great seriousness. There was never here any of that flashing humour which made the other masters suspect him of flippancy. Finding time for everything in his busy day, he was able at certain intervals to take separately for a quarter of an hour or twenty minutes the boys whom he was preparing for confirmation. He wanted to make them feel that this was the first consciously serious step in their lives; he tried to grope into the depths of their souls; he wanted to instil in them his own vehement devotion. In Philip, notwithstanding his shyness, he felt the possibility of a passion equal to his own. The boy's temperament seemed to him essentially religious. One day he broke off suddenly from the subject on which he had been talking.

"Have you thought at all what you're going to be when you grow up?" he asked.

"My uncle wants me to be ordained," said Philip.

"And you?"

Philip looked away. He was ashamed to answer that he felt himself unworthy.

"I don't know any life that's so full of happiness as ours. I wish I could make you feel what a wonderful privilege it is. One can serve God in every walk, but we stand nearer to Him. I don't want to influence you, but if you made up your mind—oh, at once—you couldn't help feeling that joy and relief which never desert one again."

Philip did not answer, but the headmaster read in his eyes that he realized already something of what he tried to indicate.

"If you go on as you are now you'll find yourself head of the school one of these days, and you ought to be pretty safe for a scholarship when you leave. Have you got anything of your own?"

"My uncle says I shall have a hundred a year when I'm twenty-one."

"You'll be rich. I had nothing."

The headmaster hesitated a moment, and then, idly drawing lines with a pencil on the blotting paper in front of him, went on.

"I'm afraid your choice of professions will be rather limited. You naturally couldn't go in for anything that required physical activity."

Philip reddened to the roots of his hair, as he always did when any reference was made to his club-foot. Mr. Perkins looked at him gravely.

"I wonder if you're not oversensitive about your misfortune. Has it ever struck you to thank God for it?"

Philip looked up quickly. His lips tightened. He remembered how for months, trusting in what they told him, he had implored God to heal him as He had healed the Leper and made the Blind to see.

"As long as you accept it rebelliously it can only cause you shame. But if you looked upon it as a cross that was given you to bear only because your shoulders were strong enough to bear it, a sign of God's favour, then it would be a source of happiness to you instead of misery."

He saw that the boy hated to discuss the matter and he let him go.

But Philip thought over all that the headmaster had said, and presently, his mind taken up entirely with the ceremony that was before him, a mystical rapture seized him. His spirit seemed to free itself from the bonds of the flesh and he seemed to be living a new life. He aspired to perfection with all the passion that was in him. He wanted to surrender himself entirely to the service of God, and he made up his mind definitely that he would be ordained. When the great day arrived, his soul deeply moved by all the preparation, by the books he had studied, and above all by the overwhelming influence of the head, he could hardly contain himself for fear and joy. One thought had tormented him. He knew that he would have to walk alone through the chancel, and he dreaded showing his limp thus obviously, not only to the whole school, who were attending the service, but also to the strangers, people from the city or parents who had come to see their sons confirmed. But when the time came he felt suddenly that he could accept the humiliation joyfully; and as he limped up the chancel, very small and insignificant beneath the lofty vaulting of the Cathedral, he offered consciously his deformity as a sacrifice to the God who loved him.

Chapter 18

But Philip could not live long in the rarefied air of the hilltops. What had happened to him when first he was seized by the religious emotion happened to him now. Because he felt so keenly the beauty of faith, because the desire for self-sacrifice burned in his heart with such a gem-like glow, his strength seemed inadequate to his ambition. He was tired out by the violence of his passion. His soul was filled on a sudden with a singular aridity. He began to forget the presence of God which had seemed so surrounding; and his religious exercises, still very punctually performed, grew merely formal. At first he blamed himself for this falling away, and the fear of hell-fire urged him to renewed vehemence; but the passion was dead, and gradually other interests distracted his thoughts.

Philip had few friends. His habit of reading isolated him: it became such a need that after being in company for some time he grew tired and restless; he was vain of the wider knowledge he had acquired from the perusal of so many books, his mind was alert, and he had not the skill to hide his contempt for his companions' stupidity. They complained that he was conceited; and, since he excelled only in matters which to them were unimportant, they asked satirically what he had to be conceited about. He was developing a sense of humour, and found that he had a knack of saying bitter things, which caught people on the raw; he said them because they amused him, hardly realizing how much they hurt, and was much offended when he found that his victims regarded him with active dislike. The humiliations he suffered when first he went to school had caused in him a shrinking from his fellows which he could never entirely overcome; he remained shy and silent. But though he did everything to alienate the sympathy of other boys he longed with all his heart for the popularity which to some was so easily accorded. These from his distance he admired extravagantly; and though he was inclined to be more sarcastic with them than with others, though he made little jokes at their expense, he would have given anything to change places with them. Indeed he would gladly have changed places with the dullest boy in the school who was whole of limb. He took to a singular habit. He would imagine that he was some boy whom he had a particular fancy for; he would throw his soul, as it were, into the other's body, talk with his voice and laugh with his laugh; he would imagine himself doing all the things the other did. It was so vivid that he seemed for a moment really to be no longer himself. In this way he enjoyed many intervals of fantastic happiness.

At the beginning of the Christmas term which followed on his confirmation Philip found himself moved into another study. One of the boys who shared it was called Rose. He was in the same form as Philip, and Philip had always looked upon him

Chapter 19

At first Philip had been too grateful for Rose's friendship to make any demands on him. He took things as they came and enjoyed life. But presently he began to resent Rose's universal amiability; he wanted a more exclusive attachment, and he claimed as a right what before he had accepted as a favour. He watched jealously Rose's companionship with others; and though he knew it was unreasonable could not help sometimes saying bitter things to him. If Rose spent an hour playing the fool in another study, Philip would receive him when he returned to his own with a sullen frown. He would sulk for a day, and he suffered more because Rose either did not notice his ill-humour or deliberately ignored it. Not seldom Philip, knowing all the time how stupid he was, would force a quarrel, and they would not speak to one another for a couple of days. But Philip could not bear to be angry with him long, and even when convinced that he was in the right, would apologize humbly. Then for a week they would be as great friends as ever. But the best was over, and Philip could see that Rose often walked with him merely from old habit or from fear of his anger; they had not so much to say to one another as at first, and Rose was often bored. Philip felt that his lameness began to irritate him.

Towards the end of the term two or three boys caught scarlet fever, and there was much talk of sending them all home in order to escape an epidemic; but the sufferers were isolated, and since no more were attacked it was supposed that the outbreak was stopped. One of the stricken was Philip. He remained in hospital through the Easter holidays, and at the beginning of the summer term was sent home to the vicarage to get a little fresh air. The Vicar, notwithstanding medical assurance that the boy was no longer infectious, received him with suspicion; he thought it very inconsiderate of the doctor to suggest that his nephew's convalescence should be spent by the seaside, and consented to have him in the house only because there was nowhere else he could go.

Philip went back to school at half-term. He had forgotten the quarrels he had had with Rose, but remembered only that he was his greatest friend. He knew that he had been silly. He made up his mind to be more reasonable. During his illness Rose had sent him in a couple of little notes, and he had ended each with the words: "Hurry up and come back." Philip thought Rose must be looking forward as much to his return as he was himself to seeing Rose.

He found that owing to the death from scarlet fever of one of the boys in the Sixth there had been some shifting in the studies and Rose was no longer in his. It was a bitter disappointment. But as soon as he arrived he burst into Rose's study. Rose was sitting at his desk, working with a boy called Hunter, and turned round crossly as Philip came in.

"Who the devil's that?" he cried. And then, seeing Philip: "Oh, it's you."

Philip stopped in embarrassment.

"I thought I'd come in and see how you were."

"We were just working."

Hunter broke into the conversation.

"When did you get back?"

"Five minutes ago."

They sat and looked at him as though he was disturbing them. They evidently expected him to go quickly. Philip reddened.

"I'll be off. You might look in when you've done," he said to Rose.

"All right."

Philip closed the door behind him and limped back to his own study. He felt frightfully hurt. Rose, far from seeming glad to see him, had looked almost put out. They might never have been more than acquaintances. Though he waited in his study, not leaving it for a moment in case just then Rose should come, his friend never appeared; and next morning when he went into prayers he saw Rose and Hunter swinging along arm in arm. What he could not see for himself others told him. He had forgotten that three months is a long time in a schoolboy's life, and though he had passed them in solitude Rose had lived in the world. Hunter had stepped into the vacant place. Philip found that Rose was quietly avoiding him. But he was not the boy to accept a situation without putting it into words; he waited till he was sure

Rose was alone in his study and went in.

"May I come in?" he asked.

Rose looked at him with an embarrassment that made him angry with Philip.

"Yes, if you want to."

"It's very kind of you," said Philip sarcastically.

"What d'you want?"

"I say, why have you been so rotten since I came back?"

"Oh, don't be an ass," said Rose.

"I don't know what you see in Hunter."

"That's my business."

Philip looked down. He could not bring himself to say what was in his heart. He was afraid of humiliating himself. Rose got up.

"I've got to go to the Gym," he said.

When he was at the door Philip forced himself to speak.

"I say, Rose, don't be a perfect beast."

"Oh, go to hell."

Rose slammed the door behind him and left Philip alone. Philip shivered with rage. He went back to his study and turned the conversation over in his mind. He hated Rose now, he wanted to hurt him, he thought of biting things he might have said to him. He brooded over the end to their friendship and fancied that others were talking of it. In his sensitiveness he saw sneers and wonderings in other fellows' manner when they were not bothering their heads with him at all. He imagined to himself what they were saying.

"After all, it wasn't likely to last long. I wonder he ever stuck

Carey at all. Blighter!"

To show his indifference he struck up a violent friendship with a boy called Sharp whom he hated and despised. He was a London boy, with a loutish air, a heavy fellow with the beginnings of a moustache on his lip and bushy eyebrows that joined one another across the bridge of his nose. He had soft hands and manners too suave for his years. He spoke with the suspicion of a cockney accent. He was one of those boys who are too slack to play games, and he exercised great ingenuity in making excuses to avoid such as were compulsory. He was regarded by boys and masters with a vague dislike, and it was from arrogance that Philip now sought his society. Sharp in a couple of terms was going to Germany for a year. He hated school, which he looked upon as an indignity to be endured till he was old enough to go out into the world. London was all he cared for, and he had many stories to tell of his doings there during the holidays. From his conversation— he spoke in a soft, deep-toned voice—there emerged the vague rumour of the London streets by night. Philip listened to him at once fascinated and repelled. With his vivid fancy he seemed to see the surging throng round the pit-door of theatres, and the glitter of cheap restaurants, bars where men, half drunk, sat on high stools talking with barmaids; and under the street lamps the mysterious passing of dark crowds bent upon pleasure. Sharp lent him cheap novels from Holywell Street, which Philip read in his cubicle with a sort of wonderful fear.

Once Rose tried to effect a reconciliation. He was a good-natured fellow, who did not like having enemies.

"I say, Carey, why are you being such a silly ass? It doesn't do you any good cutting me and all that."

"I don't know what you mean," answered Philip.

"Well, I don't see why we shouldn't talk."

"You bore me," said Philip.

"Please yourself."

Rose shrugged his shoulders and left him. Philip was very white, as he always became when he was moved, and his heart beat violently. When Rose went away he felt suddenly sick with misery. He did not know why he had answered in that fashion. He would have given anything to be friends with Rose. He hated to have quarrelled with him, and now that he saw he had given him pain he was very sorry. But at the moment he had not been master of himself. It seemed that some devil had seized him, forcing him to say bitter things against his will, even though at the time he wanted to shake hands with Rose and meet him more than halfway. The desire to wound had been too strong for him. He had wanted to revenge himself for the pain and the humiliation he had endured. It was pride: it was folly too, for he knew that Rose would not care at all, while he would suffer bitterly. The thought came to him that he would go to Rose, and say:

"I say, I'm sorry I was such a beast. I couldn't help it. Let's make it up."

But he knew he would never be able to do it. He was afraid that Rose would sneer at him. He was angry with himself, and when Sharp came in a little while afterwards he seized upon the first opportunity to quarrel with him. Philip had a fiendish instinct for discovering other people's raw spots, and was able to say things that rankled because they were true. But Sharp had the last word.

"I heard Rose talking about you to Mellor just now," he said. "Mellor said: Why didn't you kick him? It would teach him manners. And Rose said: I didn't like to. Damned cripple."

Philip suddenly became scarlet. He could not answer, for there was a lump in his throat that almost choked him.

Chapter 20

Philip was moved into the Sixth, but he hated school now with all his heart, and, having lost his ambition, cared nothing whether he did ill or well. He awoke in the morning with a sinking heart because he must go through another day of drudgery. He was tired of having to do things because he was told; and the restrictions irked him, not because they were unreasonable, but because they were restrictions. He yearned for freedom. He was weary of repeating things that he knew already and of the hammering away, for the sake of a thick-witted fellow, at something that he understood from the beginning.

With Mr. Perkins you could work or not as you chose. He was at once eager and abstracted. The Sixth Form room was in a part of the old abbey which had been restored, and it had a Gothic window: Philip tried to cheat his boredom by drawing this over and over again; and sometimes out of his head he drew the great tower of the Cathedral or the gateway that led into the precincts. He had a knack for drawing. Aunt Louisa during her youth had painted in water colours, and she had several albums filled with sketches of churches, old bridges, and picturesque cottages. They were often shown at the vicarage tea-parties. She had once given Philip a paint-box as a Christmas present, and he had started by copying her pictures. He copied them better than anyone could have expected, and presently he did little pictures of his own. Mrs. Carey encouraged him. It was a good way to keep him out of mischief, and later on his sketches would be useful for bazaars. Two or three of them had been framed and hung in his bedroom.

But one day, at the end of the morning's work, Mr. Perkins stopped him as he was lounging out of the form-room.

"I want to speak to you, Carey."

Philip waited. Mr. Perkins ran his lean fingers through his beard and looked at Philip. He seemed to be thinking over what he wanted to say.

"What's the matter with you, Carey?" he said abruptly.

Philip, flushing, looked at him quickly. But knowing him well by now, without answering, he waited for him to go on.

"I've been dissatisfied with you lately. You've been slack and inattentive. You seem to take no interest in your work. It's been slovenly and bad."

"I'm very sorry, sir," said Philip.

"Is that all you have to say for yourself?"

Philip looked down sulkily. How could he answer that he was bored to death?

"You know, this term you'll go down instead of up. I shan't give you a very good report."

Philip wondered what he would say if he knew how the report was treated. It arrived at breakfast, Mr. Carey glanced at it indifferently, and passed it over to Philip.

"There's your report. You'd better see what it says," he remarked, as he ran his fingers through the wrapper of a catalogue of second-hand books.

Philip read it.

"Is it good?" asked Aunt Louisa.

"Not so good as I deserve," answered Philip, with a smile, giving it to her.

"I'll read it afterwards when I've got my spectacles," she said.

But after breakfast Mary Ann came in to say the butcher was there, and she generally forgot.

Mr. Perkins went on.

"I'm disappointed with you. And I can't understand. I know you *can* do things if you want to, but you don't seem to want to any more. I was going to make you a monitor next term, but I think I'd better wait a bit."

Philip flushed. He did not like the thought of being passed over. He tightened his lips.

"And there's something else. You must begin thinking of your scholarship now. You won't get anything unless you start working very seriously."

Philip was irritated by the lecture. He was angry with the headmaster, and angry with himself.

"I don't think I'm going up to Oxford," he said.

"Why not? I thought your idea was to be ordained."

"I've changed my mind."

"Why?"

Philip did not answer. Mr. Perkins, holding himself oddly as he always did, like a figure in one of Perugino's pictures, drew his fingers thoughtfully through his beard. He looked at Philip as though he were trying to understand and then abruptly told him he might go.

Apparently he was not satisfied, for one evening, a week later, when Philip had to go into his study with some papers, he resumed the conversation; but this time he adopted a different method: he spoke to Philip not as a schoolmaster with a boy but as one human being with another. He did not seem to care now that Philip's work was poor, that he ran small chance against keen rivals of carrying off the scholarship necessary for him to go to Oxford: the important matter was his changed intention about his life afterwards. Mr. Perkins set himself to revive his eagerness to be ordained. With infinite skill he worked on his feelings, and this was easier since he was himself genuinely moved. Philip's change of mind caused him bitter distress, and he really thought he was throwing away his chance of happiness in life for he knew not what. His voice was very persuasive. And Philip, easily moved by the emotion of others, very emotional himself notwithstanding a placid exterior—his face, partly by nature but also from the habit of all these years at school, seldom except by his quick flushing showed what he felt—Philip was deeply touched by what the master said. He was very grateful to him for the interest he showed, and he was conscience-stricken by the grief which he felt his behaviour caused him. It was subtly flattering to know that with the whole school to think about Mr. Perkins should trouble with him, but at the same time something else in him, like another person standing at his elbow, clung desperately to two words.

"I won't. I won't. I won't."

He felt himself slipping. He was powerless against the weakness that seemed to well up in him; it was like the water that rises up in an empty bottle held over a full basin; and he set his teeth, saying the words over and over to himself.

"I won't. I won't. I won't."

At last Mr. Perkins put his hand on Philip's shoulder.

"I don't want to influence you," he said. "You must decide for yourself. Pray to Almighty God for help and guidance."

When Philip came out of the headmaster's house there was a light rain falling. He went under the archway that led to the precincts, there was not a soul there, and the rooks were silent in the elms. He walked round slowly. He felt hot, and the rain did him good. He thought over all that Mr. Perkins had said, calmly now that he was withdrawn from the fervour of his personality, and he was thankful he had not given way.

In the darkness he could but vaguely see the great mass of the Cathedral: he hated it now because of the irksomeness of the long services which he was forced to attend. The anthem was interminable, and you had to stand drearily while it was being sung; you could not hear the droning sermon, and your body twitched because you had to sit still when you wanted to move about. Then Philip thought of the two services every Sunday at Blackstable. The church was bare and cold, and there was a smell all about one of pomade and starched clothes. The curate preached once and his uncle preached once. As he grew up he had learned to know his uncle; Philip was downright and intolerant, and he could not understand that a man might sincerely say things as a clergyman which he never acted up to as a man. The deception outraged him. His uncle was a weak and selfish man, whose chief desire it was to be saved trouble.

Mr. Perkins had spoken to him of the beauty of a life dedicated to the service of God. Philip knew what sort of lives the clergy led in the corner of East Anglia which was his home. There was the Vicar of Whitestone, a parish a little way from Blackstable: he was a bachelor and to give himself something to do had lately taken up farming: the local paper constantly reported the cases he had in the county court against this one and that, labourers he would not pay their wages to or tradesmen whom he accused of cheating him; scandal said he starved his cows, and there was much talk about some general action which should be taken against him. Then there was the Vicar of Ferne, a bearded, fine figure of a man: his wife had been forced to leave him because of his cruelty, and she had filled the neighbourhood with stories of his immorality. The Vicar of Surle, a tiny hamlet by the sea, was to be seen every evening in the public house a stone's throw from his vicarage; and the churchwardens had been to Mr. Carey to ask his advice. There was not a soul for any of them to talk to except small farmers or fishermen; there were long winter evenings when the wind blew, whistling drearily through the leafless trees, and all around they saw nothing but the bare monotony of ploughed fields; and there was poverty, and there was lack of any work that seemed to matter; every kink in their characters had free play; there was nothing to restrain them; they grew narrow and eccentric: Philip knew all this, but in his young intolerance he did not offer it as an excuse. He shivered at the thought of leading such a life; he wanted to get out into the world.

Chapter 21

Mr. Perkins soon saw that his words had had no effect on Philip, and for the rest of the term ignored him. He wrote a report which was vitriolic. When it arrived and Aunt Louisa asked Philip what it was like, he answered cheerfully:

"Rotten."

"Is it?" said the Vicar. "I must look at it again."

"Do you think there's any use in my staying on at Tercanbury? I should have thought it would be better if I went to Germany for a bit."

"What has put that in your head?" said Aunt Louisa.

"Don't you think it's rather a good idea?"

Sharp had already left King's School and had written to Philip from Hanover. He was really starting life, and it made Philip more restless to think of it. He felt he could not bear another year of restraint.

"But then you wouldn't get a scholarship."

"I haven't a chance of getting one anyhow. And besides, I don't know that I particularly want to go to Oxford."

"But if you're going to be ordained, Philip?" Aunt Louisa exclaimed in dismay.

"I've given up that idea long ago."

Mrs. Carey looked at him with startled eyes, and then, used to self-restraint, she poured out another cup of tea for his uncle. They did not speak. In a moment Philip saw tears slowly falling down her cheeks. His heart was suddenly wrung because he caused her pain. In her tight black dress, made by the dressmaker down the street, with her wrinkled face and pale tired eyes, her grey hair still done in the frivolous ringlets of her youth, she was a ridiculous but strangely pathetic figure. Philip saw it for the first time.

Afterwards, when the Vicar was shut up in his study with the curate, he put his arms round her waist.

"I say, I'm sorry you're upset, Aunt Louisa," he said. "But it's no good my being ordained if I haven't a real vocation, is it?"

"I'm so disappointed, Philip," she moaned. "I'd set my heart on it. I thought you could be your uncle's curate, and then when our time came—after all, we can't last for ever, can we?—you might have taken his place."

Philip shivered. He was seized with panic. His heart beat like a pigeon in a trap beating with its wings. His aunt wept softly, her head upon his shoulder.

"I wish you'd persuade Uncle William to let me leave Tercanbury. I'm so sick of it."

But the Vicar of Blackstable did not easily alter any arrangements he had made, and it had always been intended that Philip should stay at King's School till he was eighteen, and should then go to Oxford. At all events he would not hear of Philip leaving then, for no notice had been given and the term's fee would have to be paid in any case.

"Then will you give notice for me to leave at Christmas?" said Philip, at the end of a long and often bitter conversation.

"I'll write to Mr. Perkins about it and see what he says."

"Oh, I wish to goodness I were twenty-one. It is awful to be at somebody else's beck and call."

"Philip, you shouldn't speak to your uncle like that," said Mrs. Carey gently.

"But don't you see that Perkins will want me to stay? He gets so much a head for every chap in the school."

"Why don't you want to go to Oxford?"

"What's the good if I'm not going into the Church?"

"You can't go into the Church: you're in the Church already," said the Vicar.

"Ordained then," replied Philip impatiently.

"What are you going to be, Philip?" asked Mrs. Carey.

"I don't know. I've not made up my mind. But whatever I am, it'll be useful to know foreign languages. I shall get far more out of a year in Germany than by staying on at that hole."

He would not say that he felt Oxford would be little better than a continuation of his life at school. He wished immensely to be his own master. Besides he would be known to a certain extent among old schoolfellows, and he wanted to get away from them all. He felt that his life at school had been a failure. He wanted to start fresh.

It happened that his desire to go to Germany fell in with certain ideas which had been of late discussed at Blackstable.

Sometimes friends came to stay with the doctor and brought news of the world outside; and the visitors spending August by the sea had their own way of looking at things. The Vicar had heard that there were people who did not think the old-fashioned education so useful nowadays as it had been in the past, and modern languages were gaining an importance which they had not had in his own youth. His own mind was divided, for a younger brother of his had been sent to Germany when he failed in some examination, thus creating a precedent, but since he had there died of typhoid it was impossible to look upon the experiment as other than dangerous. The result of innumerable conversations was that Philip should go back to Tercanbury for another term and then should leave. With this agreement Philip was not dissatisfied. But when he had been back a few days the headmaster spoke to him.

"I've had a letter from your uncle. It appears you want to go to Germany, and he asks me what I think about it."

Philip was astounded. He was furious with his guardian for going back on his word.

"I thought it was settled, sir," he said.

"Far from it. I've written to say I think it the greatest mistake to take you away."

Philip immediately sat down and wrote a violent letter to his uncle. He did not measure his language. He was so angry that he could not get to sleep till quite late that night, and he awoke in the early morning and began brooding over the way they had treated him. He waited impatiently for an answer. In two or three days it came. It was a mild, pained letter from Aunt Louisa, saying that he should not write such things to his uncle, who was very much distressed. He was unkind and unchristian. He must know they were only trying to do their best for him, and they were so much older than he that they must be better judges of what was good for him. Philip clenched his hands. He had heard that statement so often, and he could not see why it was true; they did not know the conditions as he did, why should they accept it as self-evident that their greater age gave them greater wisdom? The letter ended with the information that Mr. Carey had withdrawn the notice he had given.

Philip nursed his wrath till the next half-holiday. They had them on Tuesdays and Thursdays, since on Saturday afternoons they had to go to a service in the Cathedral. He stopped behind when the rest of the Sixth went out.

"May I go to Blackstable this afternoon, please, sir?" he asked.

"No," said the headmaster briefly.

"I wanted to see my uncle about something very important."

"Didn't you hear me say no?"

Philip did not answer. He went out. He felt almost sick with humiliation, the humiliation of having to ask and the humiliation of the curt refusal. He hated the headmaster now. Philip writhed under that despotism which never vouchsafed a reason for the most tyrannous act. He was too angry to care what he did, and after dinner walked down to the station, by the back ways he knew so well, just in time to catch the train to Blackstable. He walked into the vicarage and found his uncle and aunt sitting in the dining-room.

"Hullo, where have you sprung from?" said the Vicar.

It was very clear that he was not pleased to see him. He

looked a little uneasy.

"I thought I'd come and see you about my leaving. I want to know what you mean by promising me one thing when I was here, and doing something different a week after."

He was a little frightened at his own boldness, but he had made up his mind exactly what words to use, and, though his heart beat violently, he forced himself to say them.

"Have you got leave to come here this afternoon?"

"No. I asked Perkins and he refused. If you like to write and tell him I've been here you can get me into a really fine old row."

Mrs. Carey sat knitting with trembling hands. She was unused to scenes and they agitated her extremely.

"It would serve you right if I told him," said Mr. Carey.

"If you like to be a perfect sneak you can. After writing to Perkins as you did you're quite capable of it."

It was foolish of Philip to say that, because it gave the Vicar exactly the opportunity he wanted.

"I'm not going to sit still while you say impertinent things to me," he said with dignity.

He got up and walked quickly out of the room into his study. Philip heard him shut the door and lock it.

"Oh, I wish to God I were twenty-one. It is awful to be tied down like this."

Aunt Louisa began to cry quietly.

"Oh, Philip, you oughtn't to have spoken to your uncle like that. Do please go and tell him you're sorry."

"I'm not in the least sorry. He's taking a mean advantage. Of course it's just waste of money keeping me on at school, but what does he care? It's not his money. It was cruel to put me under the guardianship of people who know nothing about things."

"Philip."

Philip in his voluble anger stopped suddenly at the sound of her voice. It was heartbroken. He had not realized what bitter things he was saying.

"Philip, how can you be so unkind? You know we are only trying to do our best for you, and we know that we have no experience; it isn't as if we'd had any children of our own: that's why we consulted Mr. Perkins." Her voice broke. "I've tried to be like a mother to you. I've loved you as if you were my own son."

She was so small and frail, there was something so pathetic in her old-maidish air, that Philip was touched. A great lump came suddenly in his throat and his eyes filled with tears.

"I'm so sorry," he said. "I didn't mean to be beastly."

He knelt down beside her and took her in his arms, and kissed her wet, withered cheeks. She sobbed bitterly, and he seemed to feel on a sudden the pity of that wasted life. She had never surrendered herself before to such a display of emotion.

"I know I've not been what I wanted to be to you, Philip, but I didn't know how. It's been just as dreadful for me to have no children as for you to have no mother."

Philip forgot his anger and his own concerns, but thought only of consoling her, with broken words and clumsy little caresses. Then the clock struck, and he had to bolt off at once to catch the only train that would get him back to Tercanbury in time for call-over. As he sat in the corner of the railway carriage he saw that he had done nothing. He was angry with himself for his weakness. It was despicable to have allowed himself to be turned from his purpose by the pompous airs of the Vicar and the tears of his aunt. But as the result of he knew not what conversations between the couple another letter was written to the headmaster. Mr. Perkins read it with an impatient shrug of the shoulders. He showed it to Philip. It ran:

Dear Mr. Perkins,

Forgive me for troubling you again about my ward, but both his Aunt and I have been uneasy about him. He seems very anxious to leave school, and his Aunt thinks he is unhappy. It is very difficult for us to know what to do as we are not his parents. He does not seem to think he is doing very well and he feels it is wasting his money to stay on. I should be very much obliged if you would have a talk to him, and if he is still of the same mind perhaps it would be better if he left at Christmas as I originally intended.

Yours very truly,
William Carey.

Philip gave him back the letter. He felt a thrill of pride in his triumph. He had got his own way, and he was satisfied. His will had gained a victory over the wills of others.

"It's not much good my spending half an hour writing to your uncle if he changes his mind the next letter he gets from you," said the headmaster irritably.

Philip said nothing, and his face was perfectly placid; but he could not prevent the twinkle in his eyes. Mr. Perkins noticed it and broke into a little laugh.

"You've rather scored, haven't you?" he said.

Then Philip smiled outright. He could not conceal his exultation.

"Is it true that you're very anxious to leave?"

"Yes, sir."

"Are you unhappy here?"

Philip blushed. He hated instinctively any attempt to get into the depths of his feelings.

"Oh, I don't know, sir."

Mr. Perkins, slowly dragging his fingers through his beard, looked at him thoughtfully. He seemed to speak almost to himself.

"Of course schools are made for the average. The holes are all round, and whatever shape the pegs are they must wedge in somehow. One hasn't time to bother about anything but the average." Then suddenly he addressed himself to Philip: "Look here, I've got a suggestion to make to you. It's getting on towards the end of the term now. Another term won't kill you, and if you want to go to Germany you'd better go after Easter than after Christmas. It'll be much pleasanter in the spring than in midwinter. If at the end of the next term you still want to go I'll make no objection. What d'you say to that?"

"Thank you very much, sir."

Philip was so glad to have gained the last three months that he did not mind the extra term. The school seemed less of a prison when he knew that before Easter he would be free from it for ever. His heart danced within him. That evening in chapel he looked round at the boys, standing according to their forms, each in his due place, and he chuckled with satisfaction at the thought that soon he would never see them again. It made him regard them almost with a friendly feeling. His eyes rested on Rose. Rose took his position as a monitor very seriously: he had quite an idea of being a good influence in the school; it was his turn to read the lesson that evening, and he read it very well. Philip smiled when he thought that he would be rid of him for ever, and it would not matter in six months whether Rose was tall and straight-limbed; and where would the importance be that he was a monitor and captain of the eleven? Philip looked at the masters in their gowns. Gordon was dead, he had died of apoplexy two years before, but all the rest were there. Philip knew now what a poor lot they were, except Turner perhaps, there was something of a man in him; and he writhed at the thought of the subjection in which they had held him. In six months they would not matter either. Their praise would mean nothing to him, and he would shrug his shoulders at their censure.

Philip had learned not to express his emotions by outward signs, and shyness still tormented him, but he had often very high spirits; and then, though he limped about demurely, silent and reserved, it seemed to be hallooing in his heart. He seemed to himself to walk more lightly. All sorts of ideas danced through his head, fancies chased one another so furiously that he could not catch them; but their coming and their going filled him with exhilaration. Now, being happy, he was able to work, and during the remaining weeks of the term set himself to make up for his long neglect. His brain worked easily, and he took a keen pleasure in the activity of his intellect. He did very well in the examinations that closed the term. Mr. Perkins made only one remark: he was talking to him about an essay he had written, and, after the usual criticisms, said:

"So you've made up your mind to stop playing the fool for a bit, have you?"

He smiled at him with his shining teeth, and Philip, looking down, gave an embarrassed smile.

The half dozen boys who expected to divide between them the various prizes which were given at the end of the summer term had ceased to look upon Philip as a serious rival, but now they began to regard him with some uneasiness. He told no one that he was leaving at Easter and so was in no sense a competitor, but left them to their anxieties. He knew that Rose flattered himself on his French, for he had spent two or three holidays in France; and he expected to get the Dean's Prize for English essay; Philip got a good deal of satisfaction in watching his dismay when he saw how much better Philip was doing in these subjects than himself. Another fellow, Norton, could not go to Oxford unless he got one of the scholarships at the disposal of the school. He asked Philip if he was going in for them.

"Have you any objection?" asked Philip.

It entertained him to think that he held someone else's future in his hand. There was something romantic in getting these various rewards actually in his grasp, and then leaving them to others because he disdained them. At last the breaking-up day came, and he went to Mr. Perkins to bid him good-bye.

"You don't mean to say you really want to leave?"

Philip's face fell at the headmaster's evident surprise.

"You said you wouldn't put any objection in the way, sir," he answered.

"I thought it was only a whim that I'd better humour. I know you're obstinate and headstrong. What on earth d'you want to leave for now? You've only got another term in any case. You can get the Magdalen scholarship easily; you'll get half the prizes we've got to give."

Philip looked at him sullenly. He felt that he had been tricked; but he had the promise, and Perkins would have to stand by it.

"You'll have a very pleasant time at Oxford. You needn't decide at once what you're going to do afterwards. I wonder if you realize how delightful the life is up there for anyone who has brains."

"I've made all my arrangements now to go to Germany, sir," said Philip.

"Are they arrangements that couldn't possibly be altered?" asked Mr. Perkins, with his quizzical smile. "I shall be very sorry to lose you. In schools the rather stupid boys who work always do better than the clever boy who's idle, but when the clever boy works—why then, he does what you've done this term."

Philip flushed darkly. He was unused to compliments, and no one had ever told him he was clever. The headmaster put his hand on Philip's shoulder.

"You know, driving things into the heads of thick-witted boys is dull work, but when now and then you have the chance of teaching a boy who comes half-way towards you, who understands almost before you've got the words out of your mouth, why, then teaching is the most exhilarating thing in the world."

Philip was melted by kindness; it had never occurred to him that it mattered really to Mr. Perkins whether he went or stayed. He was touched and immensely flattered. It would be pleasant to end up his school-days with glory and then go to Oxford: in a flash there appeared before him the life which he had heard described from boys who came back to play in the O. K. S. match or in letters from the University read out in one of the studies. But he was ashamed; he would look such a fool in his own eyes if he gave in now; his uncle would chuckle at the success of the headmaster's ruse. It was rather a come-down from the dramatic surrender of all these prizes which were in his reach, because he disdained to take them, to the plain, ordinary winning of them. It only required a little more persuasion, just enough to save his self-respect, and Philip would have done anything that Mr. Perkins wished; but his face showed nothing of his conflicting emotions. It was placid and sullen.

"I think I'd rather go, sir," he said.

Mr. Perkins, like many men who manage things by their personal influence, grew a little impatient when his power was not immediately manifest. He had a great deal of work to do, and could not waste more time on a boy who seemed to him insanely obstinate.

"Very well, I promised to let you if you really wanted it, and I keep my promise. When do you go to Germany?"

Philip's heart beat violently. The battle was won, and he did not know whether he had not rather lost it.

"At the beginning of May, sir," he answered.

"Well, you must come and see us when you get back."

He held out his hand. If he had given him one more chance Philip would have changed his mind, but he seemed to look upon the matter as settled. Philip walked out of the house. His school-days were over, and he was free; but the wild exultation to which he had looked forward at that moment was not there. He walked round the precincts slowly, and a profound depression seized him. He wished now that he had not been foolish. He did not want to go, but he knew he could never bring himself to go to the headmaster and tell him he would stay. That was a humiliation he could never put upon himself. He wondered whether he had done right. He was dissatisfied with himself and with all his circumstances. He asked himself dully whether whenever you got your way you wished afterwards that you hadn't.

Chapter 22

Philip's uncle had an old friend, called Miss Wilkinson, who lived in Berlin. She was the daughter of a clergyman, and it was with her father, the rector of a village in Lincolnshire, that Mr. Carey had spent his last curacy; on his death, forced to earn her living, she had taken various situations as a governess in France and Germany. She had kept up a correspondence with Mrs. Carey, and two or three times had spent her holidays at Blackstable Vicarage, paying as was usual with the Careys' unfrequent guests a small sum for her keep. When it became clear that it was less trouble to yield to Philip's wishes than to resist them, Mrs. Carey wrote to ask her for advice. Miss Wilkinson recommended Heidelberg as an excellent place to learn German in and the house of Frau Professor Erlin as a comfortable home. Philip might live there for thirty marks a week, and the Professor himself, a teacher at the local high school, would instruct him.

Philip arrived in Heidelberg one morning in May. His things were put on a barrow and he followed the porter out of the station. The sky was bright blue, and the trees in the avenue through which they passed were thick with leaves; there was something in the air fresh to Philip, and mingled with the timidity he felt at entering on a new life, among strangers, was a great exhilaration. He was a little disconsolate that no one had come to meet him, and felt very shy when the porter left him at the front door of a big white house. An untidy lad let him in and took him into a drawing-room. It was filled with a large suite covered in green velvet, and in the middle was a round table. On this in water stood a bouquet of flowers tightly packed together in a paper frill like the bone of a mutton chop, and carefully spaced round it were books in leather bindings. There was a musty smell.

Presently, with an odour of cooking, the Frau Professor came in, a short, very stout woman with tightly dressed hair and a red face; she had little eyes, sparkling like beads, and an effusive manner. She took both Philip's hands and asked him about Miss Wilkinson, who had twice spent a few weeks with her. She spoke in German and in broken English. Philip could not make her understand that he did not know Miss Wilkinson. Then her two daughters appeared. They seemed hardly young to Philip, but perhaps they were not more than twenty-five: the elder, Thekla, was as short as her mother, with the same, rather shifty air, but with a pretty face and abundant dark hair; Anna, her younger sister, was tall and plain, but since she had a pleasant smile Philip immediately preferred her. After a few minutes of polite conversation the Frau Professor took Philip to his room and left him. It was in a turret, looking over the tops of the trees in the *Anlage*; and the bed was in an alcove, so that when you sat at the desk it had not the look of a bedroom at all. Philip unpacked his things and set out all his books. He was his own master at last.

A bell summoned him to dinner at one o'clock, and he found the Frau Professor's guests assembled in the drawing-room. He was introduced to her husband, a tall man of middle age with a large fair head, turning now to grey, and mild blue eyes. He spoke to Philip in correct, rather archaic English, having learned it from a study of the English classics, not from conversation; and it was odd to hear him use words colloquially which Philip had only met in the plays of Shakespeare. Frau Professor Erlin called her establishment a family and not a pension; but it would have required the subtlety of a metaphysician to find out exactly where the difference lay. When they sat down to dinner in a long dark apartment that led out of the drawing-room, Philip, feeling very shy, saw that there were sixteen people. The Frau Professor sat at one end and carved. The service was conducted, with a great clattering of plates, by the same clumsy lout who had opened the door for him; and though he was quick, it happened that the first persons to be served had finished before the last had received their appointed portions. The Frau Professor insisted that nothing but German should be spoken, so that Philip, even if his bashfulness had permitted him to be talkative, was forced to hold his tongue. He looked at the people among whom he was to live. By the Frau Professor sat several old ladies, but Philip did not give them much of his attention. There were two young girls, both fair and one of them very pretty, whom Philip heard addressed as Fräulein Hedwig and Fräulein Cäcilie. Fräulein Cäcilie had a long pig-tail hanging down her back. They sat side by side and chattered to one another, with smothered laughter: now and then they glanced at Philip and one of them said something in an undertone; they both giggled, and Philip blushed awkwardly, feeling that they were making fun of him. Near them sat a Chinaman, with a yellow face and an expansive smile, who was studying Western conditions at the University. He spoke so quickly, with a queer accent, that the girls could not always understand him, and then they burst out laughing. He laughed too, good-humouredly, and his almond eyes almost closed as he did so. There were two or three American men, in black coats, rather yellow and dry of skin: they were theological students; Philip heard the twang of their New England accent through their bad German, and he glanced at them with suspicion; for he had been taught to look upon Americans as wild and desperate barbarians.

Afterwards, when they had sat for a little on the stiff green velvet chairs of the drawing-room, Fräulein Anna asked Philip if he would like to go for a walk with them.

Philip accepted the invitation. They were quite a party. There were the two daughters of the Frau Professor, the two other girls, one of the American students, and Philip. Philip walked by the side of Anna and Fräulein Hedwig. He was a little fluttered. He had never known any girls. At Blackstable there were only the farmers' daughters and the girls of the local tradesmen. He knew them by name and by sight, but he was timid, and he thought they laughed at his deformity. He accepted willingly the difference which the Vicar and Mrs. Carey put between their own exalted rank and that of the farmers. The doctor had two daughters, but they were both much older than Philip and had been married to successive assistants while Philip was still a small boy. At school there had been two or three girls of more boldness than modesty whom some of the boys knew; and desperate stories, due in all probability to the masculine imagination, were told of intrigues with them; but Philip had always concealed under a lofty contempt the terror with which they filled him. His imagination and the books he had read had inspired in him a desire for the Byronic attitude; and he was torn between a morbid self-consciousness and a conviction that he owed it to himself to be gallant. He felt now that he should be bright and amusing, but his brain seemed empty and he could not for the life of him think of anything to say. Fräulein Anna, the Frau Professor's daughter, addressed herself to him frequently from a sense of duty, but the other said little: she looked at him now and then with sparkling eyes, and sometimes to his confusion laughed outright. Philip felt that she thought him perfectly ridiculous. They walked along the side of a hill among pine-trees, and their pleasant odour caused Philip a keen delight. The day was warm and cloudless. At last they came to an eminence from which they saw the valley of the Rhine spread out before them under the sun. It was a vast stretch of country, sparkling with golden light, with cities in the distance; and through it meandered the silver ribband of the river. Wide spaces are rare in the corner of Kent which Philip knew, the sea offers the only broad horizon, and the immense distance he saw now gave him a peculiar, an indescribable thrill. He felt suddenly elated. Though he did not know it, it was the first time that he had experienced, quite undiluted with foreign emotions, the sense of beauty. They sat on a bench, the three of them, for the others had gone on, and while the girls talked in rapid German, Philip, indifferent to their proximity, feasted his eyes.

"By Jove, I am happy," he said to himself unconsciously.

Chapter 23

Philip thought occasionally of the King's School at Tercanbury, and laughed to himself as he remembered what at some particular moment of the day they were doing. Now and then he dreamed that he was there still, and it gave him an extraordinary satisfaction, on awaking, to realize that he was in his little room in the turret. From his bed he could see the great cumulus clouds that hung in the blue sky. He revelled in his freedom. He could go to bed when he chose and get up when the fancy took him. There was no one to order him about. It struck him that he need not tell any more lies.

It had been arranged that Professor Erlin should teach him Latin and German; a Frenchman came every day to give him lessons in French; and the Frau Professor had recommended for mathematics an Englishman who was taking a philological degree at the university. This was a man named Wharton. Philip went to him every morning. He lived in one room on the top floor of a shabby house. It was dirty and untidy, and it was filled with a pungent odour made up of many different stinks. He was generally in bed when Philip arrived at ten o'clock, and he jumped out, put on a filthy dressing-gown and felt slippers, and, while he gave instruction, ate his simple breakfast. He was a short man, stout from excessive beer- drinking, with a heavy moustache and long, unkempt hair. He had been in Germany for five years and was become very Teutonic. He spoke with scorn of Cambridge where he had taken his degree and with horror of the life which awaited him when, having taken his doctorate in Heidelberg, he must return to England and a pedagogic career. He adored the life of the German university with its happy freedom and its jolly companionships. He was a member of a *Burschenschaft*, and promised to take Philip to a *Kneipe*. He was very poor and made no secret that the lessons he was giving Philip meant the difference between meat for his dinner and bread and cheese. Sometimes after a heavy night he had such a headache that he could not drink his coffee, and he gave his lesson with heaviness of spirit. For these occasions he kept a few bottles of beer under the bed, and one of these and a pipe would help him to bear the burden of life.

"A hair of the dog that bit him," he would say as he poured out the beer, carefully, so that the foam should not make him wait too long to drink.

Then he would talk to Philip of the university, the quarrels between the rival corps, the duels, and the merits of this and that professor. Philip learnt more of life from him than of mathematics. Sometimes Wharton would sit back with a laugh and say:

"Look here, we've not done anything today. You needn't pay me for the lesson."

"Oh, it doesn't matter," said Philip.

This was something new and very interesting, and he felt that it was of greater import than trigonometry, which he never could understand. It was like a window on life that he had a chance of peeping through, and he looked with a wildly beating heart.

"No, you can keep your dirty money," said Wharton.

"But how about your dinner?" said Philip, with a smile, for he knew exactly how his master's finances stood.

Wharton had even asked him to pay him the two shillings which the lesson cost once a week rather than once a month, since it made things less complicated.

"Oh, never mind my dinner. It won't be the first time I've dined off a bottle of beer, and my mind's never clearer than when I do."

He dived under the bed (the sheets were grey with want of washing), and fished out another bottle. Philip, who was young and did not know the good things of life, refused to share it with him, so he drank alone.

"How long are you going to stay here?" asked Wharton.

Both he and Philip had given up with relief the pretence of mathematics.

"Oh, I don't know. I suppose about a year. Then my people want me to go to Oxford."

Wharton gave a contemptuous shrug of the shoulders. It was a new experience for Philip to learn that there were persons who did not look upon that seat of learning with awe.

"What d'you want to go there for? You'll only be a glorified schoolboy. Why don't you matriculate here? A year's no good.

Spend five years here. You know, there are two good things in life, freedom of thought and freedom of action. In France you get freedom of action: you can do what you like and nobody bothers, but you must think like everybody else. In Germany you must do what everybody else does, but you may think as you choose. They're both very good things. I personally prefer freedom of thought. But in England you get neither: you're ground down by convention. You can't think as you like and you can't act as you like. That's because it's a democratic nation. I expect America's worse."

He leaned back cautiously, for the chair on which he sat had a rickety leg, and it was disconcerting when a rhetorical flourish was interrupted by a sudden fall to the floor.

"I ought to go back to England this year, but if I can scrape together enough to keep body and soul on speaking terms I shall stay another twelve months. But then I shall have to go. And I must leave all this" —he waved his arm round the dirty garret, with its unmade bed, the clothes lying on the floor, a row of empty beer bottles against the wall, piles of unbound, ragged books in every corner— "for some provincial university where I shall try and get a chair of philology. And I shall play tennis and go to tea-parties." He interrupted himself and gave Philip, very neatly dressed, with a clean collar on and his hair well-brushed, a quizzical look. "And, my God! I shall have to wash."

Philip reddened, feeling his own spruceness an intolerable reproach; for of late he had begun to pay some attention to his toilet, and he had come out from England with a pretty selection of ties.

The summer came upon the country like a conqueror. Each day was beautiful. The sky had an arrogant blue which goaded the nerves like a spur. The green of the trees in the *Anlage* was violent and crude; and the houses, when the sun caught them, had a dazzling white which stimulated till it hurt. Sometimes on his way back from Wharton Philip would sit in the shade on one of the benches in the *Anlage*, enjoying the coolness and watching the patterns of light which the sun, shining through the leaves, made on the ground. His soul danced with delight as gaily as the sunbeams. He revelled in those moments of idleness stolen from his work. Sometimes he sauntered through the streets of the old town. He looked with awe at the students of the corps, their cheeks gashed and red, who swaggered about in their coloured caps. In the afternoons he wandered about the hills with the girls in the Frau Professor's house, and sometimes they went up the river and had tea in a leafy beer-garden. In the evenings they walked round and round the *Stadtgarten*, listening to the band.

Philip soon learned the various interests of the household. Fräulein Thekla, the professor's elder daughter, was engaged to a man in England who had spent twelve months in the house to learn German, and their marriage was to take place at the end of the year. But the young man wrote that his father, an india-rubber merchant who lived in Slough, did not approve of the union, and Fräulein Thekla was often in tears. Sometimes she and her mother might be seen, with stern eyes and determined mouths, looking over the letters of the reluctant lover. Thekla painted in water colour, and occasionally she and Philip, with another of the girls to keep them company, would go out and paint little pictures. The pretty Fräulein Hedwig had amorous troubles too. She was the daughter of a merchant in Berlin and a dashing hussar had fallen in love with her, a *von* if you please; but his parents opposed a marriage with a person of her condition, and she had been sent to Heidelberg to forget him. She could never, never do this, and corresponded with him continually, and he was making every effort to induce an exasperating father to change his mind. She told all this to Philip with pretty sighs and becoming blushes, and showed him the photograph of the gay lieutenant. Philip liked her best of all the girls at the Frau Professor's, and on their walks always tried to get by her side. He blushed a great deal when the others chaffed him for his obvious preference. He made the first declaration in his life to Fräulein Hedwig, but unfortunately it was an accident, and it happened in this manner. In the evenings when they did not go out, the young women sang little songs in the green velvet drawing-room, while Fräulein Anna, who always made herself useful, industriously accompanied. Fräulein Hedwig's favourite song was called *Ich liebe dich* (I love you); and one evening after she had sung this, when Philip was standing with her on the balcony, looking at the stars, it occurred to him to make some remark about it. He began:

"*Ich liebe dich.*"

His German was halting, and he looked about for the word he wanted. The pause was infinitesimal, but before he could go on Fräulein Hedwig said:

"*Ach, Herr Carey, Sie müssen mir nicht 'du' sagen*—you mustn't talk to me in the second person singular."

Philip felt himself grow hot all over, for he would never have dared to do anything so familiar, and he could think of nothing on earth to say. It would be ungallant to explain that he was not making an observation, but merely mentioning the title of a song.

"*Entschuldigen Sie*," he said. "I beg your pardon."

"It does not matter," she whispered.

She smiled pleasantly, quietly took his hand and pressed it, then turned back into the drawing-room.

Next day he was so embarrassed that he could not speak to her, and in his shyness did all that was possible to avoid her. When he was asked to go for the usual walk he refused because, he said, he had work to do. But Fräulein Hedwig seized an opportunity to speak to him alone.

"Why are you behaving in this way?" she said kindly. "You know, I'm not angry with you for what you said last night. You can't help it if you love me. I'm flattered. But although I'm not exactly engaged to Hermann I can never love anyone else, and I look upon myself as his bride."

Philip blushed again, but he put on quite the expression of a rejected lover.

"I hope you'll be very happy," he said.

Chapter 24

Professor Erlin gave Philip a lesson every day. He made out a list of books which Philip was to read till he was ready for the final achievement of *Faust*, and meanwhile, ingeniously enough, started him on a German translation of one of the plays by Shakespeare which Philip had studied at school. It was the period in Germany of Goethe's highest fame. Notwithstanding his rather condescending attitude towards patriotism he had been adopted as the national poet, and seemed since the war of seventy to be one of the most significant glories of national unity. The enthusiastic seemed in the wildness of the *Walpurgisnacht* to hear the rattle of artillery at Gravelotte. But one mark of a writer's greatness is that different minds can find in him different inspirations; and Professor Erlin, who hated the Prussians, gave his enthusiastic admiration to Goethe because his works, Olympian and sedate, offered the only refuge for a sane mind against the onslaughts of the present generation. There was a dramatist whose name of late had been much heard at Heidelberg, and the winter before one of his plays had been given at the theatre amid the cheers of adherents and the hisses of decent people. Philip heard discussions about it at the Frau Professor's long table, and at these Professor Erlin lost his wonted calm: he beat the table with his fist, and drowned all opposition with the roar of his fine deep voice. It was nonsense and obscene nonsense. He forced himself to sit the play out, but he did not know whether he was more bored or nauseated. If that was what the theatre was coming to, then it was high time the police stepped in and closed the playhouses. He was no prude and could laugh as well as anyone at the witty immorality of a farce at the Palais Royal, but here was nothing but filth. With an emphatic gesture he held his nose and whistled through his teeth. It was the ruin of the family, the uprooting of morals, the destruction of Germany.

"*Aber, Adolf,*" said the Frau Professor from the other end of the table. "Calm yourself."

He shook his fist at her. He was the mildest of creatures and ventured upon no action of his life without consulting her.

"No, Helene, I tell you this," he shouted. "I would sooner my daughters were lying dead at my feet than see them listening to the garbage of that shameless fellow."

The play was *A Doll's House* and the author was Henrik Ibsen.

Professor Erlin classed him with Richard Wagner, but of him he spoke not with anger but with good-humoured laughter. He was a charlatan but a successful charlatan, and in that was always something for the comic spirit to rejoice in.

"*Verrückter Kerl!* A madman!" he said.

He had seen *Lohengrin* and that passed muster. It was dull, but no worse. But *Siegfried!* When he mentioned it Professor Erlin leaned his head on his hand and bellowed with laughter. Not a melody in it from beginning to end! He could imagine Richard Wagner sitting in his box and laughing till his sides ached at the sight of all the people who were taking it seriously. It was the greatest hoax of the nineteenth century. He lifted his glass of beer to his lips, threw back his head, and drank till the glass was empty. Then wiping his mouth with the back of his hand, he said:

"I tell you young people that before the nineteenth century is out Wagner will be as dead as mutton. Wagner! I would give all his works for one opera by Donizetti."

Chapter 25

The oddest of Philip's masters was his teacher of French. Monsieur Ducroz was a citizen of Geneva. He was a tall old man, with a sallow skin and hollow cheeks; his grey hair was thin and long. He wore shabby black clothes, with holes at the elbows of his coat and frayed trousers. His linen was very dirty. Philip had never seen him in a clean collar. He was a man of few words, who gave his lesson conscientiously but without enthusiasm, arriving as the clock struck and leaving on the minute. His charges were very small. He was taciturn, and what Philip learnt about him he learnt from others: it appeared that he had fought with Garibaldi against the Pope, but had left Italy in disgust when it was clear that all his efforts for freedom, by which he meant the establishment of a republic, tended to no more than an exchange of yokes; he had been expelled from Geneva for it was not known what political offences. Philip looked upon him with puzzled surprise; for he was very unlike his idea of the revolutionary: he spoke in a low voice and was extraordinarily polite; he never sat down till he was asked to; and when on rare occasions he met Philip in the street took off his hat with an elaborate gesture; he never laughed, he never even smiled. A more complete imagination than Philip's might have pictured a youth of splendid hope, for he must have been entering upon manhood in 1848 when kings, remembering their brother of France, went about with an uneasy crick in their necks; and perhaps that passion for liberty which passed through Europe, sweeping before it what of absolutism and tyranny had reared its head during the reaction from the revolution of 1789, filled no breast with a hotter fire. One might fancy him, passionate with theories of human equality and human rights, discussing, arguing, fighting behind barricades in Paris, flying before the Austrian cavalry in Milan, imprisoned here, exiled from there, hoping on and upborne ever with the word which seemed so magical, the word Liberty; till at last, broken with disease and starvation, old, without means to keep body and soul together but such lessons as he could pick up from poor students, he found himself in that little neat town under the heel of a personal tyranny greater than any in Europe. Perhaps his taciturnity hid a contempt for the human race which had abandoned the great dreams of his youth and now wallowed in sluggish ease; or perhaps these thirty years of revolution had taught him that men are unfit for liberty, and he thought that he had spent his life in the pursuit of that which was not worth the finding. Or maybe he was tired out and waited only with indifference for the release of death.

One day Philip, with the bluntness of his age, asked him if it was true he had been with Garibaldi. The old man did not seem to attach any importance to the question. He answered quite quietly in as low a voice as usual:

"*Oui, monsieur.*"

"They say you were in the Commune?"

"Do they? Shall we get on with our work?"

He held the book open and Philip, intimidated, began to translate the passage he had prepared.

One day Monsieur Ducroz seemed to be in great pain. He had been scarcely able to drag himself up the many stairs to Philip's room; and when he arrived sat down heavily, his sallow face drawn, with beads of sweat on his forehead, trying to recover himself.

"I'm afraid you're ill," said Philip.

"It's of no consequence."

But Philip saw that he was suffering, and at the end of the hour asked whether he would not prefer to give no more lessons till he was better.

"No," said the old man, in his even low voice. "I prefer to go on while I am able."

Philip, morbidly nervous when he had to make any reference to money, reddened.

"But it won't make any difference to you," he said. "I'll pay for the lessons just the same. If you wouldn't mind I'd like to give you the money for next week in advance."

Monsieur Ducroz charged eighteen pence an hour. Philip took a ten-mark piece out of his pocket and shyly put it on the table. He could not bring himself to offer it as if the old man were a beggar.

"In that case I think I won't come again till I'm better." He took the coin and, without anything more than the elaborate bow with which he always took his leave, went out.

"*Bonjour, monsieur.*"

Philip was vaguely disappointed. Thinking he had done a generous thing, he had expected that Monsieur Ducroz would overwhelm him with expressions of gratitude. He was taken aback to find that the old teacher accepted the present as though it were his due. He was so young, he did not realize how much less is the sense of obligation in those who receive favours than in those who grant them. Monsieur Ducroz appeared again five or six days later. He tottered a little more and was very weak, but seemed to have overcome the severity of the attack. He was no more communicative than he had been before. He remained mysterious, aloof, and dirty. He made no reference to his illness till after the lesson; and then, just as he was leaving, at the door, which he held open, he paused. He hesitated, as though to speak were difficult.

"If it hadn't been for the money you gave me I should have starved. It was all I had to live on."

He made his solemn, obsequious bow, and went out. Philip felt a little lump in his throat. He seemed to realize in a fashion the hopeless bitterness of the old man's struggle, and how hard life was for him when to himself it was so pleasant.

Chapter 26

Philip had spent three months in Heidelberg when one morning the Frau Professor told him that an Englishman named Hayward was coming to stay in the house, and the same evening at supper he saw a new face. For some days the family had lived in a state of excitement. First, as the result of heaven knows what scheming, by dint of humble prayers and veiled threats, the parents of the young Englishman to whom Fräulein Thekla was engaged had invited her to visit them in England, and she had set off with an album of water colours to show how accomplished she was and a bundle of letters to prove how deeply the young man had compromised himself. A week later Fräulein Hedwig with radiant smiles announced that the lieutenant of her affections was coming to Heidelberg with his father and mother. Exhausted by the importunity of their son and touched by the dowry which Fräulein Hedwig's father offered, the lieutenant's parents had consented to pass through Heidelberg to make the young woman's acquaintance. The interview was satisfactory and Fräulein Hedwig had the satisfaction of showing her lover in the *Stadtgarten* to the whole of Frau Professor Erlin's household. The silent old ladies who sat at the top of the table near the Frau Professor were in a flutter, and when Fräulein Hedwig said she was to go home at once for the formal engagement to take place, the Frau Professor, regardless of expense, said she would give a *Maibowle*. Professor Erlin prided himself on his skill in preparing this mild intoxicant, and after supper the large bowl of hock and soda, with scented herbs floating in it, and wild strawberries, was placed with solemnity on the round table in the drawing-room. Fräulein Anna teased Philip about the departure of his lady-love, and he felt very uncomfortable and rather melancholy. Fräulein Hedwig sang several songs, Fräulein Anna played the Wedding March, and the Professor sang *Die Wacht am Rhein*. Amid all this jollification Philip paid little attention to the new arrival. They had sat opposite one another at supper, but Philip was chattering busily with Fräulein Hedwig, and the stranger, knowing no German, had eaten his food in silence. Philip, observing that he wore a pale blue tie, had on that account taken a sudden dislike to him. He was a man of twenty-six, very fair, with long, wavy hair through which he passed his hand frequently with a careless gesture. His eyes were large and blue, but the blue was very pale, and they looked rather tired already. He was clean-shaven, and his mouth, notwithstanding its thin lips, was well-shaped. Fräulein Anna took an interest in physiognomy, and she made Philip notice afterwards how finely shaped was his skull, and how weak was the lower part of his face. The head, she remarked, was the head of a thinker, but the jaw lacked character. Fräulein Anna, foredoomed to a spinster's life, with her high cheek-bones and large misshapen nose, laid great stress upon character. While they talked of him he stood a little apart from the others, watching the noisy party with a good-humoured but faintly supercilious expression. He was tall and slim. He held himself with a deliberate grace. Weeks, one of the American students, seeing him alone, went up and began to talk to him. The pair were oddly contrasted: the American very neat in his black coat and pepper-and-salt trousers, thin and dried-up, with something of ecclesiastical unction already in his manner; and the Englishman in his loose tweed suit, large-limbed and slow of gesture.

Philip did not speak to the newcomer till next day. They found themselves alone on the balcony of the drawing-room before dinner. Hayward addressed him.

"You're English, aren't you?"

"Yes."

"Is the food always as bad it was last night?"

"It's always about the same."

"Beastly, isn't it?"

"Beastly."

Philip had found nothing wrong with the food at all, and in fact had eaten it in large quantities with appetite and enjoyment, but he did not want to show himself a person of so little discrimination as to think a dinner good which another thought execrable.

Fräulein Thekla's visit to England made it necessary for her sister to do more in the house, and she could not often spare the time for long walks; and Fräulein Cäcilie, with her long plait of fair hair and her little snub-nosed face, had of late shown a certain disinclination for society. Fräulein Hedwig was gone, and Weeks, the American who generally accompanied them on their rambles, had set out for a tour of South Germany. Philip was left a good deal to himself. Hayward sought his acquaintance; but Philip had an unfortunate trait: from shyness or from some atavistic inheritance of the cave-dweller, he always disliked people on first acquaintance; and it was not till he became used to them that he got over his first impression. It made him difficult of access. He received Hayward's advances very shyly, and when Hayward asked him one day to go for a walk he accepted only because he could not think of a civil excuse. He made his usual apology, angry with himself for the flushing cheeks he could not control, and trying to carry it off with a laugh.

"I'm afraid I can't walk very fast."

"Good heavens, I don't walk for a wager. I prefer to stroll. Don't you remember the chapter in *Marius* where Pater talks of the gentle exercise of walking as the best incentive to conversation?"

Philip was a good listener; though he often thought of clever things to say, it was seldom till after the opportunity to say them had passed; but Hayward was communicative; anyone more experienced than Philip might have thought he liked to hear himself talk. His supercilious attitude impressed Philip. He could not help admiring, and yet being awed by, a man who faintly despised so many things which Philip had looked upon as almost sacred. He cast down the fetish of exercise, damning with the contemptuous word *pot-hunters* all those who devoted themselves to its various forms; and Philip did not realize that he was merely putting up in its stead the other fetish of culture.

They wandered up to the castle, and sat on the terrace that overlooked the town. It nestled in the valley along the pleasant Neckar with a comfortable friendliness. The smoke from the chimneys hung over it, a pale blue haze; and the tall roofs, the spires of the churches, gave it a pleasantly medieval air. There was a homeliness in it which warmed the heart. Hayward talked of *Richard Feverel* and *Madame Bovary*, of Verlaine, Dante, and Matthew Arnold. In those days Fitzgerald's translation of Omar Khayyám was known only to the elect, and Hayward repeated it to Philip. He was very fond of reciting poetry, his own and that of others, which he did in a monotonous sing-song. By the time they reached home Philip's distrust of Hayward was changed to enthusiastic admiration.

They made a practice of walking together every afternoon, and Philip learned presently something of Hayward's circumstances. He was the son of a country judge, on whose death some time before he had inherited three hundred a year. His record at Charterhouse was so brilliant that when he went to Cambridge the Master of Trinity Hall went out of his way to express his satisfaction that he was going to that college. He prepared himself for a distinguished career. He moved in the most intellectual circles; he read Browning with enthusiasm and turned up his well-shaped nose at Tennyson; he knew all the details of Shelley's treatment of Harriet; he dabbled in the history of art (on the walls of his rooms were reproductions of pictures by G. F. Watts, Burne-Jones, and Botticelli); and he wrote not without distinction verses of a pessimistic character.

His friends told one another that he was a man of excellent gifts, and he listened to them willingly when they prophesied his future eminence. In course of time he became an authority on art and literature. He came under the influence of Newman's *Apologia*; the picturesqueness of the Roman Catholic faith appealed to his aesthetic sensibility; and it was only the fear of his father's wrath (a plain, blunt man of narrow ideas, who read Macaulay) which prevented him from "going over." When he only got a pass degree his friends were astonished; but he shrugged his shoulders and delicately insinuated that he was not the dupe of examiners. He made one feel that a first class was ever so slightly vulgar. He described one of the vivas with tolerant humour; some fellow in an outrageous collar was asking him questions in logic; it was infinitely tedious, and suddenly he noticed that he wore elastic-sided boots: it was grotesque and ridiculous; so he withdrew his mind and thought of the Gothic beauty of the Chapel at King's. But he had spent some delightful days at Cambridge; he had given better dinners than anyone he knew; and the conversation in his rooms had been often memorable. He quoted to Philip the exquisite epigram:

"They told me, Herakleitus, they told me you were dead."

And now, when he related again the picturesque little anecdote about the examiner and his boots, he laughed.

"Of course, it was folly," he said, "but it was a folly in which there was something fine."

Philip, with a little thrill, thought it magnificent.

Then Hayward went to London to read for the bar. He had charming rooms in Clement's Inn, with panelled walls, and he tried to make them look like his old rooms at the Hall. He had ambitions that were vaguely political, he described himself as a Whig, and he was put up for a club which was of Liberal but gentlemanly flavour. His idea was to practise at the Bar (he chose the Chancery side as less brutal), and get a seat for some pleasant constituency as soon as the various promises made him were carried out; meanwhile he went a great deal to the opera, and made acquaintance with a small number of charming people who admired the things that he admired. He joined a dining-club of which the motto was, The Whole, The Good, and The Beautiful. He formed a platonic friendship with a lady some years older than himself, who lived in Kensington Square; and nearly every afternoon he drank tea with her by the light of shaded candles, and talked of George Meredith and Walter Pater. It was notorious that any fool could pass the examinations of the Bar Council, and he pursued his studies in a dilatory fashion. When he was ploughed for his final he looked upon it as a personal affront. At the same time the lady in Kensington Square told him that her husband was coming home from India on leave, and was a man, though worthy in every way, of a commonplace mind, who would not understand a young man's frequent visits. Hayward felt that life was full of ugliness, his soul revolted from the thought of affronting again the cynicism of examiners, and he saw something rather splendid in kicking away the ball which lay at his feet. He was also a good deal in debt: it was difficult to live in London like a gentleman on three hundred a year; and his heart yearned for the Venice and Florence which John Ruskin had so magically described. He felt that he was unsuited to the vulgar bustle of the Bar, for he had discovered that it was not sufficient to put your name on a door to get briefs; and modern politics seemed to lack nobility. He felt himself a poet. He disposed of his rooms in Clement's Inn and went to Italy. He had spent a winter in Florence and a winter in Rome, and now was passing his second summer abroad in Germany, so that he might read Goethe in the original.

Hayward had one gift which was very precious. He had a real feeling for literature, and he could impart his own passion with an admirable fluency. He could throw himself into sympathy with a writer and see all that was best in him, and then he could talk about him with understanding. Philip had read a great deal, but he had read without discrimination everything that he happened to come across, and it was very good for him now to meet someone who could guide his taste. He borrowed books from the small lending library which the town possessed and began reading all the wonderful things that Hayward spoke of. He did not read always with enjoyment but invariably with perseverance. He was eager for self-improvement. He felt himself very ignorant and very humble. By the end of August, when Weeks returned from South Germany, Philip was completely under Hayward's influence. Hayward did not like Weeks. He deplored the American's black coat and pepper-and-salt trousers, and spoke with a scornful shrug of his New England conscience. Philip listened complacently to the abuse of a man who had gone out of his way to be kind to him, but when Weeks in his turn made disagreeable remarks about Hayward he lost his temper.

"Your new friend looks like a poet," said Weeks, with a thin smile on his careworn, bitter mouth.

"He is a poet."

"Did he tell you so? In America we should call him a pretty fair specimen of a waster."

"Well, we're not in America," said Philip frigidly.

"How old is he? Twenty-five? And he does nothing but stay in pensions and write poetry."

"You don't know him," said Philip hotly.

"Oh yes, I do: I've met a hundred and forty-seven of him."

Weeks' eyes twinkled, but Philip, who did not understand American humour, pursed his lips and looked severe. Weeks to Philip seemed a man of middle age, but he was in point of fact little more than thirty. He had a long, thin body and the scholar's stoop; his head was large and ugly; he had pale scanty hair and an earthy skin; his thin mouth and thin, long nose, and the great protuberance of his frontal bones, gave him an uncouth look. He was cold and precise in his manner, a bloodless man, without passion; but he had a curious vein of frivolity which disconcerted the serious-minded among whom his instincts naturally threw him. He was studying theology in Heidelberg, but the other theological students of his own nationality looked upon him with suspicion. He was very unorthodox, which frightened them; and his freakish humour excited their disapproval.

"How can you have known a hundred and forty-seven of him?" asked Philip seriously.

"I've met him in the Latin Quarter in Paris, and I've met him in pensions in Berlin and Munich. He lives in small hotels in Perugia and Assisi. He stands by the dozen before the Botticellis in Florence, and he sits on all the benches of the Sistine Chapel in

Rome. In Italy he drinks a little too much wine, and in Germany he drinks a great deal too much beer. He always admires the right thing whatever the right thing is, and one of these days he's going to write a great work. Think of it, there are a hundred and forty-seven great works reposing in the bosoms of a hundred and forty-seven great men, and the tragic thing is that not one of those hundred and forty-seven great works will ever be written. And yet the world goes on."

Weeks spoke seriously, but his grey eyes twinkled a little at the end of his long speech, and Philip flushed when he saw that the American was making fun of him.

"You do talk rot," he said crossly.

Chapter 27

Weeks had two little rooms at the back of Frau Erlin's house, and one of them, arranged as a parlour, was comfortable enough for him to invite people to sit in. After supper, urged perhaps by the impish humour which was the despair of his friends in Cambridge, Mass., he often asked Philip and Hayward to come in for a chat. He received them with elaborate courtesy and insisted on their sitting in the only two comfortable chairs in the room. Though he did not drink himself, with a politeness of which Philip recognized the irony, he put a couple of bottles of beer at Hayward's elbow, and he insisted on lighting matches whenever in the heat of argument Hayward's pipe went out. At the beginning of their acquaintance Hayward, as a member of so celebrated a university, had adopted a patronizing attitude towards Weeks, who was a graduate of Harvard; and when by chance the conversation turned upon the Greek tragedians, a subject upon which Hayward felt he spoke with authority, he had assumed the air that it was his part to give information rather than to exchange ideas. Weeks had listened politely, with smiling modesty, till Hayward finished;

then he asked one or two insidious questions, so innocent in appearance that Hayward, not seeing into what a quandary they led him, answered blandly; Weeks made a courteous objection, then a correction of fact, after that a quotation from some little known Latin commentator, then a reference to a German authority; and the fact was disclosed that he was a scholar. With smiling ease, apologetically, Weeks tore to pieces all that Hayward had said; with elaborate civility he displayed the superficiality of his attainments. He mocked him with gentle irony. Philip could not help seeing that Hayward looked a perfect fool, and Hayward had not the sense to hold his tongue; in his irritation, his self-assurance undaunted, he attempted to argue: he made wild statements and Weeks amicably corrected them; he reasoned falsely and Weeks proved that he was absurd: Weeks confessed that he had taught Greek Literature at Harvard. Hayward gave a laugh of scorn.

"I might have known it. Of course you read Greek like a schoolmaster," he said. "I read it like a poet."

"And do you find it more poetic when you don't quite know what it means? I thought it was only in revealed religion that a mistranslation improved the sense."

At last, having finished the beer, Hayward left Weeks' room hot and dishevelled; with an angry gesture he said to Philip:

"Of course the man's a pedant. He has no real feeling for beauty. Accuracy is the virtue of clerks. It's the spirit of the Greeks that we aim at. Weeks is like that fellow who went to hear Rubinstein and complained that he played false notes. False notes! What did they matter when he played divinely?"

Philip, not knowing how many incompetent people have found solace in these false notes, was much impressed.

Hayward could never resist the opportunity which Weeks offered him of regaining ground lost on a previous occasion, and Weeks was able with the greatest ease to draw him into a discussion. Though he could not help seeing how small his attainments were beside the American's, his British pertinacity, his wounded vanity (perhaps they are the same thing), would not allow him to give up the struggle. Hayward seemed to take a delight in displaying his ignorance, self-satisfaction, and wrongheadedness. Whenever Hayward said something which was illogical, Weeks in a few words would show the falseness of his reasoning, pause for a moment to enjoy his triumph, and then hurry on to another subject as though Christian charity impelled him to spare the vanquished foe. Philip tried sometimes to put in something to help his friend, and Weeks gently crushed him, but so kindly, differently from the way in which he answered Hayward, that even Philip, outrageously sensitive, could not feel hurt. Now and then, losing his calm as he felt himself more and more foolish, Hayward became abusive, and only the American's smiling politeness prevented the argument from degenerating into a quarrel. On these occasions when Hayward left Weeks' room he muttered angrily:

"Damned Yankee!"

That settled it. It was a perfect answer to an argument which had seemed unanswerable.

Though they began by discussing all manner of subjects in Weeks' little room eventually the conversation always turned to religion: the theological student took a professional interest in it, and Hayward welcomed a subject in which hard facts need not disconcert him; when feeling is the gauge you can snap your fingers at logic, and when your logic is weak that is very agreeable. Hayward found it difficult to explain his beliefs to Philip without a great flow of words; but it was clear (and this fell in with Philip's idea of the natural order of things) that he had been brought up in the church by law established. Though he had now given up all idea of becoming a Roman Catholic, he still looked upon that communion with sympathy. He had much to say in its praise, and he compared favourably its gorgeous ceremonies with the simple services of the Church of England. He gave Philip Newman's *Apologia* to read, and Philip, finding it very dull, nevertheless read it to the end.

"Read it for its style, not for its matter," said Hayward.

He talked enthusiastically of the music at the Oratory, and said charming things about the connection between incense and the devotional spirit. Weeks listened to him with his frigid smile.

"You think it proves the truth of Roman Catholicism that John Henry Newman wrote good English and that Cardinal Manning has a picturesque appearance?"

Hayward hinted that he had gone through much trouble with his soul. For a year he had swum in a sea of darkness. He passed his fingers through his fair, waving hair and told them that he would not for five hundred pounds endure again those agonies of mind. Fortunately he had reached calm waters at last.

"But what *do* you believe?" asked Philip, who was never satisfied with vague statements.

"I believe in the Whole, the Good, and the Beautiful."

Hayward with his loose large limbs and the fine carriage of his head looked very handsome when he said this, and he said it with an air.

"Is that how you would describe your religion in a census paper?" asked Weeks, in mild tones.

"I hate the rigid definition: it's so ugly, so obvious. If you like I will say that I believe in the church of the Duke of Wellington and Mr. Gladstone."

"That's the Church of England," said Philip.

"Oh, wise young man!" retorted Hayward, with a smile which made Philip blush, for he felt that in putting into plain words what the other had expressed in a paraphrase, he had been guilty of vulgarity. "I belong to the Church of England. But I love the gold and the silk which clothe the priest of Rome, and his celibacy, and the confessional, and purgatory; and in the darkness of an Italian cathedral, incense-laden and mysterious, I believe with all my heart in the miracle of the Mass. In Venice I have seen a fisherwoman come in, barefoot, throw down her basket of fish by her side, fall on her knees, and pray to the Madonna; and that I felt was the real faith, and I prayed and believed with her. But I believe also in Aphrodite and Apollo and the Great God Pan."

He had a charming voice, and he chose his words as he spoke; he uttered them almost rhythmically. He would have gone on, but Weeks opened a second bottle of beer.

"Let me give you something to drink."

Hayward turned to Philip with the slightly condescending gesture which so impressed the youth.

"Now are you satisfied?" he asked.

Philip, somewhat bewildered, confessed that he was.

"I'm disappointed that you didn't add a little Buddhism," said Weeks. "And I confess I have a sort of sympathy for Mahomet; I regret that you should have left him out in the cold."

Hayward laughed, for he was in a good humour with himself that evening, and the ring of his sentences still sounded pleasant in his ears. He emptied his glass.

"I didn't expect you to understand me," he answered. "With your cold American intelligence you can only adopt the critical attitude. Emerson and all that sort of thing. But what is criticism? Criticism is purely destructive; anyone can destroy, but not everyone can build up. You are a pedant, my dear fellow. The important thing is to construct: I am constructive; I am a poet."

Weeks looked at him with eyes which seemed at the same time to be quite grave and yet to be smiling brightly.

"I think, if you don't mind my saying so, you're a little drunk."

"Nothing to speak of," answered Hayward cheerfully. "And not enough for me to be unable to overwhelm you in argument. But come, I have unbosomed my soul; now tell us what your religion is."

Weeks put his head on one side so that he looked like a sparrow on a perch.

"I've been trying to find that out for years. I think I'm a Unitarian."

"But that's a dissenter," said Philip.

He could not imagine why they both burst into laughter,

Hayward uproariously, and Weeks with a funny chuckle.

"And in England dissenters aren't gentlemen, are they?" asked Weeks.

"Well, if you ask me point-blank, they're not," replied Philip rather crossly.

He hated being laughed at, and they laughed again.

"And will you tell me what a gentleman is?" asked Weeks.

"Oh, I don't know; everyone knows what it is."

"Are you a gentleman?"

No doubt had ever crossed Philip's mind on the subject, but he knew it was not a thing to state of oneself.

"If a man tells you he's a gentleman you can bet your boots he isn't," he retorted.

"Am I a gentleman?"

Philip's truthfulness made it difficult for him to answer, but he was naturally polite.

"Oh, well, you're different," he said. "You're American, aren't you?"

"I suppose we may take it that only Englishmen are gentlemen," said Weeks gravely.

Philip did not contradict him.

"Couldn't you give me a few more particulars?" asked Weeks.

Philip reddened, but, growing angry, did not care if he made himself ridiculous.

"I can give you plenty." He remembered his uncle's saying that it took three generations to make a gentleman: it was a companion proverb to the silk purse and the sow's ear. "First of all he's the son of a gentleman, and he's been to a public school and to Oxford or Cambridge."

"Edinburgh wouldn't do, I suppose?" asked Weeks.

"And he talks English like a gentleman, and he wears the right sort of things, and if he's a gentleman he can always tell if another chap's a gentleman."

It seemed rather lame to Philip as he went on, but there it was: that was what he meant by the word, and everyone he had ever known had meant that too.

"It is evident to me that I am not a gentleman," said Weeks. "I don't see why you should have been so surprised because I was a dissenter."

"I don't quite know what a Unitarian is," said Philip.

Weeks in his odd way again put his head on one side: you almost expected him to twitter.

"A Unitarian very earnestly believes in almost everything that anybody else believes, and he has a very lively sustaining faith in he doesn't quite know what."

"I don't see why you should make fun of me," said Philip. "I really want to know."

"My dear friend, I'm not making fun of you. I have arrived at that definition after years of great labour and the most anxious, nerve-racking study."

When Philip and Hayward got up to go, Weeks handed Philip a little book in a paper cover.

"I suppose you can read French pretty well by now. I wonder if this would amuse you."

Philip thanked him and, taking the book, looked at the title. It was Renan's *Vie de Jésus*.

Chapter 28

It occurred neither to Hayward nor to Weeks that the conversations which helped them to pass an idle evening were being turned over afterwards in Philip's active brain. It had never struck him before that religion was a matter upon which discussion was possible. To him it meant the Church of England, and not to believe in its tenets was a sign of wilfulness which could not fail of punishment here or hereafter. There was some doubt in his mind about the chastisement of unbelievers. It was possible that a merciful judge, reserving the flames of hell for the heathen—Mahommedans, Buddhists, and the rest—would spare Dissenters and Roman Catholics (though at the cost of how much humiliation when they were made to realize their error!), and it was also possible that He would be pitiful to those who had had no chance of learning the truth—this was reasonable enough, though such were the activities of the Missionary Society there could not be many in this condition—but if the chance had been theirs and they had neglected it (in which category were obviously Roman Catholics and Dissenters), the punishment was sure and merited. It was clear that the miscreant was in a parlous state. Perhaps Philip had not been taught it in so many words, but certainly the impression had been given him that only members of the Church of England had any real hope of eternal happiness.

One of the things that Philip had heard definitely stated was that the unbeliever was a wicked and a vicious man; but Weeks, though he believed in hardly anything that Philip believed, led a life of Christian purity. Philip had received little kindness in his life, and he was touched by the American's desire to help him: once when a cold kept him in bed for three days, Weeks nursed him like a mother. There was neither vice nor wickedness in him, but only sincerity and loving-kindness. It was evidently possible to be virtuous and unbelieving.

Also Philip had been given to understand that people adhered to other faiths only from obstinacy or self-interest: in their hearts they knew they were false; they deliberately sought to deceive others. Now, for the sake of his German he had been accustomed on Sunday mornings to attend the Lutheran service, but when Hayward arrived he began instead to go with him to Mass. He noticed that, whereas the Protestant church was nearly empty and the congregation had a listless air, the Jesuit on the other hand was crowded and the worshippers seemed to pray with all their hearts. They had not the look of hypocrites. He was surprised at the contrast; for he knew of course that the Lutherans, whose faith was closer to that of the Church of England, on that account were nearer the truth than the Roman Catholics. Most of the men—it was largely a masculine congregation—were South Germans; and he could not help saying to himself that if he had been born in South Germany he would certainly have been a Roman Catholic. He might just as well have been born in a Roman Catholic country as in England; and in England as well in a Wesleyan, Baptist, or Methodist family as in one that fortunately belonged to the church by law established. He was a little breathless at the danger he had run. Philip was on friendly terms with the little Chinaman who sat at table with him twice each day. His name was Sung. He was always smiling, affable, and polite. It seemed strange that he should frizzle in hell merely because he was a Chinaman; but if salvation was possible whatever a man's faith was, there did not seem to be any particular advantage in belonging to the Church of England.

Philip, more puzzled than he had ever been in his life, sounded Weeks. He had to be careful, for he was very sensitive to ridicule; and the acidulous humour with which the American treated the Church of England disconcerted him. Weeks only puzzled him more. He made Philip acknowledge that those South Germans whom he saw in the Jesuit church were every bit as firmly convinced of the truth of Roman Catholicism as he was of that of the Church of England, and from that he led him to admit that the Mahommedan and the Buddhist were convinced also of the truth of their respective religions. It looked as though knowing that you were right meant nothing; they all knew they were right. Weeks had no intention of undermining the boy's faith, but he was deeply interested in religion, and found it an absorbing topic of conversation. He had described his own views accurately when he said that he very earnestly disbelieved in almost everything that other people believed. Once Philip asked him a question, which he had heard his uncle put when the conversation at the vicarage had fallen upon some mildly rationalistic work which was then exciting discussion in the newspapers.

"But why should you be right and all those fellows like St. Anselm and St. Augustine be wrong?"

"You mean that they were very clever and learned men, while you have grave doubts whether I am either?" asked Weeks.

"Yes," answered Philip uncertainly, for put in that way his question seemed impertinent.

"St. Augustine believed that the earth was flat and that the sun turned round it."

"I don't know what that proves."

"Why, it proves that you believe with your generation. Your saints lived in an age of faith, when it was practically impossible to disbelieve what to us is positively incredible."

"Then how d'you know that we have the truth now?"

"I don't."

Philip thought this over for a moment, then he said:

"I don't see why the things we believe absolutely now shouldn't be just as wrong as what they believed in the past."

"Neither do I."

"Then how can you believe anything at all?"

"I don't know."

Philip asked Weeks what he thought of Hayward's religion.

"Men have always formed gods in their own image," said Weeks. "He believes in the picturesque."

Philip paused for a little while, then he said:

"I don't see why one should believe in God at all."

The words were no sooner out of his mouth than he realized that he had ceased to do so. It took his breath away like a plunge into cold water. He looked at Weeks with startled eyes. Suddenly he felt afraid. He left Weeks as quickly as he could. He wanted to be alone. It was the most startling experience that he had ever had. He tried to think it all out; it was very exciting, since his whole life seemed concerned (he thought his decision on this matter must profoundly affect its course) and a mistake might lead to eternal damnation; but the more he reflected the more convinced he was; and though during the next few weeks he read books, aids to scepticism, with eager interest it was only to confirm him in what he felt instinctively. The fact was that he had ceased to believe not for this reason or the other, but because he had not the religious temperament. Faith had been forced upon him from the outside. It was a matter of environment and example. A new environment and a new example gave him the opportunity to find himself. He put off the faith of his childhood quite simply, like a cloak that he no longer needed. At first life seemed strange and lonely without the belief which, though he never realized it, had been an unfailing support. He felt like a man who has leaned on a stick and finds himself forced suddenly to walk without assistance. It really seemed as though the days were colder and the nights more solitary. But he was upheld by the excitement; it seemed to make life a more thrilling adventure; and in a little while the stick which he had thrown aside, the cloak which had fallen from his shoulders, seemed an intolerable burden of which he had been eased. The religious exercises which for so many years had been forced upon him were part and parcel of religion to him. He thought of the collects and epistles which he had been made to learn by heart, and the long services in the Cathedral through which he had sat when every limb itched with the desire for movement; and he remembered those walks at night through muddy roads to the parish church at Blackstable, and the coldness of that bleak building; he sat with his feet like ice, his fingers numb and heavy, and all around was the sickly smell of pomatum. Oh, he had been so bored! His heart leaped when he saw he was free from all that.

He was surprised at himself because he ceased to believe so easily, and, not knowing that he felt as he did on account of the subtle workings of his inmost nature, he ascribed the certainty he had reached to his own cleverness. He was unduly pleased with himself. With youth's lack of sympathy for an attitude other than its own he despised not a little Weeks and Hayward because they were content with the vague emotion which they called God and would not take the further step which to himself seemed so obvious. One day he went alone up a certain hill so that he might see a view which, he knew not why, filled him always with wild exhilaration. It was autumn now, but often the days were cloudless still, and then the sky seemed to glow with a more splendid light: it was as though nature consciously sought to put a fuller vehemence into the remaining days of fair weather. He looked down upon the plain, a-quiver with the sun, stretching vastly before him: in the distance were the roofs of Mannheim and ever so far away the dimness of Worms. Here and there a more piercing glitter was the Rhine. The tremendous spaciousness of it was glowing with rich gold. Philip, as he stood there, his heart beating with sheer joy, thought how the tempter had stood with Jesus on a high mountain and shown him the kingdoms of the earth. To Philip, intoxicated with the beauty of the scene, it seemed that it was the whole world which was spread before him, and he was eager to step down and enjoy it. He was free from degrading fears and free from prejudice. He could go his way without the intolerable dread of hell-fire. Suddenly he realized that he had lost also that burden of responsibility which made every action of his life a matter of urgent consequence. He could breathe more freely in a lighter air. He was responsible only to himself for the things he did. Freedom! He was his own master at last. From old habit, unconsciously he thanked God that he no longer believed in Him.

Drunk with pride in his intelligence and in his fearlessness, Philip entered deliberately upon a new life. But his loss of faith made less difference in his behaviour than he expected. Though he had thrown on one side the Christian dogmas it never occurred to him to criticize the Christian ethics; he accepted the Christian virtues, and indeed thought it fine to practise them for their own sake, without a thought of reward or punishment. There was small occasion for heroism in the Frau Professor's house, but he was a little more exactly truthful than he had been, and he forced himself to be more than commonly attentive to the dull, elderly ladies who sometimes engaged him in conversation. The gentle oath, the violent adjective, which are typical of our language and which he had cultivated before as a sign of manliness, he now elaborately eschewed.

Having settled the whole matter to his satisfaction he sought to put it out of his mind, but that was more easily said than done; and he could not prevent the regrets nor stifle the misgivings which sometimes tormented him. He was so young and had so few friends that immortality had no particular attractions for him, and he was able without trouble to give up belief in it; but there was one thing which made him wretched; he told himself that he was unreasonable, he tried to laugh himself out of such pathos; but the tears really came to his eyes when he thought that he would never see again the beautiful mother whose love for him had grown more precious as the years since her death passed on. And sometimes, as though the influence of innumerable ancestors, God-fearing and devout, were working in him unconsciously, there seized him a panic fear that perhaps after all it was all true, and there was, up there behind the blue sky, a jealous God who would punish in everlasting flames the atheist. At these times his reason could offer him no help, he imagined the anguish of a physical torment which would last endlessly, he felt quite sick with fear and burst into a violent sweat. At last he would say to himself desperately:

"After all, it's not my fault. I can't force myself to believe. If there is a God after all and He punishes me because I honestly don't believe in Him I can't help it."

Chapter 29

Winter set in. Weeks went to Berlin to attend the lectures of Paulssen, and Hayward began to think of going South. The local theatre opened its doors. Philip and Hayward went to it two or three times a week with the praiseworthy intention of improving their German, and Philip found it a more diverting manner of perfecting himself in the language than listening to sermons. They found themselves in the midst of a revival of the drama. Several of Ibsen's plays were on the repertory for the winter; Sudermann's *Die Ehre* was then a new play, and on its production in the quiet university town caused the greatest excitement; it was extravagantly praised and bitterly attacked; other dramatists followed with plays written under the modern influence and Philip witnessed a series of works in which the vileness of mankind was displayed before him. He had never been to a play in his life till then (poor touring companies sometimes came to the Assembly Rooms at Blackstable, but the Vicar, partly on account of his profession, partly because he thought it would be vulgar, never went to see them) and the passion of the stage seized him. He felt a thrill the moment he got into the little, shabby, ill-lit theatre. Soon he came to know the peculiarities of the small company, and by the casting could tell at once what were the characteristics of the persons in the drama; but this made no difference to him. To him it was real life. It was a strange life, dark and tortured, in which men and women showed to remorseless eyes the evil that was in their hearts: a fair face concealed a depraved mind; the virtuous used virtue as a mask to hide their secret vice, the seeming-strong fainted within with their weakness; the honest were corrupt, the chaste were lewd. You seemed to dwell in a room where the night before an orgy had taken place: the windows had not been opened in the morning; the air was foul with the dregs of beer, and stale smoke, and flaring gas. There was no laughter. At most you sniggered at the hypocrite or the fool: the characters expressed themselves in cruel words that seemed wrung out of their hearts by shame and anguish.

Philip was carried away by the sordid intensity of it. He seemed to see the world again in another fashion, and this world too he was anxious to know. After the play was over he went to a tavern and sat in the bright warmth with Hayward to eat a sandwich and drink a glass of beer. All round were little groups of students, talking and laughing; and here and there was a family, father and mother, a couple of sons and a girl; and sometimes the girl said a sharp thing, and the father leaned back in his chair and laughed, laughed heartily. It was very friendly and innocent. There was a pleasant homeliness in the scene, but for this Philip had no eyes. His thoughts ran on the play he had just come from.

"You do feel it's life, don't you?" he said excitedly. "You

know, I don't think I can stay here much longer. I want to get to London so that I can really begin. I want to have experiences. I'm so tired of preparing for life: I want to live it now."

Sometimes Hayward left Philip to go home by himself. He would never exactly reply to Philip's eager questioning, but with a merry, rather stupid laugh, hinted at a romantic amour; he quoted a few lines of Rossetti, and once showed Philip a sonnet in which passion and purple, pessimism and pathos, were packed together on the subject of a young lady called Trude. Hayward surrounded his sordid and vulgar little adventures with a glow of poetry, and thought he touched hands with Pericles and Pheidias because to describe the object of his attentions he used the word *hetaira* instead of one of those, more blunt and apt, provided by the English language. Philip in the daytime had been led by curiosity to pass through the little street near the old bridge, with its neat white houses and green shutters, in which according to Hayward the Fräulein Trude lived; but the women, with brutal faces and painted cheeks, who came out of their doors and cried out to him, filled him with fear; and he fled in horror from the rough hands that sought to detain him. He yearned above all things for experience and felt himself ridiculous because at his age he had not enjoyed that which all fiction taught him was the most important thing in life; but he had the unfortunate gift of seeing things as they were, and the reality which was offered him differed too terribly from the ideal of his dreams.

He did not know how wide a country, arid and precipitous, must be crossed before the traveller through life comes to an acceptance of reality. It is an illusion that youth is happy, an illusion of those who have lost it; but the young know they are wretched, for they are full of the truthless ideals which have been instilled into them, and each time they come in contact with the real they are bruised and wounded. It looks as if they were victims of a conspiracy; for the books they read, ideal by the necessity of selection, and the conversation of their elders, who look back upon the past through a rosy haze of forgetfulness, prepare them for an unreal life. They must discover for themselves that all they have read and all they have been told are lies, lies, lies; and each discovery is another nail driven into the body on the cross of life. The strange thing is that each one who has gone through that bitter disillusionment adds to it in his turn, unconsciously, by the power within him which is stronger than himself. The companionship of Hayward was the worst possible thing for Philip. He was a man who saw nothing for himself, but only through a literary atmosphere, and he was dangerous because he had deceived himself into sincerity. He honestly mistook his sensuality for romantic emotion, his vacillation for the artistic temperament, and his idleness for philosophic calm. His mind, vulgar in its effort at refinement, saw everything a little larger than life size, with the outlines blurred, in a golden mist of sentimentality. He lied and never knew that he lied, and when it was pointed out to him said that lies were beautiful. He was an idealist.

Chapter 30

Philip was restless and dissatisfied. Hayward's poetic allusions troubled his imagination, and his soul yearned for romance. At least that was how he put it to himself.

And it happened that an incident was taking place in Frau Erlin's house which increased Philip's preoccupation with the matter of sex. Two or three times on his walks among the hills he had met Fräulein Cäcilie wandering by herself. He had passed her with a bow, and a few yards further on had seen the Chinaman. He thought nothing of it; but one evening on his way home, when night had already fallen, he passed two people walking very close together. Hearing his footstep, they separated quickly, and though he could not see well in the darkness he was almost certain they were Cäcilie and Herr Sung. Their rapid movement apart suggested that they had been walking arm in arm. Philip was puzzled and surprised. He had never paid much attention to Fräulein Cäcilie. She was a plain girl, with a square face and blunt features. She could not have been more than sixteen, since she still wore her long fair hair in a plait. That evening at supper he looked at her curiously; and, though of late she had talked little at meals, she addressed him.

"Where did you go for your walk today, Herr Carey?" she asked.

"Oh, I walked up towards the *Königstuhl*."

"I didn't go out," she volunteered. "I had a headache."

The Chinaman, who sat next to her, turned round.

"I'm so sorry," he said. "I hope it's better now."

Fräulein Cäcilie was evidently uneasy, for she spoke again to Philip.

"Did you meet many people on the way?"

Philip could not help reddening when he told a downright lie.

"No. I don't think I saw a living soul."

He fancied that a look of relief passed across her eyes.

Soon, however, there could be no doubt that there was something between the pair, and other people in the Frau Professor's house saw them lurking in dark places. The elderly ladies who sat at the head of the table began to discuss what was now a scandal. The Frau Professor was angry and harassed. She had done her best to see nothing. The winter was at hand, and it was not as easy a matter then as in the summer to keep her house full. Herr Sung was a good customer: he had two rooms on the ground floor, and he drank a bottle of Moselle at each meal. The Frau Professor charged him three marks a bottle and made a good profit. None of her other guests drank wine, and some of them did not even drink beer. Neither did she wish to lose Fräulein Cäcilie, whose parents were in business in South America and paid well for the Frau Professor's motherly care; and she knew that if she wrote to the girl's uncle, who lived in Berlin, he would immediately take her away. The Frau Professor contented herself with giving them both severe looks at table and, though she dared not be rude to the Chinaman, got a certain satisfaction out of incivility to Cäcilie. But the three elderly ladies were not content. Two were widows, and one, a Dutchwoman, was a spinster of masculine appearance; they paid the smallest possible sum for their pension, and gave a good deal of trouble, but they were permanent and therefore had to be put up with. They went to the Frau Professor and said that something must be done; it was disgraceful, and the house was ceasing to be respectable. The Frau Professor tried obstinacy, anger, tears, but the three old ladies routed her, and with a sudden assumption of virtuous indignation she said that she would put a stop to the whole thing.

After luncheon she took Cäcilie into her bedroom and began to talk very seriously to her; but to her amazement the girl adopted a brazen attitude; she proposed to go about as she liked; and if she chose to walk with the Chinaman she could not see it was anybody's business but her own. The Frau Professor threatened to write to her uncle.

"Then Onkel Heinrich will put me in a family in Berlin for the winter, and that will be much nicer for me. And Herr Sung will come to Berlin too."

The Frau Professor began to cry. The tears rolled down her coarse, red, fat cheeks; and Cäcilie laughed at her.

"That will mean three rooms empty all through the winter," she said.

Then the Frau Professor tried another plan. She appealed to

Fräulein Cäcilie's better nature: she was kind, sensible, tolerant; she treated her no longer as a child, but as a grown woman. She said that it wouldn't be so dreadful, but a Chinaman, with his yellow skin and flat nose, and his little pig's eyes! That's what made it so horrible. It filled one with disgust to think of it.

"*Bitte, bitte,*" said Cäcilie, with a rapid intake of the breath. "I won't listen to anything against him."

"But it's not serious?" gasped Frau Erlin.

"I love him. I love him. I love him."

"*Gott im Himmel!*"

The Frau Professor stared at her with horrified surprise; she had thought it was no more than naughtiness on the child's part, and innocent, folly; but the passion in her voice revealed everything. Cäcilie looked at her for a moment with flaming eyes, and then with a shrug of her shoulders went out of the room.

Frau Erlin kept the details of the interview to herself, and a day or two later altered the arrangement of the table. She asked Herr Sung if he would not come and sit at her end, and he with his unfailing politeness accepted with alacrity. Cäcilie took the change indifferently. But as if the discovery that the relations between them were known to the whole household made them more shameless, they made no secret now of their walks together, and every afternoon quite openly set out to wander about the hills. It was plain that they did not care what was said of them. At last even the placidity of Professor Erlin was moved, and he insisted that his wife should speak to the Chinaman. She took him aside in his turn and expostulated; he was ruining the girl's reputation, he was doing harm to the house, he must see how wrong and wicked his conduct was; but she was met with smiling denials; Herr Sung did not know what she was talking about, he was not paying any attention to Fräulein Cäcilie, he never walked with her; it was all untrue, every word of it.

"*Ach*, Herr Sung, how can you say such things? You've been seen again and again."

"No, you're mistaken. It's untrue."

He looked at her with an unceasing smile, which showed his even, little white teeth. He was quite calm. He denied everything. He denied with bland effrontery. At last the Frau Professor lost her temper and said the girl had confessed she loved him. He was not moved. He continued to smile.

"Nonsense! Nonsense! It's all untrue."

She could get nothing out of him. The weather grew very bad; there was snow and frost, and then a thaw with a long succession of cheerless days, on which walking was a poor amusement. One evening when Philip had just finished his German lesson with the Herr Professor and was standing for a moment in the drawing-room, talking to Frau Erlin, Anna came quickly in.

"Mamma, where is Cäcilie?" she said.

"I suppose she's in her room."

"There's no light in it."

The Frau Professor gave an exclamation, and she looked at her daughter in dismay. The thought which was in Anna's head had flashed across hers.

"Ring for Emil," she said hoarsely.

This was the stupid lout who waited at table and did most of the housework. He came in.

"Emil, go down to Herr Sung's room and enter without knocking. If anyone is there say you came in to see about the stove."

No sign of astonishment appeared on Emil's phlegmatic face.

He went slowly downstairs. The Frau Professor and Anna left the door open and listened. Presently they heard Emil come up again, and they called him.

"Was anyone there?" asked the Frau Professor.

"Yes, Herr Sung was there."

"Was he alone?"

The beginning of a cunning smile narrowed his mouth.

"No, Fräulein Cäcilie was there."

"Oh, it's disgraceful," cried the Frau Professor.

Now he smiled broadly.

"Fräulein Cäcilie is there every evening. She spends hours at a time there."

Frau Professor began to wring her hands.

"Oh, how abominable! But why didn't you tell me?"

"It was no business of mine," he answered, slowly shrugging his shoulders.

"I suppose they paid you well. Go away. Go."

He lurched clumsily to the door.

"They must go away, mamma," said Anna.

"And who is going to pay the rent? And the taxes are falling due. It's all very well for you to say they must go away. If they go away I can't pay the bills." She turned to Philip, with tears streaming down her face. "*Ach*, Herr Carey, you will not say what you have heard. If Fräulein Förster— " this was the Dutch spinster— "if Fräulein Förster knew she would leave at once. And if they all go we must close the house. I cannot afford to keep it."

"Of course I won't say anything."

"If she stays, I will not speak to her," said Anna.

That evening at supper Fräulein Cäcilie, redder than usual, with a look of obstinacy on her face, took her place punctually; but Herr Sung did not appear, and for a while Philip thought he was going to shirk the ordeal. At last he came, very smiling, his little eyes dancing with the apologies he made for his late arrival. He insisted as usual on pouring out the Frau Professor a glass of his Moselle, and he offered a glass to Fräulein Förster. The room was very hot, for the stove had been alight all day and the windows were seldom opened. Emil blundered about, but succeeded somehow in serving everyone quickly and with order. The three old ladies sat in silence, visibly disapproving: the Frau Professor had scarcely recovered from her tears; her husband was silent and oppressed. Conversation languished. It seemed to Philip that there was something dreadful in that gathering which he had sat with so often; they looked different under the light of the two hanging lamps from what they had ever looked before; he was vaguely uneasy. Once he caught Cäcilie's eye, and he thought she looked at him with hatred and contempt. The room was stifling. It was as though the beastly passion of that pair troubled them all; there was a feeling of Oriental depravity; a faint savour of joss-sticks, a mystery of hidden vices, seemed to make their breath heavy. Philip could feel the beating of the arteries in his forehead.

He could not understand what strange emotion distracted him; he seemed to feel something infinitely attractive, and yet he was repelled and horrified.

For several days things went on. The air was sickly with the unnatural passion which all felt about them, and the nerves of the little household seemed to grow exasperated. Only Herr Sung remained unaffected; he was no less smiling, affable, and polite than he had been before: one could not tell whether his manner was a triumph of civilization or an expression of contempt on the part of the Oriental for the vanquished West. Cäcilie was flaunting and cynical. At last even the Frau Professor could bear the position no longer. Suddenly panic seized her; for Professor Erlin with brutal frankness had suggested the possible consequences of an intrigue which was now manifest to everyone, and she saw her good name in Heidelberg and the repute of her house ruined by a scandal which could not possibly be hidden. For some reason, blinded perhaps by her interests, this possibility had never occurred to her; and now, her wits muddled by a terrible fear, she could hardly be prevented from turning the girl out of the house at once. It was due to Anna's good sense that a cautious letter was written to the uncle in Berlin suggesting that Cäcilie should be taken away.

But having made up her mind to lose the two lodgers, the Frau Professor could not resist the satisfaction of giving rein to the ill-temper she had curbed so long. She was free now to say anything she liked to Cäcilie.

"I have written to your uncle, Cäcilie, to take you away. I cannot have you in my house any longer."

Her little round eyes sparkled when she noticed the sudden whiteness of the girl's face.

"You're shameless. Shameless," she went on.

She called her foul names.

"What did you say to my uncle Heinrich, Frau Professor?" the girl asked, suddenly falling from her attitude of flaunting independence.

"Oh, he'll tell you himself. I expect to get a letter from him tomorrow."

Next day, in order to make the humiliation more public, at supper she called down the table to Cäcilie.

"I have had a letter from your uncle, Cäcilie. You are to pack your things tonight, and we will put you in the train tomorrow morning. He will meet you himself in Berlin at the Central Bahnhof."

"Very good, Frau Professor."

Herr Sung smiled in the Frau Professor's eyes, and notwithstanding her protests insisted on pouring out a glass of wine for her. The Frau Professor ate her supper with a good appetite. But she had triumphed unwisely. Just before going to bed she called the servant.

"Emil, if Fräulein Cäcilie's box is ready you had better take it downstairs tonight. The porter will fetch it before breakfast."

The servant went away and in a moment came back.

"Fräulein Cäcilie is not in her room, and her bag has gone."

With a cry the Frau Professor hurried along: the box was on the floor, strapped and locked; but there was no bag, and neither hat nor cloak. The dressing-table was empty. Breathing heavily, the

Frau Professor ran downstairs to the Chinaman's rooms, she had not moved so quickly for twenty years, and Emil called out after her to beware she did not fall; she did not trouble to knock, but burst in. The rooms were empty. The luggage had gone, and the door into the garden, still open, showed how it had been got away. In an envelope on the table were notes for the money due on the month's board and an approximate sum for extras. Groaning, suddenly overcome by her haste, the Frau Professor sank obesely on to a sofa. There could be no doubt. The pair had gone off together. Emil remained stolid and unmoved.

Chapter 31

Hayward, after saying for a month that he was going South next day and delaying from week to week out of inability to make up his mind to the bother of packing and the tedium of a journey, had at last been driven off just before Christmas by the preparations for that festival. He could not support the thought of a Teutonic merry-making. It gave him goose-flesh to think of the season's aggressive cheerfulness, and in his desire to avoid the obvious he determined to travel on Christmas Eve.

Philip was not sorry to see him off, for he was a downright person and it irritated him that anybody should not know his own mind. Though much under Hayward's influence, he would not grant that indecision pointed to a charming sensitiveness; and he resented the shadow of a sneer with which Hayward looked upon his straight ways. They corresponded. Hayward was an admirable letter-writer, and knowing his talent took pains with his letters. His temperament was receptive to the beautiful influences with which he came in contact, and he was able in his letters from Rome to put a subtle fragrance of Italy. He thought the city of the ancient Romans a little vulgar, finding distinction only in the decadence of the Empire; but the Rome of the Popes appealed to his sympathy, and in his chosen words, quite exquisitely, there appeared a Rococo beauty. He wrote of old church music and the Alban Hills, and of the languor of incense and the charm of the streets by night, in the rain, when the pavements shone and the light of the street lamps was mysterious. Perhaps he repeated these admirable letters to various friends. He did not know what a troubling effect they had upon Philip; they seemed to make his life very humdrum. With the spring Hayward grew dithyrambic. He proposed that Philip should come down to Italy. He was wasting his time at Heidelberg. The Germans were gross and life there was common: how could the soul come to her own in that prim landscape? In Tuscany the spring was scattering flowers through the land, and Philip was nineteen; let him come and they could wander through the mountain towns of Umbria. Their names sank in Philip's heart. And Cäcilie too, with her lover, had gone to Italy. When he thought of them Philip was seized with a restlessness he could not account for. He cursed his fate because he had no money to travel, and he knew his uncle would not send him more than the fifteen pounds a month which had been agreed upon. He had not managed his allowance very well. His pension and the price of his lessons left him very little over, and he had found going about with Hayward expensive. Hayward had often suggested excursions, a visit to the play, or a bottle of wine, when Philip had come to the end of his month's money; and with the folly of his age he had been unwilling to confess he could not afford an extravagance.

Luckily Hayward's letters came seldom, and in the intervals Philip settled down again to his industrious life. He had matriculated at the university and attended one or two courses of lectures. Kuno Fischer was then at the height of his fame and during the winter had been lecturing brilliantly on Schopenhauer. It was Philip's introduction to philosophy. He had a practical mind and moved uneasily amid the abstract; but he found an unexpected fascination in listening to metaphysical disquisitions; they made him breathless; it was a little like watching a tight-rope dancer doing perilous feats over an abyss; but it was very exciting. The pessimism of the subject attracted his youth; and he believed that the world he was about to enter was a place of pitiless woe and of darkness. That made him none the less eager to enter it; and when, in due course, Mrs. Carey, acting as the correspondent for his guardian's views, suggested that it was time for him to come back to England, he agreed with enthusiasm. He must make up his mind now what he meant to do. If he left Heidelberg at the end of July they could talk things over during August, and it would be a good time to make arrangements.

The date of his departure was settled, and Mrs. Carey wrote to him again. She reminded him of Miss Wilkinson, through whose kindness he had gone to Frau Erlin's house at Heidelberg, and told him that she had arranged to spend a few weeks with them at Blackstable. She would be crossing from Flushing on such and such a day, and if he travelled at the same time he could look after her and come on to Blackstable in her company. Philip's shyness immediately made him write to say that he could not leave till a day or two afterwards. He pictured himself looking out for

Miss Wilkinson, the embarrassment of going up to her and asking if it were she (and he might so easily address the wrong person and be snubbed), and then the difficulty of knowing whether in the train he ought to talk to her or whether he could ignore her and read his book.

At last he left Heidelberg. For three months he had been thinking of nothing but the future; and he went without regret. He never knew that he had been happy there. Fräulein Anna gave him a copy of *Der Trompeter von Säckingen* and in return he presented her with a volume of William Morris. Very wisely neither of them ever read the other's present.

Chapter 32

Philip was surprised when he saw his uncle and aunt. He had never noticed before that they were quite old people. The Vicar received him with his usual, not unamiable, indifference. He was a little stouter, a little balder, a little greyer. Philip saw how insignificant he was. His face was weak and self-indulgent. Aunt Louisa took him in her arms and kissed him; and tears of happiness flowed down her cheeks. Philip was touched and embarrassed; he had not known with what a hungry love she cared for him.

"Oh, the time has seemed long since you've been away, Philip," she cried.

She stroked his hands and looked into his face with glad eyes.

"You've grown. You're quite a man now."

There was a very small moustache on his upper lip. He had bought a razor and now and then with infinite care shaved the down off his smooth chin.

"We've been so lonely without you." And then shyly, with a

little break in her voice, she asked: "You are glad to come back to your home, aren't you?"

"Yes, rather."

She was so thin that she seemed almost transparent, the arms she put round his neck were frail bones that reminded you of chicken bones, and her faded face was oh! so wrinkled. The grey curls which she still wore in the fashion of her youth gave her a queer, pathetic look; and her little withered body was like an autumn leaf, you felt it might be blown away by the first sharp wind. Philip realized that they had done with life, these two quiet little people: they belonged to a past generation, and they were waiting there patiently, rather stupidly, for death; and he, in his vigour and his youth, thirsting for excitement and adventure, was appalled at the waste. They had done nothing, and when they went it would be just as if they had never been. He felt a great pity for Aunt Louisa, and he loved her suddenly because she loved him.

Then Miss Wilkinson, who had kept discreetly out of the way till the Careys had had a chance of welcoming their nephew, came into the room.

"This is Miss Wilkinson, Philip," said Mrs. Carey.

"The prodigal has returned," she said, holding out her hand. "I have brought a rose for the prodigal's buttonhole."

With a gay smile she pinned to Philip's coat the flower she had just picked in the garden. He blushed and felt foolish. He knew that Miss Wilkinson was the daughter of his Uncle William's last rector, and he had a wide acquaintance with the daughters of clergymen. They wore ill-cut clothes and stout boots. They were generally dressed in black, for in Philip's early years at Blackstable homespuns had not reached East Anglia, and the ladies of the clergy did not favour colours. Their hair was done very untidily, and they smelt aggressively of starched linen. They considered the feminine graces unbecoming and looked the same whether they were old or young. They bore their religion arrogantly. The closeness of their connection with the church made them adopt a slightly dictatorial attitude to the rest of mankind.

Miss Wilkinson was very different. She wore a white muslin gown stamped with gay little bunches of flowers, and pointed, high-heeled shoes, with open-work stockings. To Philip's inexperience it seemed that she was wonderfully dressed; he did not see that her frock was cheap and showy. Her hair was elaborately dressed, with a neat curl in the middle of the forehead: it was very black, shiny, and hard, and it looked as though it could never be in the least disarranged. She had large black eyes and her nose was slightly aquiline; in profile she had somewhat the look of a bird of prey, but full face she was prepossessing. She smiled a great deal, but her mouth was large and when she smiled she tried to hide her teeth, which were big and rather yellow. But what embarrassed Philip most was that she was heavily powdered; he had very strict views on feminine behaviour and did not think a lady ever powdered; but of course Miss Wilkinson was a lady because she was a clergyman's daughter, and a clergyman was a gentleman.

Philip made up his mind to dislike her thoroughly. She spoke with a slight French accent; and he did not know why she should, since she had been born and bred in the heart of England. He thought her smile affected, and the coy sprightliness of her manner irritated him. For two or three days he remained silent and hostile, but Miss Wilkinson apparently did not notice it. She was very affable. She addressed her conversation almost exclusively to him, and there was something flattering in the way she appealed constantly to his sane judgment. She made him laugh too, and Philip could never resist people who amused him: he had a gift now and then of saying neat things; and it was pleasant to have an appreciative listener. Neither the Vicar nor Mrs. Carey had a sense of humour, and they never laughed at anything he said. As he grew used to Miss Wilkinson, and his shyness left him, he began to like her better; he found the French accent picturesque; and at a garden party which the doctor gave she was very much better dressed than anyone else. She wore a blue foulard with large white spots, and Philip was tickled at the sensation it caused.

"I'm certain they think you're no better than you should be," he told her, laughing.

"It's the dream of my life to be taken for an abandoned hussy," she answered.

One day when Miss Wilkinson was in her room he asked Aunt Louisa how old she was.

"Oh, my dear, you should never ask a lady's age; but she's certainly too old for you to marry."

The Vicar gave his slow, obese smile.

"She's no chicken, Louisa," he said. "She was nearly grown up when we were in Lincolnshire, and that was twenty years ago. She wore a pigtail hanging down her back."

"She may not have been more than ten," said Philip.

"She was older than that," said Aunt Louisa.

"I think she was nearer twenty," said the Vicar.

"Oh, no, William. Sixteen or seventeen at the outside."

"That would make her well over thirty," said Philip.

At that moment Miss Wilkinson tripped downstairs, singing a song by Benjamin Goddard. She had put her hat on, for she and Philip were going for a walk, and she held out her hand for him to button her glove. He did it awkwardly. He felt embarrassed but gallant. Conversation went easily between them now, and as they strolled along they talked of all manner of things. She told Philip about Berlin, and he told her of his year in Heidelberg. As he spoke, things which had appeared of no importance gained a new interest: he described the people at Frau Erlin's house; and to the conversations between Hayward and Weeks, which at the time seemed so significant, he gave a little twist, so that they looked absurd. He was flattered at Miss Wilkinson's laughter.

"I'm quite frightened of you," she said. "You're so sarcastic."

Then she asked him playfully whether he had not had any love affairs at Heidelberg. Without thinking, he frankly answered that he had not; but she refused to believe him.

"How secretive you are!" she said. "At your age is it likely?"

He blushed and laughed.

"You want to know too much," he said.

"Ah, I thought so," she laughed triumphantly. "Look at him blushing."

He was pleased that she should think he had been a sad dog, and he changed the conversation so as to make her believe he had all sorts of romantic things to conceal. He was angry with himself that he had not. There had been no opportunity.

Miss Wilkinson was dissatisfied with her lot. She resented having to earn her living and told Philip a long story of an uncle of her mother's, who had been expected to leave her a fortune but had married his cook and changed his will. She hinted at the luxury of her home and compared her life in Lincolnshire, with horses to ride and carriages to drive in, with the mean dependence of her present state. Philip was a little puzzled when he mentioned this afterwards to Aunt Louisa, and she told him that when she knew the Wilkinsons they had never had anything more than a pony and a dog-cart; Aunt Louisa had heard of the rich uncle, but as he was married and had children before Emily was born she could never have had much hope of inheriting his fortune. Miss Wilkinson had little good to say of Berlin, where she was now in a situation. She complained of the vulgarity of German life, and compared it bitterly with the brilliance of Paris, where she had spent a number of years. She did not say how many. She had been governess in the family of a fashionable portrait-painter, who had married a Jewish wife of means, and in their house she had met many distinguished people. She dazzled Philip with their names. Actors from the Comédie Française had come to the house frequently, and Coquelin, sitting next her at dinner, had told her he had never met a foreigner who spoke such perfect French. Alphonse Daudet had come also, and he had given her a copy of *Sapho*: he had promised to write her name in it, but she had forgotten to remind him. She treasured the volume none the less and she would lend it to Philip. Then there was Maupassant. Miss Wilkinson with a rippling laugh looked at Philip knowingly. What a man, but what a writer! Hayward had talked of Maupassant, and his reputation was not unknown to Philip.

"Did he make love to you?" he asked.

The words seemed to stick funnily in his throat, but he asked them nevertheless. He liked Miss Wilkinson very much now, and was thrilled by her conversation, but he could not imagine anyone making love to her.

"What a question!" she cried. "Poor Guy, he made love to every woman he met. It was a habit that he could not break himself of."

She sighed a little, and seemed to look back tenderly on the past.

"He was a charming man," she murmured.

A greater experience than Philip's would have guessed from these words the probabilities of the encounter: the distinguished writer invited to luncheon *en famille*, the governess coming in sedately with the two tall girls she was teaching; the introduction:

"*Notre Miss Anglaise.*"

"*Mademoiselle.*"

And the luncheon during which the *Miss Anglaise* sat silent while the distinguished writer talked to his host and hostess.

But to Philip her words called up much more romantic fancies.

"Do tell me all about him," he said excitedly.

"There's nothing to tell," she said truthfully, but in such a manner as to convey that three volumes would scarcely have contained the lurid facts. "You mustn't be curious."

She began to talk of Paris. She loved the boulevards and

the Bois. There was grace in every street, and the trees in the Champs-Élysées had a distinction which trees had not elsewhere. They were sitting on a stile now by the high-road, and Miss Wilkinson looked with disdain upon the stately elms in front of them. And the theatres: the plays were brilliant, and the acting was incomparable. She often went with Madame Foyot, the mother of the girls she was educating, when she was trying on clothes.

"Oh, what a misery to be poor!" she cried. "These beautiful things, it's only in Paris they know how to dress, and not to be able to afford them! Poor Madame Foyot, she had no figure. Sometimes the dressmaker used to whisper to me: 'Ah, Mademoiselle, if she only had your figure.'"

Philip noticed then that Miss Wilkinson had a robust form, and was proud of it.

"Men are so stupid in England. They only think of the face. The French, who are a nation of lovers, know how much more important the figure is."

Philip had never thought of such things before, but he observed now that Miss Wilkinson's ankles were thick and ungainly. He withdrew his eyes quickly.

"You should go to France. Why don't you go to Paris for a year? You would learn French, and it would—*déniaiser* you."

"What is that?" asked Philip.

She laughed slyly.

"You must look it out in the dictionary. Englishmen do not know how to treat women. They are so shy. Shyness is ridiculous in a man. They don't know how to make love. They can't even tell a woman she is charming without looking foolish."

Philip felt himself absurd. Miss Wilkinson evidently expected him to behave very differently; and he would have been delighted to say gallant and witty things, but they never occurred to him; and when they did he was much too afraid of making a fool of himself to say them.

"Oh, I love Paris," sighed Miss Wilkinson. "But I had to go to Berlin. I was with the Foyots till the girls married, and then I could get nothing to do, and I had the chance of this post in Berlin. They're relations of Madame Foyot, and I accepted. I had a tiny apartment in the Rue Bréda, on the *cinquiéme:* it wasn't at all respectable. You know about the Rue Bréda—*ces dames,* you know."

Philip nodded, not knowing at all what she meant, but vaguely suspecting, and anxious she should not think him too ignorant.

"But I didn't care. *Je suis libre, n'est-ce pas?*" She was very fond of speaking French, which indeed she spoke well. "Once I had such a curious adventure there."

She paused a little and Philip pressed her to tell it.

"You wouldn't tell me yours in Heidelberg," she said.

"They were so unadventurous," he retorted.

"I don't know what Mrs. Carey would say if she knew the sort of things we talk about together."

"You don't imagine I shall tell her."

"Will you promise?"

When he had done this, she told him how an art student who had a room on the floor above her—but she interrupted herself.

"Why don't you go in for art? You paint so prettily."

"Not well enough for that."

"That is for others to judge. *Je m'y connais*, and I believe you have the making of a great artist."

"Can't you see Uncle William's face if I suddenly told him I wanted to go to Paris and study art?"

"You're your own master, aren't you?"

"You're trying to put me off. Please go on with the story."

Miss Wilkinson, with a little laugh, went on. The art student had passed her several times on the stairs, and she had paid no particular attention. She saw that he had fine eyes, and he took off his hat very politely. And one day she found a letter slipped under her door. It was from him. He told her that he had adored her for months, and that he waited about the stairs for her to pass. Oh, it was a charming letter! Of course she did not reply, but what woman could help being flattered? And next day there was another letter! It was wonderful, passionate, and touching. When next she met him on the stairs she did not know which way to look. And every day the letters came, and now he begged her to see him. He said he would come in the evening, *vers neuf heures*, and she did not know what to do. Of course it was impossible, and he might ring and ring, but she would never open the door; and then while she was waiting for the tinkling of the bell, all nerves, suddenly he stood before her. She had forgotten to shut the door when she came in.

"*C'était une fatalité.*"

"And what happened then?" asked Philip.

"That is the end of the story," she replied, with a ripple of laughter.

Philip was silent for a moment. His heart beat quickly, and strange emotions seemed to be hustling one another in his heart. He saw the dark staircase and the chance meetings, and he admired the boldness of the letters—oh, he would never have dared to do that—and then the silent, almost mysterious entrance. It seemed to him the very soul of romance.

"What was he like?"

"Oh, he was handsome. *Charmant garçon.*"

"Do you know him still?"

Philip felt a slight feeling of irritation as he asked this.

"He treated me abominably. Men are always the same. You're heartless, all of you."

"I don't know about that," said Philip, not without embarrassment.

"Let us go home," said Miss Wilkinson.

Chapter 33

Philip could not get Miss Wilkinson's story out of his head. It was clear enough what she meant, even though she cut it short, and he was a little shocked. That sort of thing was all very well for married women, he had read enough French novels to know that in France it was indeed the rule, but Miss Wilkinson was English and unmarried; her father was a clergyman. Then it struck him that the art student probably was neither the first nor the last of her lovers, and he gasped: he had never looked upon Miss Wilkinson like that; it seemed incredible that anyone should make love to her. In his ingenuousness he doubted her story as little as he doubted what he read in books, and he was angry that such wonderful things never happened to him. It was humiliating that if Miss Wilkinson insisted upon his telling her of his adventures in Heidelberg he would have nothing to tell. It was true that he had some power of invention, but he was not sure whether he could persuade her that he was steeped in vice; women were full of intuition, he had read that, and she might easily discover that he was fibbing. He blushed scarlet as he thought of her laughing up her sleeve.

Miss Wilkinson played the piano and sang in a rather tired voice; but her songs, Massenet, Benjamin Goddard and Augusta Holmes, were new to Philip; and together they spent many hours at the piano. One day she wondered if he had a voice and insisted on trying it. She told him he had a pleasant baritone and offered to give him lessons. At first with his usual bashfulness he refused, but she insisted, and then every morning at a convenient time after breakfast she gave him an hour's lesson. She had a natural gift for teaching, and it was clear that she was an excellent governess. She had method and firmness. Though her French accent was so much part of her that it remained, all the mellifluousness of her manner left her when she was engaged in teaching. She put up with no nonsense. Her voice became a little peremptory, and instinctively she suppressed inattention and corrected slovenliness. She knew what she was about and put Philip to scales and exercises.

When the lesson was over she resumed without effort her seductive smiles, her voice became again soft and winning, but Philip could not so easily put away the pupil as she the pedagogue; and this impression conflicted with the feelings her stories had aroused in him. He looked at her more narrowly. He liked her much better in the evening than in the morning. In the morning she was rather lined and the skin of her neck was just a little rough. He wished she would hide it, but the weather was very warm just then and she wore blouses which were cut low. She was very fond of white; in the morning it did not suit her. At night she often looked very attractive, she put on a gown which was almost a dinner dress, and she wore a chain of garnets round her neck; the lace about her bosom and at her elbows gave her a pleasant softness, and the scent she wore (at Blackstable no one used anything but *eau-de-Cologne*, and that only on Sundays or when suffering from a sick headache) was troubling and exotic. She really looked very young then.

Philip was much exercised over her age. He added twenty and seventeen together, and could not bring them to a satisfactory total. He asked Aunt Louisa more than once why she thought Miss Wilkinson was thirty-seven: she didn't look more than thirty, and everyone knew that foreigners aged more rapidly than English women; Miss Wilkinson had lived so long abroad that she might almost be called a foreigner. He personally wouldn't have thought her more than twenty-six.

"She's more than that," said Aunt Louisa.

Philip did not believe in the accuracy of the Careys' statements. All they distinctly remembered was that Miss Wilkinson had not got her hair up the last time they saw her in Lincolnshire. Well, she might have been twelve then: it was so long ago and the Vicar was always so unreliable. They said it was twenty years ago, but people used round figures, and it was just as likely to be eighteen years, or seventeen. Seventeen and twelve were only twenty-nine, and hang it all, that wasn't old, was it? Cleopatra was forty-eight when Antony threw away the world for her sake.

It was a fine summer. Day after day was hot and cloudless; but the heat was tempered by the neighbourhood of the sea, and there was a pleasant exhilaration in the air, so that one was excited and not oppressed by the August sunshine. There was a pond in the garden in which a fountain played; water-lilies grew in it and goldfish sunned themselves on the surface. Philip and Miss Wilkinson used to take rugs and cushions there after dinner and lie on the lawn in the shade of a tall hedge of roses. They talked and read all the afternoon. They smoked cigarettes, which the Vicar did not allow in the house; he thought smoking a disgusting habit, and used frequently to say that it was disgraceful for anyone to grow a slave to a habit. He forgot that he was himself a slave to afternoon tea.

One day Miss Wilkinson gave Philip *La Vie de Bohême*. She had found it by accident when she was rummaging among the books in the Vicar's study. It had been bought in a lot with something Mr. Carey wanted and had remained undiscovered for ten years.

Philip began to read Murger's fascinating, ill-written, absurd masterpiece, and fell at once under its spell. His soul danced with joy at that picture of starvation which is so good-humoured, of squalor which is so picturesque, of sordid love which is so romantic, of bathos which is so moving. Rodolphe and Mimi, Musette and Schaunard! They wander through the grey streets of the Latin Quarter, finding refuge now in one attic, now in another, in their quaint costumes of Louis Philippe, with their tears and their smiles, happy-go-lucky and reckless. Who can resist them? It is only when you return to the book with a sounder judgment that you find how gross their pleasures were, how vulgar their minds; and you feel the utter worthlessness, as artists and as human beings, of that gay procession. Philip was enraptured.

"Don't you wish you were going to Paris instead of London?" asked MissWilkinson, smiling at his enthusiasm.

"It's too late now even if I did," he answered.

During the fortnight he had been back from Germany there had been much discussion between himself and his uncle about his future. He had refused definitely to go to Oxford, and now that there was no chance of his getting scholarships even Mr. Carey came to the conclusion that he could not afford it. His entire fortune had consisted of only two thousand pounds, and though it had been invested in mortgages at five per cent, he had not been able to live on the interest. It was now a little reduced. It would be absurd to spend two hundred a year, the least he could live on at a university, for three years at Oxford which would lead him no nearer to earning his living. He was anxious to go straight to London. Mrs. Carey thought there were only four professions for a gentleman, the Army, the Navy, the Law, and the Church. She had added medicine because her brother-in-law practised it, but did not forget that in her young days no one ever considered the doctor a gentleman. The first two were out of the question, and Philip was firm in his refusal to be ordained. Only the law remained. The local doctor had suggested that many gentlemen now went in for engineering, but Mrs. Carey opposed the idea at once.

"I shouldn't like Philip to go into trade," she said.

"No, he must have a profession," answered the Vicar.

"Why not make him a doctor like his father?"

"I should hate it," said Philip.

Mrs. Carey was not sorry. The Bar seemed out of the

question, since he was not going to Oxford, for the Careys were under the impression that a degree was still necessary for success in that calling; and finally it was suggested that he should become articled to a solicitor. They wrote to the family lawyer, Albert Nixon, who was co-executor with the Vicar of Blackstable for the late Henry Carey's estate, and asked him whether he would take Philip. In a day or two the answer came back that he had not a vacancy, and was very much opposed to the whole scheme; the profession was greatly overcrowded, and without capital or connections a man had small chance of becoming more than a managing clerk; he suggested, however, that Philip should become a chartered accountant. Neither the Vicar nor his wife knew in the least what this was, and Philip had never heard of anyone being a chartered accountant; but another letter from the solicitor explained that the growth of modern businesses and the increase of companies had led to the formation of many firms of accountants to examine the books and put into the financial affairs of their clients an order which old-fashioned methods had lacked. Some years before a Royal Charter had been obtained, and the profession was becoming every year more respectable, lucrative, and important. The chartered accountants whom Albert Nixon had employed for thirty years happened to have a vacancy for an articled pupil, and would take Philip for a fee of three hundred pounds. Half of this would be returned during the five years the articles lasted in the form of salary. The prospect was not exciting, but Philip felt that he must decide on something, and the thought of living in London overbalanced the slight shrinking he felt. The Vicar of Blackstable wrote to ask Mr. Nixon whether it was a profession suited to a gentleman; and Mr. Nixon replied that, since the Charter, men were going into it who had been to public schools and a university; moreover, if Philip disliked the work and after a year wished to leave, Herbert Carter, for that was the accountant's name, would return half the money paid for the articles. This settled it, and it was arranged that Philip should start work on the fifteenth of September.

"I have a full month before me," said Philip.

"And then you go to freedom and I to bondage," returned Miss Wilkinson.

Her holidays were to last six weeks, and she would be leaving Blackstable only a day or two before Philip.

"I wonder if we shall ever meet again," she said.

"I don't know why not."

"Oh, don't speak in that practical way. I never knew anyone so unsentimental."

Philip reddened. He was afraid that Miss Wilkinson would think him a milksop: after all she was a young woman, sometimes quite pretty, and he was getting on for twenty; it was absurd that they should talk of nothing but art and literature. He ought to make love to her. They had talked a good deal of love. There was the art student in the Rue Bréda, and then there was the painter in whose family she had lived so long in Paris: he had asked her to sit for him, and started to make love to her so violently that she was forced to invent excuses not to sit to him again. It was clear enough that Miss Wilkinson was used to attentions of that sort. She looked very nice now in a large straw hat: it was hot that afternoon, the hottest day they had had, and beads of sweat stood in a line on her upper lip. He called to mind Fräulein Cäcilie and Herr Sung. He had never thought of Cäcilie in an amorous way, she was exceedingly plain; but now, looking back, the affair seemed very romantic. He had a chance of romance too. Miss Wilkinson was practically French, and that added zest to a possible adventure. When he thought of it at night in bed, or when he sat by himself in the garden reading a book, he was thrilled by it; but when he saw Miss Wilkinson it seemed less picturesque.

At all events, after what she had told him, she would not be surprised if he made love to her. He had a feeling that she must think it odd of him to make no sign: perhaps it was only his fancy, but once or twice in the last day or two he had imagined that there was a suspicion of contempt in her eyes.

"A penny for your thoughts," said Miss Wilkinson, looking at him with a smile.

"I'm not going to tell you," he answered.

He was thinking that he ought to kiss her there and then. He wondered if she expected him to do it; but after all he didn't see how he could without any preliminary business at all. She would just think him mad, or she might slap his face; and perhaps she would complain to his uncle. He wondered how Herr Sung had started with Fräulein Cäcilie. It would be beastly if she told his uncle: he knew what his uncle was, he would tell the doctor and Josiah Graves; and he would look a perfect fool. Aunt Louisa kept on saying that Miss Wilkinson was thirty-seven if she was a day; he shuddered at the thought of the ridicule he would be exposed to; they would say she was old enough to be his mother.

"Twopence for your thoughts," smiled Miss Wilkinson.

"I was thinking about you," he answered boldly.

That at all events committed him to nothing.

"What were you thinking?"

"Ah, now you want to know too much."

"Naughty boy!" said Miss Wilkinson.

There it was again! Whenever he had succeeded in working himself up she said something which reminded him of the governess. She called him playfully a naughty boy when he did not sing his exercises to her satisfaction. This time he grew quite sulky.

"I wish you wouldn't treat me as if I were a child."

"Are you cross?"

"Very."

"I didn't mean to."

She put out her hand and he took it. Once or twice lately when they shook hands at night he had fancied she slightly pressed his hand, but this time there was no doubt about it.

He did not quite know what he ought to say next. Here at last was his chance of an adventure, and he would be a fool not to take it; but it was a little ordinary, and he had expected more glamour. He had read many descriptions of love, and he felt in himself none of that uprush of emotion which novelists described; he was not carried off his feet in wave upon wave of passion; nor was Miss Wilkinson the ideal: he had often pictured to himself the great violet eyes and the alabaster skin of some lovely girl, and he had thought of himself burying his face in the rippling masses of her auburn hair. He could not imagine himself burying his face in Miss Wilkinson's hair, it always struck him as a little sticky. All the same it would be very satisfactory to have an intrigue, and he thrilled with the legitimate pride he would enjoy in his conquest. He owed it to himself to seduce her. He made up his mind to kiss Miss Wilkinson; not then, but in the evening; it would be easier in the dark, and after he had kissed her the rest would follow. He would kiss her that very evening. He swore an oath to that effect.

He laid his plans. After supper he suggested that they should take a stroll in the garden. Miss Wilkinson accepted, and they sauntered side by side. Philip was very nervous. He did not know why, but the conversation would not lead in the right direction; he had decided that the first thing to do was to put his arm round her waist; but he could not suddenly put his arm round her waist when she was talking of the regatta which was to be held next week. He led her artfully into the darkest parts of the garden, but having arrived there his courage failed him. They sat on a bench, and he had really made up his mind that here was his opportunity when Miss Wilkinson said she was sure there were earwigs and insisted on moving. They walked round the garden once more, and Philip promised himself he would take the plunge before they arrived at that bench again; but as they passed the house, they saw Mrs. Carey standing at the door.

"Hadn't you young people better come in? I'm sure the night air isn't good for you."

"Perhaps we had better go in," said Philip. "I don't want you to catch cold."

He said it with a sigh of relief. He could attempt nothing more that night. But afterwards, when he was alone in his room, he was furious with himself. He had been a perfect fool. He was certain that Miss Wilkinson expected him to kiss her, otherwise she wouldn't have come into the garden. She was always saying that only Frenchmen knew how to treat women. Philip had read French novels. If he had been a Frenchman he would have seized her in his arms and told her passionately that he adored her; he would have pressed his lips on her *nuque*. He did not know why Frenchmen always kissed ladies on the *nuque*. He did not himself see anything so very attractive in the nape of the neck. Of course it was much easier for Frenchmen to do these things; the language was such an aid; Philip could never help feeling that to say passionate things in English sounded a little absurd. He wished now that he had never undertaken the siege of Miss Wilkinson's virtue; the first fortnight had been so jolly, and now he was wretched; but he was determined not to give in, he would never respect himself again if he did, and he made up his mind irrevocably that the next night he would kiss her without fail.

Next day when he got up he saw it was raining, and his first thought was that they would not be able to go into the garden that evening. He was in high spirits at breakfast. Miss Wilkinson sent Mary Ann in to say that she had a headache and would remain in bed. She did not come down till tea-time, when she appeared in a becoming wrapper and a pale face; but she was quite recovered by supper, and the meal was very cheerful. After prayers she said she would go straight to bed, and she kissed Mrs. Carey. Then she turned to Philip.

"Good gracious!" she cried. "I was just going to kiss you too."

"Why don't you?" he said.

She laughed and held out her hand. She distinctly pressed his.

The following day there was not a cloud in the sky, and the garden was sweet and fresh after the rain. Philip went down to the beach to bathe and when he came home ate a magnificent dinner. They were having a tennis party at the vicarage in the afternoon and Miss Wilkinson put on her best dress. She certainly knew how to wear her clothes, and Philip could not help noticing how elegant she looked beside the curate's wife and the doctor's married daughter. There were two roses in her waistband. She sat in a garden chair by the side of the lawn, holding a red parasol over herself, and the light on her face was very becoming. Philip was fond of tennis. He served well and as he ran clumsily played close to the net: notwithstanding his club-foot he was quick, and it was difficult to get a ball past him. He was pleased because he won all his sets. At tea he lay down at Miss Wilkinson's feet, hot and panting.

"Flannels suit you," she said. "You look very nice this afternoon."

He blushed with delight.

"I can honestly return the compliment. You look perfectly ravishing."

She smiled and gave him a long look with her black eyes.

After supper he insisted that she should come out.

"Haven't you had enough exercise for one day?"

"It'll be lovely in the garden tonight. The stars are all out."

He was in high spirits.

"D'you know, Mrs. Carey has been scolding me on your

account?" said Miss Wilkinson, when they were sauntering through the kitchen garden. "She says I mustn't flirt with you."

"Have you been flirting with me? I hadn't noticed it."

"She was only joking."

"It was very unkind of you to refuse to kiss me last night."

"If you saw the look your uncle gave me when I said what I did!"

"Was that all that prevented you?"

"I prefer to kiss people without witnesses."

"There are no witnesses now."

Philip put his arm round her waist and kissed her lips. She only laughed a little and made no attempt to withdraw. It had come quite naturally. Philip was very proud of himself. He said he would, and he had. It was the easiest thing in the world. He wished he had done it before. He did it again.

"Oh, you mustn't," she said.

"Why not?"

"Because I like it," she laughed.

Chapter 34

Next day after dinner they took their rugs and cushions to the fountain, and their books; but they did not read. Miss Wilkinson made herself comfortable and she opened the red sunshade. Philip was not at all shy now, but at first she would not let him kiss her.

"It was very wrong of me last night," she said. "I couldn't sleep, I felt I'd done so wrong."

"What nonsense!" he cried. "I'm sure you slept like a top."

"What do you think your uncle would say if he knew?"

"There's no reason why he should know."

He leaned over her, and his heart went pit-a-pat.

"Why d'you want to kiss me?"

He knew he ought to reply: "Because I love you." But he could not bring himself to say it.

"Why do you think?" he asked instead.

She looked at him with smiling eyes and touched his face with the tips of her fingers.

"How smooth your face is," she murmured.

"I want shaving awfully," he said.

It was astonishing how difficult he found it to make romantic speeches. He found that silence helped him much more than words. He could look inexpressible things. Miss Wilkinson sighed.

"Do you like me at all?"

"Yes, awfully."

When he tried to kiss her again she did not resist. He pretended to be much more passionate than he really was, and he succeeded in playing a part which looked very well in his own eyes.

"I'm beginning to be rather frightened of you," said Miss Wilkinson.

"You'll come out after supper, won't you?" he begged.

"Not unless you promise to behave yourself."

"I'll promise anything."

He was catching fire from the flame he was partly simulating, and at tea-time he was obstreperously merry. Miss Wilkinson looked at him nervously.

"You mustn't have those shining eyes," she said to him afterwards. "What will your Aunt Louisa think?"

"I don't care what she thinks."

Miss Wilkinson gave a little laugh of pleasure. They had no sooner finished supper than he said to her:

"Are you going to keep me company while I smoke a cigarette?"

"Why don't you let Miss Wilkinson rest?" said Mrs. Carey. "You must remember she's not as young as you."

"Oh, I'd like to go out, Mrs. Carey," she said, rather acidly.

"After dinner walk a mile, after supper rest a while," said the Vicar.

"Your aunt is very nice, but she gets on my nerves sometimes," said Miss Wilkinson, as soon as they closed the side door behind them.

Philip threw away the cigarette he had just lighted, and flung his arms round her. She tried to push him away.

"You promised you'd be good, Philip."

"You didn't think I was going to keep a promise like that?"

"Not so near the house, Philip," she said. "Supposing someone should come out suddenly?"

He led her to the kitchen garden where no one was likely to come, and this time Miss Wilkinson did not think of earwigs. He kissed her passionately. It was one of the things that puzzled him that he did not like her at all in the morning, and only moderately in the afternoon, but at night the touch of her hand thrilled him. He said things that he would never have thought himself capable of saying; he could certainly never have said them in the broad light of day; and he listened to himself with wonder and satisfaction.

"How beautifully you make love," she said.

That was what he thought himself.

"Oh, if I could only say all the things that burn my heart!" he murmured passionately.

It was splendid. It was the most thrilling game he had ever played; and the wonderful thing was that he felt almost all he said. It was only that he exaggerated a little. He was tremendously interested and excited in the effect he could see it had on her. It was obviously with an effort that at last she suggested going in.

"Oh, don't go yet," he cried.

"I must," she muttered. "I'm frightened."

He had a sudden intuition what was the right thing to do then.

"I can't go in yet. I shall stay here and think. My cheeks are burning. I want the night-air. Good night."

He held out his hand seriously, and she took it in silence. He thought she stifled a sob. Oh, it was magnificent! When, after a decent interval during which he had been rather bored in the dark garden by himself, he went in, he found that Miss Wilkinson had already gone to bed.

After that things were different between them. The next day and the day after Philip showed himself an eager lover. He was deliciously flattered to discover that Miss Wilkinson was in love with him: she told him so in English, and she told him so in French. She paid him compliments. No one had ever informed him before that his eyes were charming and that he had a sensual mouth. He had never bothered much about his personal appearance, but now, when occasion presented, he looked at himself in the glass with satisfaction. When he kissed her it was wonderful to feel the passion that seemed to thrill her soul. He kissed her a good deal, for he found it easier to do that than to say the things he instinctively felt she expected of him. It still made him feel a fool to say he worshipped her. He wished there were someone to whom he could boast a little, and he would willingly have discussed minute points of his conduct. Sometimes she said things that were enigmatic, and he was puzzled. He wished

Hayward had been there so that he could ask him what he thought she meant, and what he had better do next. He could not make up his mind whether he ought to rush things or let them take their time. There were only three weeks more.

"I can't bear to think of that," she said. "It breaks my heart. And then perhaps we shall never see one another again."

"If you cared for me at all, you wouldn't be so unkind to me," he whispered.

"Oh, why can't you be content to let it go on as it is? Men are always the same. They're never satisfied."

And when he pressed her, she said:

"But don't you see it's impossible. How can we here?"

He proposed all sorts of schemes, but she would not have anything to do with them.

"I daren't take the risk. It would be too dreadful if your aunt found out."

A day or two later he had an idea which seemed brilliant.

"Look here, if you had a headache on Sunday evening and offered to stay at home and look after the house, Aunt Louisa would go to church."

Generally Mrs. Carey remained in on Sunday evening in order to allow Mary Ann to go to church, but she would welcome the opportunity of attending evensong.

Philip had not found it necessary to impart to his relations the change in his views on Christianity which had occurred in Germany; they could not be expected to understand; and it seemed less trouble to go to church quietly. But he only went in the morning. He regarded this as a graceful concession to the prejudices of society and his refusal to go a second time as an adequate assertion of free thought.

When he made the suggestion, Miss Wilkinson did not speak for a moment, then shook her head.

"No, I won't," she said.

But on Sunday at tea-time she surprised Philip.

"I don't think I'll come to church this evening," she said suddenly. "I've really got a dreadful headache."

Mrs. Carey, much concerned, insisted on giving her some "drops" which she was herself in the habit of using. Miss Wilkinson thanked her, and immediately after tea announced that she would go to her room and lie down.

"Are you sure there's nothing you'll want?" asked Mrs. Carey anxiously.

"Quite sure, thank you."

"Because, if there isn't, I think I'll go to church. I don't often have the chance of going in the evening."

"Oh yes, do go."

"I shall be in," said Philip. "If Miss Wilkinson wants anything, she can always call me."

"You'd better leave the drawing-room door open, Philip, so that if Miss Wilkinson rings, you'll hear."

"Certainly," said Philip.

So after six o'clock Philip was left alone in the house with Miss Wilkinson. He felt sick with apprehension. He wished with all his heart that he had not suggested the plan; but it was too late now; he must take the opportunity which he had made. What would Miss Wilkinson think of him if he did not! He went into the hall and listened. There was not a sound. He wondered if Miss Wilkinson really had a headache. Perhaps she had forgotten his suggestion. His heart beat painfully. He crept up the stairs as softly as he could, and he stopped with a start when they creaked. He stood outside Miss Wilkinson's room and listened; he put his hand on the knob of the door-handle. He waited. It seemed to him that he waited for at least five minutes, trying to make up his mind; and his hand trembled. He would willingly have bolted, but he was afraid of the remorse which he knew would seize him. It was like getting on the highest diving-board in a swimming-bath; it looked nothing from below, but when you got up there and stared down at the water your heart sank; and the only thing that forced you to dive was the shame of coming down meekly by the steps you had climbed up. Philip screwed up his courage. He turned the handle softly and walked in. He seemed to himself to be trembling like a leaf.

Miss Wilkinson was standing at the dressing-table with her back to the door, and she turned round quickly when she heard it open.

"Oh, it's you. What d'you want?"

She had taken off her skirt and blouse, and was standing in her petticoat. It was short and only came down to the top of her boots; the upper part of it was black, of some shiny material, and there was a red flounce. She wore a camisole of white calico with short arms. She looked grotesque. Philip's heart sank as he stared at her; she had never seemed so unattractive; but it was too late now. He closed the door behind him and locked it.

Chapter 35

Philip woke early next morning. His sleep had been restless; but when he stretched his legs and looked at the sunshine that slid through the Venetian blinds, making patterns on the floor, he sighed with satisfaction. He was delighted with himself. He began to think of Miss Wilkinson. She had asked him to call her Emily, but, he knew not why, he could not; he always thought of her as Miss Wilkinson. Since she chid him for so addressing her, he avoided using her name at all. During his childhood he had often heard a sister of Aunt Louisa, the widow of a naval officer, spoken of as Aunt Emily. It made him uncomfortable to call Miss Wilkinson by that name, nor could he think of any that would have suited her better. She had begun as Miss Wilkinson, and it seemed inseparable from his impression of her. He frowned a little: somehow or other he saw her now at her worst; he could not forget his dismay when she turned round and he saw her in her camisole and the short petticoat; he remembered the slight roughness of her skin and the sharp, long lines on the side of the neck. His triumph was short-lived. He reckoned out her age again, and he did not see how she could be less than forty. It made the affair ridiculous. She was plain and old. His quick fancy showed her to him, wrinkled, haggard, made-up, in those frocks which were too showy for her position and too young for her years. He shuddered; he felt suddenly that he never wanted to see her again; he could not bear the thought of kissing her. He was horrified with himself. Was that love?

He took as long as he could over dressing in order to put back the moment of seeing her, and when at last he went into the dining-room it was with a sinking heart. Prayers were over, and they were sitting down at breakfast.

"Lazy bones," Miss Wilkinson cried gaily.

He looked at her and gave a little gasp of relief. She was sitting with her back to the window. She was really quite nice. He wondered why he had thought such things about her. His self-satisfaction returned to him.

He was taken aback by the change in her. She told him in a voice thrilling with emotion immediately after breakfast that she loved him; and when a little later they went into the drawing-room for his singing lesson and she sat down on the music-stool she put up her face in the middle of a scale and said:

"*Embrasse-moi.*"

When he bent down she flung her arms round his neck. It was slightly uncomfortable, for she held him in such a position that he felt rather choked.

"*Ah, je t'aime. Je t'aime. Je t'aime,*" she cried, with her extravagantly French accent.

Philip wished she would speak English.

"I say, I don't know if it's struck you that the gardener's quite likely to pass the window any minute."

"*Ah, je m'en fiche du jardinier. Je m'en refiche, et je m'en contrefiche.*"

Philip thought it was very like a French novel, and he did not know why it slightly irritated him.

At last he said:

"Well, I think I'll tootle along to the beach and have a dip."

"Oh, you're not going to leave me this morning—of all mornings?"

Philip did not quite know why he should not, but it did not matter.

"Would you like me to stay?" he smiled.

"Oh, you darling! But no, go. Go. I want to think of you mastering the salt sea waves, bathing your limbs in the broad ocean."

He got his hat and sauntered off.

"What rot women talk!" he thought to himself.

But he was pleased and happy and flattered. She was evidently frightfully gone on him. As he limped along the high street of Blackstable he looked with a tinge of superciliousness at the people he passed. He knew a good many to nod to, and as he gave them a smile of recognition he thought to himself, if they only knew! He did want someone to know very badly. He thought he would write to Hayward, and in his mind composed the letter. He would talk of the garden and the roses, and the little French governess, like an exotic flower amongst them, scented and perverse: he would say she was French, because—well, she had lived in France so long that she almost was, and besides it would be shabby to give the whole thing away too exactly, don't you know; and he would tell Hayward how he had seen her first in her pretty muslin dress and of the flower she had given him. He made a delicate idyll of it: the sunshine and the sea gave it passion and magic, and the stars added poetry, and the old vicarage garden was a fit and exquisite setting. There was something Meredithian about it: it was not quite Lucy Feverel and not quite Clara Middleton; but it was inexpressibly charming. Philip's heart beat quickly. He was so delighted with his fancies that he began thinking of them again as soon as he crawled back, dripping and cold, into his bathing-machine. He thought of the object of his affections. She had the most adorable little nose and large brown eyes—he would describe her to Hayward—and masses of soft brown hair, the sort of hair it was delicious to bury your face in, and a skin which was like ivory and sunshine, and her cheek was like a red, red rose. How old was she? Eighteen perhaps, and he called her Musette. Her laughter was like a rippling brook, and her voice was so soft, so low, it was the sweetest music he had ever heard.

"What *are* you thinking about?"

Philip stopped suddenly. He was walking slowly home.

"I've been waving at you for the last quarter of a mile. You *are* absent-minded."

Miss Wilkinson was standing in front of him, laughing at his surprise.

"I thought I'd come and meet you."

"That's awfully nice of you," he said.

"Did I startle you?"

"You did a bit," he admitted.

He wrote his letter to Hayward all the same. There were eight pages of it.

The fortnight that remained passed quickly, and though each evening, when they went into the garden after supper, Miss Wilkinson remarked that one day more had gone, Philip was in too cheerful spirits to let the thought depress him. One night Miss Wilkinson suggested that it would be delightful if she could exchange her situation in Berlin for one in London. Then they could see one another constantly. Philip said it would be very jolly, but the prospect aroused no enthusiasm in him; he was looking forward to a wonderful life in London, and he preferred not to be hampered. He spoke a little too freely of all he meant to do, and allowed Miss Wilkinson to see that already he was longing to be off.

"You wouldn't talk like that if you loved me," she cried.

He was taken aback and remained silent.

"What a fool I've been," she muttered.

To his surprise he saw that she was crying. He had a tender heart, and hated to see anyone miserable.

"Oh, I'm awfully sorry. What have I done? Don't cry."

"Oh, Philip, don't leave me. You don't know what you mean to me. I have such a wretched life, and you've made me so happy."

He kissed her silently. There really was anguish in her tone, and he was frightened. It had never occurred to him that she meant what she said quite, quite seriously.

"I'm awfully sorry. You know I'm frightfully fond of you. I wish you would come to London."

"You know I can't. Places are almost impossible to get, and I hate English life."

Almost unconscious that he was acting a part, moved by her distress, he pressed her more and more. Her tears vaguely flattered him, and he kissed her with real passion.

But a day or two later she made a real scene. There was a tennis-party at the vicarage, and two girls came, daughters of a retired major in an Indian regiment who had lately settled in Blackstable. They were very pretty, one was Philip's age and the other was a year or two younger. Being used to the society of young men (they were full of stories of hill-stations in India, and at that time the stories of Rudyard Kipling were in every hand) they began to chaff Philip gaily; and he, pleased with the novelty—the young ladies at Blackstable treated the Vicar's nephew with a certain seriousness—was gay and jolly. Some devil within him prompted him to start a violent flirtation with them both, and as he was the only young man there, they were quite willing to meet him halfway. It happened that they played tennis quite well and Philip was tired of pat-ball with Miss Wilkinson (she had only begun to play when she came to Blackstable), so when he arranged the sets after tea he suggested that Miss Wilkinson should play against the curate's wife, with the curate as her partner; and he would play later with the newcomers. He sat down by the elder Miss O'Connor and said to her in an undertone:

"We'll get the duffers out of the way first, and then we'll have a jolly set afterwards."

Apparently Miss Wilkinson overheard him, for she threw down her racket, and, saying she had a headache, went away. It was plain to everyone that she was offended. Philip was annoyed that she should make the fact public. The set was arranged without her, but presently Mrs. Carey called him.

"Philip, you've hurt Emily's feelings. She's gone to her room and she's crying."

"What about?"

"Oh, something about a duffer's set. Do go to her, and say you didn't mean to be unkind, there's a good boy."

"All right."

He knocked at Miss Wilkinson's door, but receiving no answer went in. He found her lying face downwards on her bed, weeping. He touched her on the shoulder.

"I say, what on earth's the matter?"

"Leave me alone. I never want to speak to you again."

"What have I done? I'm awfully sorry if I've hurt your feelings. I didn't mean to. I say, do get up."

"Oh, I'm so unhappy. How could you be cruel to me? You know I hate that stupid game. I only play because I want to play with you."

She got up and walked towards the dressing-table, but after a quick look in the glass sank into a chair. She made her handkerchief into a ball and dabbed her eyes with it.

"I've given you the greatest thing a woman can give a man— oh, what a fool I was! —and you have no gratitude. You must be quite heartless. How could you be so cruel as to torment me by flirting with those vulgar girls. We've only got just over a week. Can't you even give me that?"

Philip stood over her rather sulkily. He thought her behaviour childish. He was vexed with her for having shown her ill-temper before strangers.

"But you know I don't care twopence about either of the O'Connors. Why on earth should you think I do?"

Miss Wilkinson put away her handkerchief. Her tears had made marks on her powdered face, and her hair was somewhat disarranged. Her white dress did not suit her very well just then. She looked at Philip with hungry, passionate eyes.

"Because you're twenty and so's she," she said hoarsely. "And I'm old."

Philip reddened and looked away. The anguish of her tone made him feel strangely uneasy. He wished with all his heart that he had never had anything to do with Miss Wilkinson.

"I don't want to make you unhappy," he said awkwardly.

"You'd better go down and look after your friends. They'll wonder what has become of you."

"All right."

He was glad to leave her.

The quarrel was quickly followed by a reconciliation, but the few days that remained were sometimes irksome to Philip. He wanted to talk of nothing but the future, and the future invariably reduced Miss Wilkinson to tears. At first her weeping affected him, and feeling himself a beast he redoubled his protestations of undying passion; but now it irritated him: it would have been all very well if she had been a girl, but it was silly of a grown-up woman to cry so much. She never ceased reminding him that he was under a debt of gratitude to her which he could never repay. He was willing to acknowledge this, since she made a point of it, but he did not really know why he should be any more grateful to her than she to him. He was expected to show his sense of obligation in ways which were rather a nuisance: he had been a good deal used to solitude, and it was a necessity to him sometimes; but Miss Wilkinson looked upon it as an unkindness if he was not always at her beck and call. The Miss O'Connors asked them both to tea, and Philip would have liked to go, but Miss Wilkinson said she only had five days more and wanted him entirely to herself. It was flattering, but a bore. Miss Wilkinson told him stories of the exquisite delicacy of Frenchmen when they stood in the same relation to fair ladies as he to Miss Wilkinson. She praised their courtesy, their passion for self-sacrifice, their perfect tact. Miss Wilkinson seemed to want a great deal.

Philip listened to her enumeration of the qualities which must be possessed by the perfect lover, and he could not help feeling a certain satisfaction that she lived in Berlin.

"You will write to me, won't you? Write to me every day. I want to know everything you're doing. You must keep nothing from me."

"I shall be awfully busy," he answered. "I'll write as often as I can."

She flung her arms passionately round his neck. He was embarrassed sometimes by the demonstrations of her affection. He would have preferred her to be more passive. It shocked him a little that she should give him so marked a lead: it did not tally altogether with his prepossessions about the modesty of the feminine temperament.

At length the day came on which Miss Wilkinson was to go, and she came down to breakfast, pale and subdued, in a serviceable travelling dress of black and white check. She looked a very competent governess. Philip was silent too, for he did not quite know what to say that would fit the circumstance; and he was terribly afraid that, if he said something flippant, Miss Wilkinson would break down before his uncle and make a scene. They had said their last good-bye to one another in the garden the night before, and Philip was relieved that there was now no opportunity for them to be alone. He remained in the dining-room after breakfast in case Miss Wilkinson should insist on kissing him on the stairs. He did not want Mary Ann, now a woman hard upon middle age with a sharp tongue, to catch them in a compromising position. Mary Ann did not like Miss Wilkinson and called her an old cat. Aunt Louisa was not very well and could not come to the station, but the Vicar and Philip saw her off. Just as the train was leaving she leaned out and kissed Mr. Carey.

"I must kiss you too, Philip," she said.

"All right," he said, blushing.

He stood up on the step and she kissed him quickly. The train started, and Miss Wilkinson sank into the corner of her carriage and wept disconsolately. Philip, as he walked back to the vicarage, felt a distinct sensation of relief.

"Well, did you see her safely off?" asked Aunt Louisa, when they got in.

"Yes, she seemed rather weepy. She insisted on kissing me and Philip."

"Oh, well, at her age it's not dangerous." Mrs. Carey pointed to the sideboard. "There's a letter for you, Philip. It came by the second post."

It was from Hayward and ran as follows:

My dear boy,

I answer your letter at once. I ventured to read it to a great friend of mine, a charming woman whose help and sympathy have been very precious to me, a woman withal with a real feeling for art and literature; and we agreed that it was charming. You wrote from your heart and you do not know the delightful naïveté which is in every line. And because you love you write like a poet. Ah, dear boy, that is the real thing: I felt the glow of your young passion, and your prose was musical from the sincerity of your emotion. You must be happy! I wish I could have been present unseen in that enchanted garden while you wandered hand in hand, like Daphnis and Chloe, amid the flowers. I can see you, my Daphnis, with the light of young love in your eyes, tender, enraptured, and ardent; while Chloe in your arms, so young and soft and fresh, vowing she would ne'er consent—consented. Roses and violets and honeysuckle! Oh, my friend, I envy you. It is so good to think that your first love should have been pure poetry. Treasure the moments; for the immortal gods have given you the Greatest Gift of All, and it will be a sweet, sad memory till your dying day. You will never again enjoy that careless rapture. First love is best love; and she is beautiful and you are young, and all the world is yours. I felt my pulse go faster when with your adorable simplicity you told me that you buried your face in her long hair. I am sure that it is that exquisite chestnut which seems just touched with gold. I would have you sit under a leafy tree side by side, and read together Romeo and Juliet; and then I would have you fall on your knees and on my behalf kiss the ground on which her foot has left its imprint; then tell her it is the homage of a poet to her radiant youth and to your love for her.

Yours always,
G. Etheridge Hayward.

"What damned rot!" said Philip, when he finished the letter.

Miss Wilkinson, oddly enough, had suggested that they should read *Romeo and Juliet* together; but Philip had firmly declined. Then, as he put the letter in his pocket, he felt a queer little pang of bitterness because reality seemed so different from the ideal.

Chapter 36

A few days later Philip went to London. The curate had recommended rooms in Barnes, and these Philip engaged by letter at fourteen shillings a week. He reached them in the evening; and the landlady, a funny little old woman with a shrivelled body and a deeply wrinkled face, had prepared high tea for him. Most of the sitting-room was taken up by the sideboard and a square table; against one wall was a sofa covered with horsehair, and by the fireplace an armchair to match; there was a white antimacassar over the back of it, and on the seat, because the springs were broken, a hard cushion.

After having his tea he unpacked and arranged his books, then he sat down and tried to read; but he was depressed. The silence in the street made him slightly uncomfortable, and he felt very much alone.

Next day he got up early. He put on his tailcoat and the tall hat which he had worn at school; but it was very shabby, and he made up his mind to stop at the stores on his way to the office and buy a new one. When he had done this he found himself in plenty of time and so walked along the Strand. The office of Messrs Herbert Carter & Co. was in a little street off Chancery Lane, and he had to ask his way two or three times. He felt that people were staring at him a great deal, and once he took off his hat to see whether by chance the label had been left on. When he arrived he knocked at the door; but no one answered, and looking at his watch he found it was barely half past nine; he supposed he was too early. He went away and ten minutes later returned to find an office boy, with a long nose, pimply face, and a Scotch accent, opening the door. Philip asked for Mr. Herbert Carter. He had not come yet.

"When will he be here?"

"Between ten and half past."

"I'd better wait," said Philip.

"What are you wanting?" asked the office boy.

Philip was nervous, but tried to hide the fact by a jocose manner.

"Well, I'm going to work here if you have no objection."

"Oh, you're the new articled clerk? You'd better come in. Mr. Goodworthy'll be here in a while."

Philip walked in, and as he did so saw the office boy—he was about the same age as Philip and called himself a junior clerk—look at his foot. He flushed and, sitting down, hid it behind the other. He looked round the room. It was dark and very dingy. It was lit by a skylight. There were three rows of desks in it and against them high stools. Over the chimney-piece was a dirty engraving of a prize-fight. Presently a clerk came in and then another; they glanced at Philip and in an undertone asked the office boy (Philip found his name was Macdougal) who he was. A whistle blew, and Macdougal got up.

"Mr. Goodworthy's come. He's the managing clerk. Shall I tell him you're here?"

"Yes, please," said Philip.

The office boy went out and in a moment returned.

"Will you come this way?"

Philip followed him across the passage and was shown into a room, small and barely furnished, in which a little, thin man was standing with his back to the fireplace. He was much below the middle height, but his large head, which seemed to hang loosely on his body, gave him an odd ungainliness. His features were wide and flattened, and he had prominent, pale eyes; his thin hair was sandy; he wore whiskers that grew unevenly on his face, and in places where you would have expected the hair to grow thickly there was no hair at all. His skin was pasty and yellow. He held out his hand to Philip, and when he smiled showed badly decayed teeth. He spoke with a patronizing and at the same time a timid air, as though he sought to assume an importance which he did not feel. He said he hoped Philip would like the work; there was a good deal of drudgery about it, but when you got used to it, it was interesting; and one made money, that was the chief thing, wasn't it? He laughed with his odd mixture of superiority and shyness.

"Mr. Carter will be here presently," he said. "He's a little late on Monday mornings sometimes. I'll call you when he comes. In the meantime I must give you something to do. Do you know anything about book-keeping or accounts?"

"I'm afraid not," answered Philip.

"I didn't suppose you would. They don't teach you things at school that are much use in business, I'm afraid." He considered for a moment. "I think I can find you something to do."

He went into the next room and after a little while came out with a large cardboard box. It contained a vast number of letters in great disorder, and he told Philip to sort them out and arrange them alphabetically according to the names of the writers.

"I'll take you to the room in which the articled clerk generally sits. There's a very nice fellow in it. His name is Watson. He's a son of Watson, Crag, and Thompson—you know—the brewers. He's spending a year with us to learn business."

Mr. Goodworthy led Philip through the dingy office, where now six or eight clerks were working, into a narrow room behind. It had been made into a separate apartment by a glass partition, and here they found Watson sitting back in a chair, reading *The Sportsman*. He was a large, stout young man, elegantly dressed, and he looked up as Mr. Goodworthy entered. He asserted his position by calling the managing clerk Goodworthy. The managing clerk objected to the familiarity, and pointedly called him Mr. Watson, but Watson, instead of seeing that it was a rebuke, accepted the title as a tribute to his gentlemanliness.

"I see they've scratched Rigoletto," he said to Philip, as soon as they were left alone.

"Have they?" said Philip, who knew nothing about horse-racing.

He looked with awe upon Watson's beautiful clothes. His tailcoat fitted him perfectly, and there was a valuable pin artfully stuck in the middle of an enormous tie. On the chimney-piece rested his tall hat; it was saucy and bell-shaped and shiny. Philip felt himself very shabby. Watson began to talk of hunting—it was such an infernal bore having to waste one's time in an infernal office, he would only be able to hunt on Saturdays—and shooting: he had ripping invitations all over the country and of course he had to refuse them. It was infernal luck, but he wasn't going to put up with it long; he was only in this internal hole for a year, and then he was going into the business, and he would hunt four days a week and get all the shooting there was.

"You've got five years of it, haven't you?" he said, waving his arm round the tiny room.

"I suppose so," said Philip.

"I daresay I shall see something of you. Carter does our accounts, you know."

Philip was somewhat overpowered by the young gentleman's condescension. At Blackstable they had always looked upon brewing with civil contempt, the Vicar made little jokes about the beerage, and it was a surprising experience for Philip to discover that Watson was such an important and magnificent fellow. He had been to Winchester and to Oxford, and his conversation impressed the fact upon one with frequency. When he discovered the details of Philip's education his manner became more patronizing still.

"Of course, if one doesn't go to a public school those sort of schools are the next best thing, aren't they?"

Philip asked about the other men in the office.

"Oh, I don't bother about them much, you know," said

Watson. "Carter's not a bad sort. We have him to dine now and then. All the rest are awful bounders."

Presently Watson applied himself to some work he had in hand, and Philip set about sorting his letters. Then Mr. Goodworthy came in to say that Mr. Carter had arrived. He took Philip into a large room next door to his own. There was a big desk in it, and a couple of big armchairs; a Turkey carpet adorned the floor, and the walls were decorated with sporting prints. Mr. Carter was sitting at the desk and got up to shake hands with Philip. He was dressed in a long frock coat. He looked like a military man; his moustache was waxed, his grey hair was short and neat, he held himself upright, he talked in a breezy way, he lived at Enfield. He was very keen on games and the good of the country. He was an officer in the Hertfordshire Yeomanry and chairman of the Conservative Association. When he was told that a local magnate had said no one would take him for a City man, he felt that he had not lived in vain. He talked to Philip in a pleasant, off-hand fashion. Mr. Goodworthy would look after him. Watson was a nice fellow, perfect gentleman, good sportsman—did Philip hunt? Pity, *the* sport for gentlemen. Didn't have much chance of hunting now, had to leave that to his son. His son was at Cambridge, he'd sent him to Rugby, fine school Rugby, nice class of boys there, in a couple of years his son would be articled, that would be nice for Philip, he'd like his son, thorough sportsman. He hoped Philip would get on well and like the work, he mustn't miss his lectures, they were getting up the tone of the profession, they wanted gentlemen in it. Well, well, Mr. Goodworthy was there. If he wanted to know anything Mr. Goodworthy would tell him. What was his handwriting like? Ah, well, Mr. Goodworthy would see about that.

Philip was overwhelmed by so much gentlemanliness: in East Anglia they knew who were gentlemen and who weren't, but the gentlemen didn't talk about it.

Chapter 37

At first the novelty of the work kept Philip interested. Mr. Carter dictated letters to him, and he had to make fair copies of statements of accounts.

Mr. Carter preferred to conduct the office on gentlemanly lines; he would have nothing to do with typewriting and looked upon shorthand with disfavour: the office boy knew shorthand, but it was only Mr. Goodworthy who made use of his accomplishment. Now and then Philip with one of the more experienced clerks went out to audit the accounts of some firm: he came to know which of the clients must be treated with respect and which were in low water. Now and then long lists of figures were given him to add up. He attended lectures for his first examination. Mr. Goodworthy repeated to him that the work was dull at first, but he would grow used to it. Philip left the office at six and walked across the river to Waterloo. His supper was waiting for him when he reached his lodgings and he spent the evening reading. On Saturday afternoons he went to the National Gallery. Hayward had recommended to him a guide which had been compiled out of Ruskin's works, and with this in hand he went industriously through room after room: he read carefully what the critic had said about a picture and then in a determined fashion set himself to see the same things in it. His Sundays were difficult to get through. He knew no one in London and spent them by himself. Mr. Nixon, the solicitor, asked him to spend a Sunday at Hampstead, and Philip passed a happy day with a set of exuberant strangers; he ate and drank a great deal, took a walk on the heath, and came away with a general invitation to come again whenever he liked; but he was morbidly afraid of being in the way, so waited for a formal invitation. Naturally enough it never came, for with numbers of friends of their own the Nixons did not think of the lonely, silent boy whose claim upon their hospitality was so small. So on Sundays he got up late and took a walk along the tow-path. At Barnes the river is muddy, dingy, and tidal; it has neither the graceful charm of the Thames above the locks nor the romance of the crowded stream below London Bridge. In the afternoon he walked about the common; and that is grey and dingy too; it is neither country nor town; the gorse is stunted; and all about is the litter of civilization. He went to a play every Saturday night and stood cheerfully for an hour or more at the gallery-door. It was not worth while to go back to Barnes for the interval between the closing of the Museum and his meal in an A. B. C. shop, and the time hung heavily on his hands. He strolled up Bond Street or through the Burlington Arcade, and when he was tired went and sat down in the Park or in wet weather in the public library in St. Martin's Lane. He looked at the people walking about and envied them because they had friends; sometimes his envy turned to hatred because they were happy and he was miserable. He had never imagined that it was possible to be so lonely in a great city. Sometimes when he was standing at the gallery-door the man next to him would attempt a conversation; but Philip had the country boy's suspicion of strangers and answered in such a way as to prevent any further acquaintance. After the play was over, obliged to keep to himself all he thought about it, he hurried across the bridge to Waterloo. When he got back to his rooms, in which for economy no fire had been lit, his heart sank. It was horribly cheerless. He began to loathe his lodgings and the long solitary evenings he spent in them. Sometimes he felt so lonely that he could not read, and then he sat looking into the fire hour after hour in bitter wretchedness.

He had spent three months in London now, and except for that one Sunday at Hampstead had never talked to anyone but his fellow-clerks. One evening Watson asked him to dinner at a restaurant and they went to a music hall together; but he felt shy and uncomfortable. Watson talked all the time of things he did not care about, and while he looked upon Watson as a Philistine he could not help admiring him. He was angry because Watson obviously set no store on his culture, and with his way of taking himself at the estimate at which he saw others held him he began to despise the acquirements which till then had seemed to him not unimportant. He felt for the first time the humiliation of poverty. His uncle sent him fourteen pounds a month and he had had to buy a good many clothes. His evening suit cost him five guineas. He had not dared tell Watson that it was bought in the Strand. Watson said there was only one tailor in London.

"I suppose you don't dance," said Watson, one day, with a glance at Philip's club-foot.

"No," said Philip.

"Pity. I've been asked to bring some dancing men to a ball. I could have introduced you to some jolly girls."

Once or twice, hating the thought of going back to Barnes, Philip had remained in town, and late in the evening wandered through the West End till he found some house at which there was a party. He stood among the little group of shabby people, behind the footmen, watching the guests arrive, and he listened to the music that floated through the window. Sometimes, notwithstanding the cold, a couple came on to the balcony and stood for a moment to get some fresh air, and Philip, imagining that they were in love with one another, turned away and limped along the street with a heavy heart. He would never be able to stand in that man's place. He felt that no woman could ever really look upon him without distaste for his deformity.

That reminded him of Miss Wilkinson. He thought of her without satisfaction. Before parting they had made an arrangement that she should write to Charing Cross Post Office till he was able to send her an address, and when he went there he found three letters from her. She wrote on blue paper with violet ink, and she wrote in French. Philip wondered why she could not write in English like a sensible woman, and her passionate expressions, because they reminded him of a French novel, left him cold. She upbraided him for not having written, and when he answered he excused himself by saying that he had been busy. He did not quite know how to start the letter. He could not bring himself to use *dearest* or *darling*, and he hated to address her as Emily, so finally he began with the word *dear*. It looked odd, standing by itself, and rather silly, but he made it do. It was the first love letter he had ever written, and he was conscious of its tameness; he felt that he should say all sorts of vehement things, how he thought of her every minute of the day and how he longed to kiss her beautiful hands and how he trembled at the thought of her red lips, but some inexplicable modesty prevented him; and instead he told her of his new rooms and his office. The answer came by return of post, angry, heart-broken, reproachful: how could he be so cold? Did he not know that she hung on his letters? She had given him all that a woman could give, and this was her reward. Was he tired of her already? Then, because he did not reply for several days, Miss Wilkinson bombarded him with letters. She could not bear his unkindness, she waited for the post, and it never brought her his letter, she cried herself to sleep night after night, she was looking so ill that everyone remarked on it: if he did not love her why did he not say so? She added that she could not live without him, and the only thing was for her to commit suicide. She told him he was cold and selfish and ungrateful. It was all in French, and Philip knew that she wrote in that language to show off, but he was worried all the same. He did not want to make her unhappy. In a little while she wrote that she could not bear the separation any longer, she would arrange to come over to London for Christmas. Philip wrote back that he would like nothing better, only he had already an engagement to spend Christmas with friends in the country, and he did not see how he could break it. She answered that she did not wish to force herself on him, it was quite evident that he did not wish to see her; she was deeply hurt, and she never thought he would repay with such cruelty all her kindness. Her letter was touching, and Philip thought he saw marks of her tears on the paper; he wrote an impulsive reply saying that he was dreadfully sorry and imploring her to come; but it was with relief that he received her answer in which she said that she found it would be impossible for her to get away. Presently when her letters came his heart sank: he delayed opening them, for he knew what they would contain, angry reproaches and pathetic appeals; they would make him feel a perfect beast, and yet he did not see with what he had to blame himself. He put off his answer from day to day, and then another letter would come, saying she was ill and lonely and miserable.

"I wish to God I'd never had anything to do with her," he said.

He admired Watson because he arranged these things so easily. The young man had been engaged in an intrigue with a girl who played in touring companies, and his account of the affair filled Philip with envious amazement. But after a time Watson's young affections changed, and one day he described the rupture to Philip.

"I thought it was no good making any bones about it, so I just told her I'd had enough of her," he said.

"Didn't she make an awful scene?" asked Philip.

"The usual thing, you know, but I told her it was no good trying on that sort of thing with me."

"Did she cry?"

"She began to, but I can't stand women when they cry, so I

said she'd better hook it."

Philip's sense of humour was growing keener with advancing years.

"And did she hook it?" he asked, smiling.

"Well, there wasn't anything else for her to do, was there?"

Meanwhile the Christmas holidays approached. Mrs. Carey had been ill all through November, and the doctor suggested that she and the Vicar should go to Cornwall for a couple of weeks round Christmas so that she should get back her strength. The result was that Philip had nowhere to go, and he spent Christmas Day in his lodgings. Under Hayward's influence he had persuaded himself that the festivities that attend this season were vulgar and barbaric, and he made up his mind that he would take no notice of the day; but when it came, the jollity of all around affected him strangely. His landlady and her husband were spending the day with a married daughter, and to save trouble Philip announced that he would take his meals out. He went up to London towards midday and ate a slice of turkey and some Christmas pudding by himself at Gatti's, and since he had nothing to do afterwards went to Westminster Abbey for the afternoon service. The streets were almost empty, and the people who went along had a preoccupied look; they did not saunter but walked with some definite goal in view, and hardly anyone was alone. To Philip they all seemed happy. He felt himself more solitary than he had ever done in his life. His intention had been to kill the day somehow in the streets and then dine at a restaurant, but he could not face again the sight of cheerful people, talking, laughing, and making merry; so he went back to Waterloo, and on his way through the Westminster

Bridge Road bought some ham and a couple of mince pies and went back to Barnes. He ate his food in his lonely little room and spent the evening with a book. His depression was almost intolerable.

When he was back at the office it made him very sore to listen to Watson's account of the short holiday. They had had some jolly girls staying with them, and after dinner they had cleared out the drawing-room and had a dance.

"I didn't get to bed till three and I don't know how I got there then. By George, I was squiffy."

At last Philip asked desperately:

"How does one get to know people in London?"

Watson looked at him with surprise and with a slightly contemptuous amusement.

"Oh, I don't know, one just knows them. If you go to dances you soon get to know as many people as you can do with."

Philip hated Watson, and yet he would have given anything to change places with him. The old feeling that he had had at school came back to him, and he tried to throw himself into the other's skin, imagining what life would be if he were Watson.

Chapter 38

At the end of the year there was a great deal to do. Philip went to various places with a clerk named Thompson and spent the day monotonously calling out items of expenditure, which the other checked; and sometimes he was given long pages of figures to add up. He had never had a head for figures, and he could only do this slowly. Thompson grew irritated at his mistakes. His fellow-clerk was a long, lean man of forty, sallow, with black hair and a ragged moustache; he had hollow cheeks and deep lines on each side of his nose. He took a dislike to Philip because he was an articled clerk. Because he could put down three hundred guineas and keep himself for five years Philip had the chance of a career; while he, with his experience and ability, had no possibility of ever being more than a clerk at thirty-five shillings a week. He was a cross-grained man, oppressed by a large family, and he resented the superciliousness which he fancied he saw in Philip. He sneered at Philip because he was better educated than himself, and he mocked at Philip's pronunciation; he could not forgive him because he spoke without a cockney accent, and when he talked to him sarcastically exaggerated his aitches. At first his manner was merely gruff and repellent, but as he discovered that Philip had no gift for accountancy he took pleasure in humiliating him; his attacks were gross and silly, but they wounded Philip, and in self-defence he assumed an attitude of superiority which he did not feel.

"Had a bath this morning?" Thompson said when Philip came to the office late, for his early punctuality had not lasted.

"Yes, haven't you?"

"No, I'm not a gentleman, I'm only a clerk. I have a bath on Saturday night."

"I suppose that's why you're more than usually disagreeable on Monday."

"Will you condescend to do a few sums in simple addition today? I'm afraid it's asking a great deal from a gentleman who knows Latin and Greek."

"Your attempts at sarcasm are not very happy."

But Philip could not conceal from himself that the other clerks, ill-paid and uncouth, were more useful than himself. Once or twice Mr. Goodworthy grew impatient with him.

"You really ought to be able to do better than this by now," he said. "You're not even as smart as the office boy."

Philip listened sulkily. He did not like being blamed, and it humiliated him, when, having been given accounts to make fair copies of, Mr. Goodworthy was not satisfied and gave them to another clerk to do. At first the work had been tolerable from its novelty, but now it grew irksome; and when he discovered that he had no aptitude for it, he began to hate it. Often, when he should have been doing something that was given him, he wasted his time drawing little pictures on the office note-paper. He made sketches of Watson in every conceivable attitude, and Watson was impressed by his talent. It occurred to him to take the drawings home, and he came back next day with the praises of his family.

"I wonder you didn't become a painter," he said. "Only of course there's no money in it."

It chanced that Mr. Carter two or three days later was dining with the Watsons, and the sketches were shown him. The following morning he sent for Philip. Philip saw him seldom and stood in some awe of him.

"Look here, young fellow, I don't care what you do out of office hours, but I've seen those sketches of yours and they're on office paper, and Mr. Goodworthy tells me you're slack. You won't do any good as a chartered accountant unless you look alive. It's a fine profession, and we're getting a very good class of men in it, but it's a profession in which you have to…" he looked for the termination of his phrase, but could not find exactly what he wanted, so finished rather tamely, "in which you have to look alive."

Perhaps Philip would have settled down but for the agreement that if he did not like the work he could leave after a year, and get back half the money paid for his articles. He felt that he was fit for something better than to add up accounts, and it was humiliating that he did so ill something which seemed contemptible. The vulgar scenes with Thompson got on his nerves. In March Watson ended his year at the office and Philip, though he did not care for him, saw him go with regret. The fact that the other clerks disliked them equally, because they belonged to a class a little higher than their own, was a bond of union. When Philip thought that he must spend over four years more with that dreary set of fellows his heart sank. He had expected wonderful things from London and it had given him nothing. He hated it now. He did not know a soul, and he had no idea how he was to get to know anyone. He was tired of going everywhere by himself. He began to feel that he could not stand much more of such a life. He would lie in bed at night and think of the joy of never seeing again that dingy office or any of the men in it, and of getting away from those drab lodgings.

A great disappointment befell him in the spring. Hayward had announced his intention of coming to London for the season, and Philip had looked forward very much to seeing him again. He had read so much lately and thought so much that his mind was full of ideas which he wanted to discuss, and he knew nobody who was willing to interest himself in abstract things. He was quite excited at the thought of talking his fill with someone, and he was wretched when Hayward wrote to say that the spring was lovelier than ever he had known it in Italy, and he could not bear to tear himself away. He went on to ask why Philip did not come. What was the use of squandering the days of his youth in an office when the world was beautiful? The letter proceeded.

> *I wonder you can bear it. I think of Fleet Street and Lincoln's Inn now with a shudder of disgust. There are only two things in the world that make life worth living, love and art. I cannot imagine you sitting in an office over a ledger, and do*

you wear a tall hat and an umbrella and a little black bag? My
feeling is that one should look upon life as an adventure, one
should burn with the hard, gem-like flame, and one should take
risks, one should expose oneself to danger. Why do you not go
to Paris and study art? I always thought you had talent.

The suggestion fell in with the possibility that Philip for
some time had been vaguely turning over in his mind. It startled
him at first, but he could not help thinking of it, and in the
constant rumination over it he found his only escape from the
wretchedness of his present state. They all thought he had talent;
at Heidelberg they had admired his water colours, Miss Wilkinson
had told him over and over again that they were charming; even
strangers like the Watsons had been struck by his sketches. *La Vie
de Bohème* had made a deep impression on him. He had brought it
to London and when he was most depressed he had only to read
a few pages to be transported into those charming attics where
Rodolphe and the rest of them danced and loved and sang. He
began to think of Paris as before he had thought of London, but
he had no fear of a second disillusion; he yearned for romance
and beauty and love, and Paris seemed to offer them all. He had
a passion for pictures, and why should he not be able to paint as
well as anybody else? He wrote to Miss Wilkinson and asked her
how much she thought he could live on in Paris. She told him
that he could manage easily on eighty pounds a year, and she
enthusiastically approved of his project. She told him he was too
good to be wasted in an office. Who would be a clerk when he
might be a great artist, she asked dramatically, and she besought

Philip to believe in himself: that was the great thing. But Philip had a cautious nature. It was all very well for Hayward to talk of taking risks, he had three hundred a year in gilt-edged securities; Philip's entire fortune amounted to no more than eighteen hundred pounds. He hesitated.

Then it chanced that one day Mr. Goodworthy asked him suddenly if he would like to go to Paris. The firm did the accounts for a hotel in the Faubourg St. Honoré, which was owned by an English company, and twice a year Mr. Goodworthy and a clerk went over. The clerk who generally went happened to be ill, and a press of work prevented any of the others from getting away. Mr. Goodworthy thought of Philip because he could best be spared, and his articles gave him some claim upon a job which was one of the pleasures of the business. Philip was delighted.

"You'll 'ave to work all day," said Mr. Goodworthy, "but we get our evenings to ourselves, and Paris is Paris." He smiled in a knowing way. "They do us very well at the hotel, and they give us all our meals, so it don't cost one anything. That's the way I like going to Paris, at other people's expense."

When they arrived at Calais and Philip saw the crowd of gesticulating porters his heart leaped.

"This is the real thing," he said to himself.

He was all eyes as the train sped through the country; he adored the sand dunes, their colour seemed to him more lovely than anything he had ever seen; and he was enchanted with the canals and the long lines of poplars. When they got out of the Gare du Nord, and trundled along the cobbled streets in a ramshackle, noisy cab, it seemed to him that he was breathing a new air so intoxicating that he could hardly restrain himself from shouting aloud. They were met at the door of the hotel by the manager, a stout, pleasant man, who spoke tolerable English; Mr. Goodworthy was an old friend and he greeted them effusively; they dined in his private room with his wife, and to Philip it seemed that he had never eaten anything so delicious as the *beefsteak aux pommes*, nor drunk such nectar as the *vin ordinaire*, which were set before them.

To Mr. Goodworthy, a respectable householder with excellent principles, the capital of France was a paradise of the joyously obscene. He asked the manager next morning what there was to be seen that was "thick." He thoroughly enjoyed these visits of his to Paris; he said they kept you from growing rusty. In the evenings, after their work was over and they had dined, he took Philip to the Moulin Rouge and the Folies Bergères. His little eyes twinkled and his face wore a sly, sensual smile as he sought out the pornographic. He went into all the haunts which were specially arranged for the foreigner, and afterwards said that a nation could come to no good which permitted that sort of thing. He nudged Philip when at some revue a woman appeared with practically nothing on, and pointed out to him the most strapping of the courtesans who walked about the hall. It was a vulgar Paris that he showed Philip, but Philip saw it with eyes blinded with illusion. In the early morning he would rush out of the hotel and go to the Champs-Élysées, and stand at the Place de la Concorde. It was June, and Paris was silvery with the delicacy of the air. Philip felt his heart go out to the people. Here he thought at last was romance.

They spent the inside of a week there, leaving on Sunday, and when Philip late at night reached his dingy rooms in Barnes his mind was made up; he would surrender his articles, and go to Paris to study art; but so that no one should think him unreasonable he determined to stay at the office till his year was up. He was to have his holiday during the last fortnight in August, and when he went away he would tell Herbert Carter that he had no intention of returning. But though Philip could force himself to go to the office every day he could not even pretend to show any interest in the work. His mind was occupied with the future. In the middle of July there was nothing much to do and he escaped a good deal by pretending he had to go to lectures for his first examination. The time he got in this way he spent in the National Gallery. He read books about Paris and books about painting. He was steeped in Ruskin. He read many of Vasari's lives of the painters. He liked that story of Correggio, and he fancied himself standing before some great masterpiece and crying: *Anch'io son' pittore.* His hesitation had left him now, and he was convinced that he had in him the makings of a great painter.

"After all, I can only try," he said to himself. "The great thing in life is to take risks."

At last came the middle of August. Mr. Carter was spending the month in Scotland, and the managing clerk was in charge of the office. Mr. Goodworthy had seemed pleasantly disposed to Philip since their trip to Paris, and now that Philip knew he was so soon to be free, he could look upon the funny little man with tolerance.

"You're going for your holiday tomorrow, Carey?" he said to

him in the evening.

All day Philip had been telling himself that this was the last time he would ever sit in that hateful office.

"Yes, this is the end of my year."

"I'm afraid you've not done very well. Mr. Carter's very dissatisfied with you."

"Not nearly so dissatisfied as I am with Mr. Carter," returned Philip cheerfully.

"I don't think you should speak like that, Carey."

"I'm not coming back. I made the arrangement that if I didn't like accountancy Mr. Carter would return me half the money I paid for my articles and I could chuck it at the end of a year."

"You shouldn't come to such a decision hastily."

"For ten months I've loathed it all, I've loathed the work, I've loathed the office, I loathe London. I'd rather sweep a crossing than spend my days here."

"Well, I must say, I don't think you're very fitted for accountancy."

"Good-bye," said Philip, holding out his hand. "I want to thank you for your kindness to me. I'm sorry if I've been troublesome. I knew almost from the beginning I was no good."

"Well, if you really do make up your mind it is good-bye. I don't know what you're going to do, but if you're in the neighbourhood at any time come in and see us."

Philip gave a little laugh.

"I'm afraid it sounds very rude, but I hope from the bottom of my heart that I shall never set eyes on any of you again."

Chapter 39

The Vicar of Blackstable would have nothing to do with the scheme which Philip laid before him. He had a great idea that one should stick to whatever one had begun. Like all weak men he laid an exaggerated stress on not changing one's mind.

"You chose to be an accountant of your own free will," he said.

"I just took that because it was the only chance I saw of getting up to town. I hate London, I hate the work, and nothing will induce me to go back to it."

Mr. and Mrs. Carey were frankly shocked at Philip's idea of being an artist. He should not forget, they said, that his father and mother were gentlefolk, and painting wasn't a serious profession; it was Bohemian, disreputable, immoral. And then Paris!

"So long as I have anything to say in the matter, I shall not allow you to live in Paris," said the Vicar firmly.

It was a sink of iniquity. The scarlet woman and she of Babylon flaunted their vileness there; the cities of the plain were not more wicked.

"You've been brought up like a gentleman and Christian, and I should be false to the trust laid upon me by your dead father and mother if I allowed you to expose yourself to such temptation."

"Well, I know I'm not a Christian and I'm beginning to doubt whether I'm a gentleman," said Philip.

The dispute grew more violent. There was another year before Philip took possession of his small inheritance, and during that time Mr. Carey proposed only to give him an allowance if he remained at the office. It was clear to Philip that if he meant not to continue with accountancy he must leave it while he could still get back half the money that had been paid for his articles. The Vicar would not listen. Philip, losing all reserve, said things to wound and irritate.

"You've got no right to waste my money," he said at last. "After all it's my money, isn't it? I'm not a child. You can't prevent me from going to Paris if I make up my mind to. You can't force me to go back to London."

"All I can do is to refuse you money unless you do what I think fit."

"Well, I don't care, I've made up my mind to go to Paris. I shall sell my clothes, and my books, and my father's jewellery."

Aunt Louisa sat by in silence, anxious and unhappy: she saw that Philip was beside himself, and anything she said then would but increase his anger. Finally the Vicar announced that he wished to hear nothing more about it and with dignity left the room. For the next three days neither Philip nor he spoke to one another. Philip wrote to Hayward for information about Paris, and made up his mind to set out as soon as he got a reply. Mrs. Carey turned the matter over in her mind incessantly; she felt that Philip included her in the hatred he bore her husband, and the thought tortured her. She loved him with all her heart. At length she spoke to him; she listened attentively while he poured out all his disillusionment of London and his eager ambition for the future.

"I may be no good, but at least let me have a try. I can't be a worse failure than I was in that beastly office. And I feel that I *can* paint. I know I've got it in me."

She was not so sure as her husband that they did right in thwarting so strong an inclination. She had read of great painters whose parents had opposed their wish to study, the event had shown with what folly; and after all it was just as possible for a painter to lead a virtuous life to the glory of God as for a chartered accountant.

"I'm so afraid of your going to Paris," she said piteously. "It wouldn't be so bad if you studied in London."

"If I'm going in for painting I must do it thoroughly, and it's only in Paris that you can get the real thing."

At his suggestion Mrs. Carey wrote to the solicitor, saying that Philip was discontented with his work in London, and asking what he thought of a change. Mr. Nixon answered as follows:

Dear Mrs. Carey,

I have seen Mr. Herbert Carter, and I am afraid I must tell you that Philip has not done so well as one could have wished. If he is very strongly set against the work, perhaps it is better that he should take the opportunity there is now to break his articles. I am naturally very disappointed, but as you know you can take a horse to the water, but you can't make him drink.

Yours very sincerely,

Albert Nixon.

The letter was shown to the Vicar, but served only to increase his obstinacy. He was willing enough that Philip should take up some other profession, he suggested his father's calling, medicine, but nothing would induce him to pay an allowance if Philip went to Paris.

"It's a mere excuse for self-indulgence and sensuality," he said.

"I'm interested to hear you blame self-indulgence in others," retorted Philip acidly.

But by this time an answer had come from Hayward, giving the name of a hotel where Philip could get a room for thirty francs a month and enclosing a note of introduction to the *massière* of a school. Philip read the letter to Mrs. Carey and told her he proposed to start on the first of September.

"But you haven't got any money?" she said.

"I'm going into Tercanbury this afternoon to sell the jewellery."

He had inherited from his father a gold watch and chain, two or three rings, some links, and two pins. One of them was a pearl and might fetch a considerable sum.

"It's a very different thing, what a thing's worth and what it'll fetch," said Aunt Louisa.

Philip smiled, for this was one of his uncle's stock phrases.

"I know, but at the worst I think I can get a hundred pounds

273

on the lot, and that'll keep me till I'm twenty-one."

Mrs. Carey did not answer, but she went upstairs, put on her little black bonnet, and went to the bank. In an hour she came back. She went to Philip, who was reading in the drawing-room, and handed him an envelope.

"What's this?" he asked.

"It's a little present for you," she answered, smiling shyly.

He opened it and found eleven five-pound notes and a little paper sack bulging with sovereigns.

"I couldn't bear to let you sell your father's jewellery. It's the money I had in the bank. It comes to very nearly a hundred pounds."

Philip blushed, and, he knew not why, tears suddenly filled his eyes.

"Oh, my dear, I can't take it," he said. "It's most awfully good of you, but I couldn't bear to take it."

When Mrs. Carey was married she had three hundred pounds, and this money, carefully watched, had been used by her to meet any unforeseen expense, any urgent charity, or to buy Christmas and birthday presents for her husband and for Philip. In the course of years it had diminished sadly, but it was still with the Vicar a subject for jesting. He talked of his wife as a rich woman and he constantly spoke of the "nest egg."

"Oh, please take it, Philip. I'm so sorry I've been extravagant, and there's only that left. But it'll make me so happy if you'll accept it."

"But you'll want it," said Philip.

"No, I don't think I shall. I was keeping it in case your

uncle died before me. I thought it would be useful to have a little something I could get at immediately if I wanted it, but I don't think I shall live very much longer now."

"Oh, my dear, don't say that. Why, of course you're going to live for ever. I can't possibly spare you."

"Oh, I'm not sorry." Her voice broke and she hid her eyes, but in a moment, drying them, she smiled bravely. "At first, I used to pray to God that He might not take me first, because I didn't want your uncle to be left alone, I didn't want him to have all the suffering, but now I know that it wouldn't mean so much to your uncle as it would mean to me. He wants to live more than I do, I've never been the wife he wanted, and I daresay he'd marry again if anything happened to me. So I should like to go first. You don't think it's selfish of me, Philip, do you? But I couldn't bear it if he went."

Philip kissed her wrinkled, thin cheek. He did not know why the sight he had of that overwhelming love made him feel strangely ashamed. It was incomprehensible that she should care so much for a man who was so indifferent, so selfish, so grossly self-indulgent; and he divined dimly that in her heart she knew his indifference and his selfishness, knew them and loved him humbly all the same.

"You will take the money, Philip?" she said, gently stroking his hand. "I know you can do without it, but it'll give me so much happiness. I've always wanted to do something for you. You see, I never had a child of my own, and I've loved you as if you were my son. When you were a little boy, though I knew it was wicked, I used to wish almost that you might be ill, so that I could nurse you day and night. But you were only ill once and then it was at school. I should so like to help you. It's the only chance I shall ever have. And perhaps some day when you're a great artist you won't forget me, but you'll remember that I gave you your start."

"It's very good of you," said Philip. "I'm very grateful."

A smile came into her tired eyes, a smile of pure happiness.

"Oh, I'm so glad."

Chapter 40

A few days later Mrs. Carey went to the station to see Philip off. She stood at the door of the carriage, trying to keep back her tears. Philip was restless and eager. He wanted to be gone.

"Kiss me once more," she said.

He leaned out of the window and kissed her. The train started, and she stood on the wooden platform of the little station, waving her handkerchief till it was out of sight. Her heart was dreadfully heavy, and the few hundred yards to the vicarage seemed very, very long. It was natural enough that he should be eager to go, she thought, he was a boy and the future beckoned to him; but she—she clenched her teeth so that she should not cry. She uttered a little inward prayer that God would guard him, and keep him out of temptation, and give him happiness and good fortune.

But Philip ceased to think of her a moment after he had settled down in his carriage. He thought only of the future. He had written to Mrs. Otter, the *massière* to whom Hayward had given him an introduction, and had in his pocket an invitation to tea on the following day. When he arrived in Paris he had his luggage put on a cab and trundled off slowly through the gay streets, over the bridge, and along the narrow ways of the Latin Quarter. He had taken a room at the Hôtel des Deux Écoles, which was in a shabby street off the Boulevard du Montparnasse; it was convenient for Amitrano's School, at which he was going to work. A waiter took his box up five flights of stairs, and Philip was shown into a tiny room, fusty from unopened windows, the greater part of which was taken up by a large wooden bed with a canopy over it of red rep; there were heavy curtains on the windows of the same dingy material; the chest of drawers served also as a washing-stand; and there was a massive wardrobe of the style which is connected with the good King Louis Philippe. The wallpaper was discoloured with age; it was dark grey, and there could be vaguely seen on it garlands of brown leaves. To Philip the room seemed quaint and charming.

Though it was late he felt too excited to sleep and, going out, made his way into the boulevard and walked towards the light. This led him to the station; and the square in front of it, vivid with arc-lamps, noisy with the yellow trams that seemed to cross it in all directions, made him laugh aloud with joy. There were cafés all round, and by chance, thirsty and eager to get a nearer sight of the crowd, Philip installed himself at a little table outside the Café de Versailles. Every other table was taken, for it was a fine night; and Philip looked curiously at the people, here little family groups, there a knot of men with odd-shaped hats and beards talking loudly and gesticulating; next to him were two men who looked like painters with women who Philip hoped were not their lawful wives; behind him he heard Americans loudly arguing on art. His soul was thrilled. He sat till very late, tired out but too happy to move, and when at last he went to bed he was wide awake; he listened to the manifold noise of Paris.

Next day about tea-time he made his way to the Lion de Belfort, and in a new street that led out of the Boulevard Raspail found Mrs. Otter. She was an insignificant woman of thirty, with a provincial air and a deliberately ladylike manner; she introduced him to her mother. He discovered presently that she had been studying in Paris for three years and later that she was separated from her husband. She had in her small drawing-room one or two portraits which she had painted, and to Philip's inexperience they seemed extremely accomplished.

"I wonder if I shall ever be able to paint as well as that," he said to her.

"Oh, I expect so," she replied, not without self-satisfaction. "You can't expect to do everything all at once, of course."

She was very kind. She gave him the address of a shop where he could get a portfolio, drawing-paper, and charcoal.

"I shall be going to Amitrano's about nine tomorrow, and if you'll be there then I'll see that you get a good place and all that sort of thing."

She asked him what he wanted to do, and Philip felt that he should not let her see how vague he was about the whole matter.

"Well, first I want to learn to draw," he said.

"I'm so glad to hear you say that. People always want to do things in such a hurry. I never touched oils till I'd been here for two years, and look at the result."

She gave a glance at the portrait of her mother, a sticky piece of painting that hung over the piano.

"And if I were you, I would be very careful about the people you get to know. I wouldn't mix myself up with any foreigners. I'm very careful myself."

Philip thanked her for the suggestion, but it seemed to him odd. He did not know that he particularly wanted to be careful.

"We live just as we would if we were in England," said Mrs. Otter's mother, who till then had spoken little. "When we came here we brought all our own furniture over."

Philip looked round the room. It was filled with a massive suite, and at the window were the same sort of white lace curtains which Aunt Louisa put up at the vicarage in summer. The piano was draped in Liberty silk and so was the chimney-piece. Mrs. Otter followed his wandering eye.

"In the evening when we close the shutters one might really feel one was in England."

"And we have our meals just as if we were at home," added her mother. "A meat breakfast in the morning and dinner in the middle of the day."

When he left Mrs. Otter Philip went to buy drawing materials; and next morning at the stroke of nine, trying to seem self-assured, he presented himself at the school. Mrs. Otter was already there, and she came forward with a friendly smile. He had been anxious about the reception he would have as a *nouveau*, for he had read a good deal of the rough joking to which a newcomer was exposed at some of the studios; but Mrs. Otter had reassured him.

"Oh, there's nothing like that here," she said. "You see, about half our students are ladies, and they set a tone to the place."

The studio was large and bare, with grey walls, on which were pinned the studies that had received prizes. A model was sitting in a chair with a loose wrap thrown over her, and about a dozen men and women were standing about, some talking and others still working on their sketch. It was the first rest of the model.

"You'd better not try anything too difficult at first," said Mrs. Otter. "Put your easel here. You'll find that's the easiest pose."

Philip placed an easel where she indicated, and Mrs. Otter introduced him to a young woman who sat next to him.

"Mr. Carey—Miss Price. Mr. Carey's never studied before, you won't mind helping him a little just at first, will you?" Then she turned to the model. "*La Pose.*"

The model threw aside the paper she had been reading, *La Petite République*, and sulkily, throwing off her gown, got on to the stand. She stood, squarely on both feet, with her hands clasped behind her head.

"It's a stupid pose," said Miss Price. "I can't imagine why they chose it."

When Philip entered, the people in the studio looked at him curiously, and the model gave him an indifferent glance, but now they ceased to pay any attention to him. Philip, with his beautiful sheet of paper in front of him, stared awkwardly at the model. He did not know how to begin. He had never seen a naked woman before. She was not young and her breasts were shrivelled. She had colourless, fair hair that fell over her forehead untidily, and her face was covered with large freckles. He glanced at Miss Price's work. She had only been working on it two days, and it looked as though she had had trouble; her paper was in a mess from constant rubbing out, and to Philip's eyes the figure looked strangely distorted.

"I should have thought I could do as well as that," he said to himself.

He began on the head, thinking that he would work slowly downwards, but, he could not understand why, he found it infinitely more difficult to draw a head from the model than to draw one from his imagination. He got into difficulties. He glanced at Miss Price. She was working with vehement gravity. Her brow was wrinkled with eagerness, and there was an anxious look in her eyes. It was hot in the studio, and drops of sweat stood on her forehead. She was a girl of twenty-six, with a great deal of dull gold hair; it was handsome hair, but it was carelessly done, dragged back from her forehead and tied in a hurried knot. She had a large face, with broad, flat features and small eyes; her skin was pasty, with a singular unhealthiness of tone, and there was no colour in the cheeks. She had an unwashed tone, and you could not help wondering if she slept in her clothes. She was serious and silent. When the next pause came, she stepped back to look at her work.

"I don't know why I'm having so much bother," she said. "But I mean to get it right." She turned to Philip. "How are you getting on?"

"Not at all," he answered, with a rueful smile.

She looked at what he had done.

"You can't expect to do anything that way. You must take measure-ments. And you must square out your paper."

She showed him rapidly how to set about the business. Philip was impressed by her earnestness, but repelled by her want of charm. He was grateful for the hints she gave him and set to work again. Meanwhile other people had come in, mostly men, for the women always arrived first, and the studio for the time of year (it was early yet) was fairly full. Presently there came in a young man with thin, black hair, an enormous nose, and a face so long that it reminded you of a horse. He sat down next to Philip and nodded across him to Miss Price.

"You're very late," she said. "Are you only just up?"

"It was such a splendid day, I thought I'd lie in bed and think how beautiful it was out."

Philip smiled, but Miss Price took the remark seriously.

"That seems a funny thing to do, I should have thought it would be more to the point to get up and enjoy it."

"The way of the humorist is very hard," said the young man gravely.

He did not seem inclined to work. He looked at his canvas; he was working in colour, and had sketched in the day before the model who was posing. He turned to Philip.

"Have you just come out from England?"

"Yes."

"How did you find your way to Amitrano's?"

"It was the only school I knew of."

"I hope you haven't come with the idea that you will learn anything here which will be of the smallest use to you."

"It's the best school in Paris," said Miss Price. "It's the only one where they take art seriously."

"Should art be taken seriously?" the young man asked; and

since Miss Price replied only with a scornful shrug, he added: "But the point is, all schools are bad. They are academical, obviously. Why this is less injurious than most is that the teaching is more incompetent than elsewhere. Because you learn nothing...."

"But why d'you come here then?" interrupted Philip.

"I see the better course, but do not follow it. Miss Price, who is cultured, will remember the Latin of that."

"I wish you would leave me out of your conversation, Mr. Clutton," said Miss Price brusquely.

"The only way to learn to paint," he went on, imperturbable, "is to take a studio, hire a model, and just fight it out for yourself."

"That seems a simple thing to do," said Philip.

"It only needs money," replied Clutton.

He began to paint, and Philip looked at him from the corner of his eye. He was long and desperately thin; his huge bones seemed to protrude from his body; his elbows were so sharp that they appeared to jut out through the arms of his shabby coat. His trousers were frayed at the bottom, and on each of his boots was a clumsy patch. Miss Price got up and went over to Philip's easel.

"If Mr. Clutton will hold his tongue for a moment, I'll just help you a little," she said.

"Miss Price dislikes me because I have humour," said Clutton, looking meditatively at his canvas, "but she detests me because I have genius."

He spoke with solemnity, and his colossal, misshapen nose made what he said very quaint. Philip was obliged to laugh, but Miss Price grew darkly red with anger.

"You're the only person who has ever accused you of genius."

"Also I am the only person whose opinion is of the least value to me."

Miss Price began to criticize what Philip had done. She talked glibly of anatomy and construction, planes and lines, and of much else which Philip did not understand. She had been at the studio a long time and knew the main points which the masters insisted upon, but though she could show what was wrong with Philip's work she could not tell him how to put it right.

"It's awfully kind of you to take so much trouble with me," said Philip.

"Oh, it's nothing," she answered, flushing awkwardly. "People did the same for me when I first came, I'd do it for anyone."

"Miss Price wants to indicate that she is giving you the advantage of her knowledge from a sense of duty rather than on account of any charms of your person," said Clutton.

Miss Price gave him a furious look, and went back to her own drawing. The clock struck twelve, and the model with a cry of relief stepped down from the stand.

Miss Price gathered up her things.

"Some of us go to Gravier's for lunch," she said to Philip, with a look at Clutton. "I always go home myself."

"I'll take you to Gravier's if you like," said Clutton.

Philip thanked him and made ready to go. On his way out Mrs. Otter asked him how he had been getting on.

"Did Fanny Price help you?" she asked. "I put you there because I know she can do it if she likes. She's a disagreeable, ill-natured girl, and she can't draw herself at all, but she knows the ropes, and she can be useful to a newcomer if she cares to take the trouble."

On their way down the street Clutton said to him:

"You've made an impression on Fanny Price. You'd better look out."

Philip laughed. He had never seen anyone on whom he wished less to make an impression. They came to the cheap little restaurant at which several of the students ate, and Clutton sat down at a table at which three or four men were already seated. For a franc, they got an egg, a plate of meat, cheese, and a small bottle of wine. Coffee was extra. They sat on the pavement, and yellow trams passed up and down the boulevard with a ceaseless ringing of bells.

"By the way, what's your name?" said Clutton, as they took their seats.

"Carey."

"Allow me to introduce an old and trusted friend, Carey by name," said Clutton gravely. "Mr. Flanagan, Mr. Lawson."

They laughed and went on with their conversation. They talked of a thousand things, and they all talked at once. No one paid the smallest attention to anyone else. They talked of the places they had been to in the summer, of studios, of the various schools; they mentioned names which were unfamiliar to Philip: Monet, Manet, Renoir, Pissarro, Degas. Philip listened with all his ears, and though he felt a little out of it, his heart leaped with exultation. The time flew. When Clutton got up he said:

"I expect you'll find me here this evening if you care to come. You'll find this about the best place for getting dyspepsia at the lowest cost in the Quarter."

Chapter 41

Philip walked down the Boulevard du Montparnasse. It was not at all like the Paris he had seen in the spring during his visit to do the accounts of the Hôtel St. Georges—he thought already of that part of his life with a shudder—but reminded him of what he thought a provincial town must be. There was an easy-going air about it, and a sunny spaciousness which invited the mind to day-dreaming. The trimness of the trees, the vivid whiteness of the houses, the breadth, were very agreeable; and he felt himself already thoroughly at home. He sauntered along, staring at the people; there seemed an elegance about the most ordinary, workmen with their broad red sashes and their wide trousers, little soldiers in dingy, charming uniforms. He came presently to the Avenue de l'Observatoire, and he gave a sigh of pleasure at the magnificent, yet so graceful, vista. He came to the gardens of the Luxembourg: children were playing, nurses with long ribbons walked slowly two by two, busy men passed through with satchels under their arms, youths strangely dressed. The scene was formal and dainty; nature was arranged and ordered, but so exquisitely, that nature unordered and unarranged seemed barbaric. Philip was enchanted. It excited him to stand on that spot of which he had read so much; it was classic ground to him; and he felt the awe and the delight which some old don might feel when for the first time he looked on the smiling plain of Sparta.

As he wandered he chanced to see Miss Price sitting by herself on a bench. He hesitated, for he did not at that moment want to see anyone, and her uncouth way seemed out of place amid the happiness he felt around him; but he had divined her sensitiveness to affront, and since she had seen him thought it would be polite to speak to her.

"What are you doing here?" she said, as he came up.

"Enjoying myself. Aren't you?"

"Oh, I come here every day from four to five. I don't think one does any good if one works straight through."

"May I sit down for a minute?" he said.

"If you want to."

"That doesn't sound very cordial," he laughed.

"I'm not much of a one for saying pretty things."

Philip, a little disconcerted, was silent as he lit a cigarette.

"Did Clutton say anything about my work?" she asked suddenly.

"No, I don't think he did," said Philip.

"He's no good, you know. He thinks he's a genius, but he isn't. He's too lazy, for one thing. Genius is an infinite capacity for taking pains. The only thing is to peg away. If one only makes up one's mind badly enough to do a thing one can't help doing it."

She spoke with a passionate strenuousness which was rather

striking. She wore a sailor hat of black straw, a white blouse which was not quite clean, and a brown skirt. She had no gloves on, and her hands wanted washing. She was so unattractive that Philip wished he had not begun to talk to her. He could not make out whether she wanted him to stay or go.

"I'll do anything I can for you," she said all at once, without reference to anything that had gone before. "I know how hard it is."

"Thank you very much," said Philip, then in a moment: "Won't you come and have tea with me somewhere?"

She looked at him quickly and flushed. When she reddened her pasty skin acquired a curiously mottled look, like strawberries and cream that had gone bad.

"No, thanks. What d'you think I want tea for? I've only just had lunch."

"I thought it would pass the time," said Philip.

"If you find it long you needn't bother about me, you know. I don't mind being left alone."

At that moment two men passed, in brown velveteens, enormous trousers, and basque caps. They were young, but both wore beards.

"I say, are those art students?" said Philip. "They might have stepped out of the *Vie de Bohème*."

"They're Americans," said Miss Price scornfully. "Frenchmen haven't worn things like that for thirty years, but the Americans from the Far West buy those clothes and have themselves photographed the day after they arrive in Paris. That's about as near to art as they ever get. But it doesn't matter to them, they've all got money."

Philip liked the daring picturesqueness of the Americans' costume; he thought it showed the romantic spirit. Miss Price asked him the time.

"I must be getting along to the studio," she said. "Are you going to the sketch classes?"

Philip did not know anything about them, and she told him that from five to six every evening a model sat, from whom anyone who liked could go and draw at the cost of fifty centimes. They had a different model every day, and it was very good practice.

"I don't suppose you're good enough yet for that. You'd better wait a bit."

"I don't see why I shouldn't try. I haven't got anything else to do."

They got up and walked to the studio. Philip could not tell from her manner whether Miss Price wished him to walk with her or preferred to walk alone. He remained from sheer embarrassment, not knowing how to leave her; but she would not talk; she answered his questions in an ungracious manner.

A man was standing at the studio door with a large dish into which each person as he went in dropped his half franc. The studio was much fuller than it had been in the morning, and there was not the preponderance of English and Americans; nor were women there in so large a proportion. Philip felt the assemblage was more the sort of thing he had expected. It was very warm, and the air quickly grew fetid. It was an old man who sat this time, with a vast grey beard, and Philip tried to put into practice the little he had learned in the morning; but he made a poor job of it; he realized that he could not draw nearly as well as he thought. He glanced enviously at one or two sketches of men who sat near him, and wondered whether he would ever be able to use the charcoal with that mastery. The hour passed quickly. Not wishing to press himself upon Miss Price he sat down at some distance from her, and at the end, as he passed her on his way out, she asked brusquely how he had got on.

"Not very well," he smiled.

"If you'd condescended to come and sit near me I could have given you some hints. I suppose you thought yourself too grand."

"No, it wasn't that. I was afraid you'd think me a nuisance."

"When I do that I'll tell you sharp enough."

Philip saw that in her uncouth way she was offering him help.

"Well, tomorrow I'll just force myself upon you."

"I don't mind," she answered.

Philip went out and wondered what he should do with himself till dinner. He was eager to do something characteristic. *Absinthe!* Of course it was indicated, and so, sauntering towards the station, he seated himself outside a café and ordered it. He drank with nausea and satisfaction. He found the taste disgusting, but the moral effect magnificent; he felt every inch an art student; and since he drank on an empty stomach his spirits presently grew very high. He watched the crowds, and felt all men were his brothers. He was happy. When he reached Gravier's the table at which Clutton sat was full, but as soon as he saw Philip limping along he called out to him. They made room. The dinner was frugal: a plate of soup, a dish of meat, fruit, cheese, and half a bottle of wine; but Philip paid no attention to what he ate. He took note of the men at the table. Flanagan was there again: he was an American, a short snub-nosed youth with a jolly face and a laughing mouth. He wore a Norfolk jacket of bold pattern, a blue stock round his neck, and a tweed cap of fantastic shape. At that time Impressionism reigned in the Latin Quarter, but its victory over the older schools was still recent; and Carolus-Duran, Bouguereau, and their like were set up against Manet, Monet, and Degas. To appreciate these was still a sign of grace. Whistler was an influence strong with the English and his compatriots, and the discerning collected Japanese prints. The old masters were tested by new standards. The esteem in which Raphael had been for centuries held was a matter of derision to wise young men. They offered to give all his works for Velasquez's head of Philip IV in the National Gallery. Philip found that a discussion on art was raging. Lawson, whom he had met at luncheon, sat opposite to him. He was a thin youth with a freckled face and red hair. He had very bright green eyes. As Philip sat down he fixed them on him and remarked suddenly:

"Raphael was only tolerable when he painted other people's pictures. When he painted Peruginos or Pinturichios he was charming; when he painted Raphaels he was," with a scornful shrug, "Raphael."

Lawson spoke so aggressively that Philip was taken aback, but he was not obliged to answer because Flanagan broke in impatiently.

"Oh, to hell with art!" he cried. "Let's get ginny."

"You were ginny last night, Flanagan," said Lawson.

"Nothing to what I mean to be tonight," he answered. "Fancy being in Paris and thinking of nothing but art all the time." He spoke with a broad Western accent. "My, it is good to be alive." He gathered himself together and then banged his fist on the table. "To hell with art, I say."

"You not only say it, but you say it with tiresome iteration," said Clutton severely.

There was another American at the table. He was dressed like those fine fellows whom Philip had seen that afternoon in the Luxembourg. He had a handsome face, thin, ascetic, with dark eyes; he wore his fantastic garb with the dashing air of a buccaneer. He had a vast quantity of dark hair which fell constantly over his eyes, and his most frequent gesture was to throw back his head dramatically to get some long wisp out of the way. He began to talk of the *Olympia* by Manet, which then hung in the Luxembourg.

"I stood in front of it for an hour today, and I tell you it's not a good picture."

Lawson put down his knife and fork. His green eyes flashed fire, he gasped with rage; but he could be seen imposing calm upon himself.

"It's very interesting to hear the mind of the untutored savage," he said. "Will you tell us why it isn't a good picture?"

Before the American could answer someone else broke in vehemently.

"D'you mean to say you can look at the painting of that flesh and say it's not good?"

"I don't say that. I think the right breast is very well painted."

293

"The right breast be damned," shouted Lawson. "The whole thing's a miracle of painting."

He began to describe in detail the beauties of the picture, but at this table at Gravier's they who spoke at length spoke for their own edification. No one listened to him. The American interrupted angrily.

"You don't mean to say you think the head's good?"

Lawson, white with passion now, began to defend the head; but Clutton, who had been sitting in silence with a look on his face of good-humoured scorn, broke in.

"Give him the head. We don't want the head. It doesn't affect the picture."

"All right, I'll give you the head," cried Lawson. "Take the head and be damned to you."

"What about the black line?" cried the American, triumphantly pushing back a wisp of hair which nearly fell in his soup. "You don't see a black line round objects in nature."

"Oh, God, send down fire from heaven to consume the blasphemer," said Lawson. "What has nature got to do with it? No one knows what's in nature and what isn't! The world sees nature through the eyes of the artist. Why, for centuries it saw horses jumping a fence with all their legs extended, and by Heaven, sir, they were extended. It saw shadows black until Monet discovered they were coloured, and by Heaven, sir, they were black. If we choose to surround objects with a black line, the world will see the black line, and there will be a black line; and if we paint grass red and cows blue, it'll see them red and blue, and, by Heaven, they will be red and blue."

"To hell with art," murmured Flanagan. "I want to get ginny."

Lawson took no notice of the interruption.

"Now look here, when *Olympia* was shown at the Salon, Zola—amid the jeers of the Philistines and the hisses of the *pompiers*, the academicians, and the public—Zola said: 'I look forward to the day when Manet's picture will hang in the Louvre opposite the *Odalisque* of Ingres, and it will not be the *Odalisque* which will gain by comparison.' It'll be there. Every day I see the time grow nearer. In ten years the *Olympia* will be in the Louvre."

"Never," shouted the American, using both hands now with a sudden desperate attempt to get his hair once for all out of the way. "In ten years that picture will be dead. It's only a fashion of the moment. No picture can live that hasn't got something which that picture misses by a million miles."

"And what is that?"

"Great art can't exist without a moral element."

"Oh God!" cried Lawson furiously. "I knew it was that. He wants morality." He joined his hands and held them towards Heaven in supplication. "Oh, Christopher Columbus, Christopher Columbus, what did you do when you discovered America?"

"Ruskin says…"

But before he could add another word, Clutton rapped with the handle of his knife imperiously on the table.

"Gentlemen," he said in a stern voice, and his huge nose positively wrinkled with passion, "a name has been mentioned which I never thought to hear again in decent society. Freedom of speech is all very well, but we must observe the limits of common propriety. You may talk of Bouguereau if you will: there is a cheerful disgustingness in the sound which excites laughter; but let us not sully our chaste lips with the names of J. Ruskin, G. F. Watts, or E. B. Jones."

"Who was Ruskin, anyway?" asked Flanagan.

"He was one of the Great Victorians. He was a master of English style."

"Ruskin's style—a thing of shreds and purple patches," said Lawson. "Besides, damn the Great Victorians. Whenever I open a paper and see Death of a Great Victorian, I thank Heaven there's one more of them gone. Their only talent was longevity, and no artist should be allowed to live after he's forty; by then a man has done his best work, all he does after that is repetition. Don't you think it was the greatest luck in the world for them that Keats, Shelley, Bonnington, and Byron died early? What a genius we should think Swinburne if he had perished on the day the first series of *Poems and Ballads* was published!"

The suggestion pleased, for no one at the table was more than twenty-four, and they threw themselves upon it with gusto. They were unanimous for once. They elaborated. Someone proposed a vast bonfire made out of the works of the Forty Academicians into which the Great Victorians might be hurled on their fortieth birthday. The idea was received with acclamation. Carlyle and Ruskin, Tennyson, Browning, G. F. Watts, E. B. Jones, Dickens, Thackeray, they were hurried into the flames; Mr. Gladstone, John Bright, and Cobden; there was a moment's discussion about George Meredith, but Matthew Arnold and Emerson were given up cheerfully. At last came Walter Pater.

"Not Walter Pater," murmured Philip.

Lawson stared at him for a moment with his green eyes and then nodded.

"You're quite right, Walter Pater is the only justification for *Mona Lisa*. D'you know Cronshaw? He used to know Pater."

"Who's Cronshaw?" asked Philip.

"Cronshaw's a poet. He lives here. Let's go to the Lilas."

La Closerie des Lilas was a café to which they often went in the evening after dinner, and here Cronshaw was invariably to be found between the hours of nine at night and two in the morning. But Flanagan had had enough of intellectual conversation for one evening, and when Lawson made his suggestion, turned to Philip.

"Oh gee, let's go where there are girls," he said. "Come to the Gaîté Montparnasse, and we'll get ginny."

"I'd rather go and see Cronshaw and keep sober," laughed Philip.

Chapter 42

There was a general disturbance. Flanagan and two or three more went on to the music hall, while Philip walked slowly with Clutton and Lawson to the Closerie des Lilas.

"You must go to the Gaîté Montparnasse," said Lawson to him. "It's one of the loveliest things in Paris. I'm going to paint it one of these days."

Philip, influenced by Hayward, looked upon music halls with scornful eyes, but he had reached Paris at a time when their artistic possibilities were just discovered. The peculiarities of lighting, the masses of dingy red and tarnished gold, the heaviness of the shadows and the decorative lines, offered a new theme; and half the studios in the Quarter contained sketches made in one or other of the local theatres. Men of letters, following in the painters' wake, conspired suddenly to find artistic value in the turns; and red-nosed comedians were lauded to the skies for their sense of character; fat female singers, who had bawled obscurely for twenty years, were discovered to possess inimitable drollery; there were those who found an aesthetic delight in performing dogs; while others exhausted their vocabulary to extol the distinction of conjurers and trick cyclists. The crowd too, under another influence, was become an object of sympathetic interest. With Hayward, Philip had disdained humanity in the mass; he adopted the attitude of one who wraps himself in solitariness and watches with disgust the antics of the vulgar; but Clutton and Lawson talked of the multitude with enthusiasm. They described the seething throng that filled the various fairs of Paris, the sea of faces, half seen in the glare of acetylene, half hidden in the darkness, and the blare of trumpets, the hooting of whistles, the hum of voices. What they said was new and strange to Philip. They told him about Cronshaw.

"Have you ever read any of his work?"

"No," said Philip.

"It came out in *The Yellow Book*."

They looked upon him, as painters often do writers, with contempt because he was a layman, with tolerance because he practised an art, and with awe because he used a medium in which themselves felt ill at ease.

"He's an extraordinary fellow. You'll find him a bit disappointing at first, he only comes out at his best when he's drunk."

"And the nuisance is," added Clutton, "that it takes him a devil of a time to get drunk."

When they arrived at the café Lawson told Philip that they would have to go in. There was hardly a bite in the autumn air, but Cronshaw had a morbid fear of draughts and even in the warmest weather sat inside.

"He knows everyone worth knowing," Lawson explained. "He knew Pater and Oscar Wilde, and he knows Mallarmé and all those fellows."

The object of their search sat in the most sheltered corner of the café, with his coat on and the collar turned up. He wore his hat pressed well down on his forehead so that he should avoid cold air. He was a big man, stout but not obese, with a round face, a small moustache, and little, rather stupid eyes. His head did not seem quite big enough for his body. It looked like a pea uneasily poised on an egg. He was playing dominoes with a Frenchman, and greeted the newcomers with a quiet smile; he did not speak, but as if to make room for them pushed away the little pile of saucers on the table which indicated the number of drinks he had already consumed. He nodded to Philip when he was introduced to him, and went on with the game. Philip's knowledge of the language was small, but he knew enough to tell that Cronshaw, although he had lived in Paris for several years, spoke French execrably.

At last he leaned back with a smile of triumph.

"*Je vous ai battu,*" he said, with an abominable accent. "*Garçong!*"

He called the waiter and turned to Philip.

"Just out from England? See any cricket?"

Philip was a little confused at the unexpected question.

"Cronshaw knows the averages of every first-class cricketer for the last twenty years," said Lawson, smiling.

The Frenchman left them for friends at another table, and Cronshaw, with the lazy enunciation which was one of his peculiarities, began to discourse on the relative merits of Kent and Lancashire. He told them of the last test match he had seen and described the course of the game wicket by wicket.

"That's the only thing I miss in Paris," he said, as he finished the *bock* which the waiter had brought. "You don't get any cricket."

Philip was disappointed, and Lawson, pardonably anxious to show off one of the celebrities of the Quarter, grew impatient. Cronshaw was taking his time to wake up that evening, though the saucers at his side indicated that he had at least made an honest attempt to get drunk. Clutton watched the scene with amusement. He fancied there was something of affectation in Cronshaw's minute knowledge of cricket; he liked to tantalize people by talking to them of things that obviously bored them; Clutton threw in a question.

"Have you seen Mallarmé lately?"

Cronshaw looked at him slowly, as if he were turning the inquiry over in his mind, and before he answered rapped on the marble table with one of the saucers.

"Bring my bottle of whiskey," he called out. He turned again to Philip. "I keep my own bottle of whiskey. I can't afford to pay fifty centimes for every thimbleful."

The waiter brought the bottle, and Cronshaw held it up to the light.

"They've been drinking it. Waiter, who's been helping himself to my whiskey?"

"*Mais personne, Monsieur Cronshaw.*"

"I made a mark on it last night, and look at it."

"Monsieur made a mark, but he kept on drinking after that. At that rate Monsieur wastes his time in making marks."

The waiter was a jovial fellow and knew Cronshaw intimately. Cronshaw gazed at him.

"If you give me your word of honour as a nobleman and a gentleman that nobody but I has been drinking my whiskey, I'll accept your statement."

This remark, translated literally into the crudest French, sounded very funny, and the lady at the *comptoir* could not help laughing.

"*Il est impayable,*" she murmured.

Cronshaw, hearing her, turned a sheepish eye upon her—she was stout, matronly, and middle-aged—and solemnly kissed his hand to her. She shrugged her shoulders.

"Fear not, madam," he said heavily. "I have passed the age when I am tempted by forty-five and gratitude."

He poured himself out some whiskey and water, and slowly drank it. He wiped his mouth with the back of his hand.

"He talked very well."

Lawson and Clutton knew that Cronshaw's remark was an answer to the question about Mallarmé. Cronshaw often went to the gatherings on Tuesday evenings when the poet received men of letters and painters, and discoursed with subtle oratory on any subject that was suggested to him. Cronshaw had evidently been there lately.

"He talked very well, but he talked nonsense. He talked about art as though it were the most important thing in the world."

"If it isn't, what are we here for?" asked Philip.

"What you're here for I don't know. It is no business of mine. But art is a luxury. Men attach importance only to self-preservation and the propagation of their species. It is only when these instincts are satisfied that they consent to occupy themselves with the entertainment which is provided for them by writers, painters, and poets."

Cronshaw stopped for a moment to drink. He had pondered for twenty years the problem whether he loved liquor because it made him talk or whether he loved conversation because it made him thirsty.

Then he said: "I wrote a poem yesterday."

Without being asked he began to recite it, very slowly, marking the rhythm with an extended forefinger. It was possibly a very fine poem, but at that moment a young woman came in. She had scarlet lips, and it was plain that the vivid colour of her cheeks was not due to the vulgarity of nature; she had blackened her eyelashes and eyebrows, and painted both eyelids a bold blue, which was continued to a triangle at the corner of the eyes. It was fantastic and amusing. Her dark hair was done over her ears in the fashion made popular by Mlle Cléo de Merode. Philip's eyes wandered to her, and Cronshaw having finished the recitation of his verses, smiled upon him indulgently.

"You were not listening," he said.

"Oh yes, I was."

"I do not blame you, for you have given an apt illustration of the statement I just made. What is art beside love? I respect and applaud your indifference to fine poetry when you can contemplate the meretricious charms of this young person."

She passed by the table at which they were sitting, and he took her arm.

"Come and sit by my side, dear child, and let us play the divine comedy of love."

"*Fichez-moi la paix,*" she said, and pushing him on one side continued her perambulation.

"Art," he continued, with a wave of the hand, "is merely the refuge which the ingenious have invented, when they were supplied with food and women, to escape the tediousness of life."

Cronshaw filled his glass again, and began to talk at length. He spoke with rotund delivery. He chose his words carefully. He mingled wisdom and nonsense in the most astounding manner, gravely making fun of his hearers at one moment, and at the next playfully giving them sound advice. He talked of art, and literature, and life. He was by turns devout and obscene, merry and lachrymose. He grew remarkably drunk, and then he began to recite poetry, his own and Milton's, his own and Shelley's, his own and Kit Marlowe's.

At last Lawson, exhausted, got up to go home.

"I shall go too," said Philip.

Clutton, the most silent of them all, remained behind listening, with a sardonic smile on his lips, to Cronshaw's maunderings. Lawson accompanied Philip to his hotel and then bade him good night. But when Philip got to bed he could not sleep. All these new ideas that had been flung before him carelessly seethed in his brain. He was tremendously excited. He felt in himself great powers. He had never before been so self-confident.

"I know I shall be a great artist," he said to himself. "I feel it in me."

A thrill passed through him as another thought came, but even to himself he would not put it into words:

"By George, I believe I've got genius."

He was in fact very drunk, but as he had not taken more than one glass of beer, it could have been due only to a more dangerous intoxicant than alcohol.

Chapter 43

On Tuesdays and Fridays masters spent the morning at Amitrano's, criticizing the work done. In France the painter earns little unless he paints portraits and is patronized by rich Americans; and men of reputation are glad to increase their incomes by spending two or three hours once a week at one of the numerous studios where art is taught. Tuesday was the day upon which Michel Rollin came to Amitrano's. He was an elderly man, with a white beard and a florid complexion, who had painted a number of decorations for the State, but these were an object of derision to the students he instructed: he was a disciple of Ingres, impervious to the progress of art and angrily impatient with that *tas de farceurs* whose names were Manet, Degas, Monet, and Sisley; but he was an excellent teacher, helpful, polite, and encouraging. Foinet, on the other hand, who visited the studio on Fridays, was a difficult man to get on with. He was a small, shrivelled person, with bad teeth and a bilious air, an untidy grey beard, and savage eyes; his voice was high and his tone sarcastic. He had had pictures bought by the Luxembourg, and at twenty-five looked forward to a great career; but his talent was due to youth rather than to personality, and for twenty years he had done nothing but repeat the landscape which had brought him his early success. When he was reproached with monotony, he answered:

"Corot only painted one thing. Why shouldn't I?"

He was envious of everyone else's success, and had a peculiar, personal loathing of the impressionists; for he looked upon his own failure as due to the mad fashion which had attracted the public, *sale bête*, to their works. The genial disdain of Michel Rollin, who called them impostors, was answered by him with vituperation, of which *crapule* and *canaille* were the least violent items; he amused himself with abuse of their private lives, and with sardonic humour, with blasphemous and obscene detail, attacked the legitimacy of their births and the purity of their conjugal relations: he used an Oriental imagery and an Oriental emphasis to accentuate his ribald scorn. Nor did he conceal his contempt for the students whose work he examined. By them he was hated and feared; the women by his brutal sarcasm he reduced often to tears, which again aroused his ridicule; and he remained at the studio, notwithstanding the protests of those who suffered too bitterly from his attacks, because there could be no doubt that he was one of the best masters in Paris. Sometimes the old model who kept the school ventured to remonstrate with him, but his expostulations quickly gave way before the violent insolence of the painter to abject apologies.

It was Foinet with whom Philip first came in contact. He was already in the studio when Philip arrived. He went round from easel to easel, with Mrs. Otter, the *massière*, by his side to interpret his remarks for the benefit of those who could not understand French. Fanny Price, sitting next to Philip, was working feverishly. Her face was sallow with nervousness, and every now and then she stopped to wipe her hands on her blouse, for they were hot with anxiety. Suddenly she turned to Philip with an anxious look, which she tried to hide by a sullen frown.

"D'you think it's good?" she asked, nodding at her drawing.

Philip got up and looked at it. He was astounded; he felt she must have no eye at all; the thing was hopelessly out of drawing.

"I wish I could draw half as well myself," he answered.

"You can't expect to, you've only just come. It's a bit too much to expect that you should draw as well as I do. I've been here two years."

Fanny Price puzzled Philip. Her conceit was stupendous. Philip had already discovered that everyone in the studio cordially disliked her; and it was no wonder, for she seemed to go out of her way to wound people.

"I complained to Mrs. Otter about Foinet," she said now. "The last two weeks he hasn't looked at my drawings. He spends about half an hour on Mrs. Otter because she's the *massière*. After all I pay as much as anybody else, and I suppose my money's as good as theirs. I don't see why I shouldn't get as much attention as anybody else."

She took up her charcoal again, but in a moment put it down with a groan.

"I can't do any more now. I'm so frightfully nervous."

She looked at Foinet, who was coming towards them with Mrs. Otter. Mrs. Otter, meek, mediocre, and self-satisfied, wore an air of importance. Foinet sat down at the easel of an untidy little Englishwoman called Ruth Chalice. She had the fine black eyes, languid but passionate, the thin face, ascetic but sensual, the skin like old ivory, which under the influence of Burne-Jones were cultivated at that time by young ladies in Chelsea. Foinet seemed in a pleasant mood; he did not say much to her, but with quick, determined strokes of her charcoal pointed out her errors. Miss Chalice beamed with pleasure when he rose. He came to Clutton, and by this time Philip was nervous too, but Mrs. Otter had promised to make things easy for him. Foinet stood for a moment in front of Clutton's work, biting his thumb silently, then absent-mindedly spat out upon the canvas the little piece of skin which he had bitten off.

"That's a fine line," he said at last, indicating with his thumb what pleased him. "You're beginning to learn to draw."

Clutton did not answer, but looked at the master with his usual air of sardonic indifference to the world's opinion.

"I'm beginning to think you have at least a trace of talent."

Mrs. Otter, who did not like Clutton, pursed her lips. She did not see anything out of the way in his work. Foinet sat down and went into technical details. Mrs. Otter grew rather tired of standing. Clutton did not say anything, but nodded now and then, and Foinet felt with satisfaction that he grasped what he said and the reasons of it; most of them listened to him, but it was clear they never understood. Then Foinet got up and came to Philip.

"He only arrived two days ago," Mrs. Otter hurried to explain. "He's a beginner. He's never studied before."

"*Ça se voit*," the master said. "One sees that."

He passed on, and Mrs. Otter murmured to him:

"This is the young lady I told you about."

He looked at her as though she were some repulsive animal, and his voice grew more rasping.

"It appears that you do not think I pay enough attention to you. You have been complaining to the *massière*. Well, show me this work to which you wish me to give attention."

Fanny Price coloured. The blood under her unhealthy skin seemed to be of a strange purple. Without answering she pointed to the drawing on which she had been at work since the beginning of the week. Foinet sat down.

"Well, what do you wish me to say to you? Do you wish me to tell you it is good? It isn't. Do you wish me to tell you it is well drawn? It isn't. Do you wish me to say it has merit? It hasn't. Do you wish me to show you what is wrong with it? It is all wrong. Do you wish me to tell you what to do with it? Tear it up. Are you satisfied now?"

Miss Price became very white. She was furious because he had said all this before Mrs. Otter. Though she had been in France so long and could understand French well enough, she could hardly speak two words.

"He's got no right to treat me like that. My money's as good as anyone else's. I pay him to teach me. That's not teaching me."

"What does she say? What does she say?" asked Foinet.

Mrs. Otter hesitated to translate, and Miss Price repeated in execrable French.

"*Je vous paye pour m'apprendre.*"

His eyes flashed with rage, he raised his voice and shook his fist.

"*Mais, nom de Dieu*, I can't teach you. I could more easily teach a camel." He turned to Mrs. Otter. "Ask her, does she do this for amusement, or does she expect to earn money by it?"

"I'm going to earn my living as an artist," Miss Price answered.

"Then it is my duty to tell you that you are wasting your time. It would not matter that you have no talent, talent does not run about the streets in these days, but you have not the beginning of an aptitude. How long have you been here? A child of five after two lessons would draw better than you do. I only say one thing to you, give up this hopeless attempt. You're more likely to earn your living as a *bonne à tout faire* than as a painter. Look."

He seized a piece of charcoal and it broke as he applied it to the paper. He cursed, and with the stump drew great firm lines. He drew rapidly and spoke at the same time, spitting out the words with venom.

"Look, those arms are not the same length. That knee, it's grotesque. I tell you a child of five. You see, she's not standing on her legs. That foot!"

With each word the angry pencil made a mark, and in a moment the drawing upon which Fanny Price had spent so much time and eager trouble was unrecognizable, a confusion of lines and smudges. At last he flung down the charcoal and stood up.

"Take my advice, Mademoiselle, try dressmaking." He looked at his watch. "It's twelve. *À la semaine prochaine, messieurs.*"

Miss Price gathered up her things slowly. Philip waited behind after the others to say to her something consolatory. He could think of nothing but:

"I say, I'm awfully sorry. What a beast that man is!"

She turned on him savagely.

"Is that what you're waiting about for? When I want your sympathy I'll ask for it. Please get out of my way."

She walked past him, out of the studio, and Philip, with a shrug of the shoulders, limped along to Gravier's for luncheon.

"It served her right," said Lawson, when Philip told him what had happened. "Ill-tempered slut."

Lawson was very sensitive to criticism and, in order to avoid it, never went to the studio when Foinet was coming.

"I don't want other people's opinion of my work," he said. "I know myself if it's good or bad."

"You mean you don't want other people's bad opinion of your work," answered Clutton dryly.

In the afternoon Philip thought he would go to the Luxembourg to see the pictures, and walking through the garden he saw Fanny Price sitting in her accustomed seat. He was sore at the rudeness with which she had met his well-meant attempt to say something pleasant, and passed as though he had not caught sight of her. But she got up at once and came towards him.

"Are you trying to cut me?" she said.

"No, of course not. I thought perhaps you didn't want to be spoken to."

"Where are you going?"

"I wanted to have a look at the Manet, I've heard so much about it."

"Would you like me to come with you? I know the

Luxembourg rather well. I could show you one or two good things."

He understood that, unable to bring herself to apologize directly, she made this offer as amends.

"It's awfully kind of you. I should like it very much."

"You needn't say yes if you'd rather go alone," she said suspiciously.

"I wouldn't."

They walked towards the gallery. Caillebotte's collection had lately been placed on view, and the student for the first time had the opportunity to examine at his ease the works of the impressionists. Till then it had been possible to see them only at Durand-Ruel's shop in the Rue Lafitte (and the dealer, unlike his fellows in England, who adopt towards the painter an attitude of superiority, was always pleased to show the shabbiest student whatever he wanted to see), or at his private house, to which it was not difficult to get a card of admission on Tuesdays, and where you might see pictures of world-wide reputation. Miss Price led Philip straight up to Manet's *Olympia*. He looked at it in astonished silence.

"Do you like it?" asked Miss Price.

"I don't know," he answered helplessly.

"You can take it from me that it's the best thing in the gallery except perhaps Whistler's portrait of his mother."

She gave him a certain time to contemplate the masterpiece and then took him to a picture representing a railway station.

"Look, here's a Monet," she said. "It's the Gare St. Lazare."

"But the railway lines aren't parallel," said Philip.

"What does that matter?" she asked, with a haughty air.

Philip felt ashamed of himself. Fanny Price had picked up the glib chatter of the studios and had no difficulty in impressing Philip with the extent of her knowledge. She proceeded to explain the pictures to him, superciliously but not without insight, and showed him what the painters had attempted and what he must look for. She talked with much gesticulation of the thumb, and Philip, to whom all she said was new, listened with profound but bewildered interest. Till now he had worshipped Watts and Burne-Jones. The pretty colour of the first, the affected drawing of the second, had entirely satisfied his aesthetic sensibilities. Their vague idealism, the suspicion of a philosophical idea which underlay the titles they gave their pictures, accorded very well with the functions of art as from his diligent perusal of Ruskin he understood it; but here was something quite different: here was no moral appeal; and the contemplation of these works could help no one to lead a purer and a higher life. He was puzzled.

At last he said: "You know, I'm simply dead. I don't think I can absorb anything more profitably. Let's go and sit down on one of the benches."

"It's better not to take too much art at a time," Miss Price answered.

When they got outside he thanked her warmly for the trouble she had taken.

"Oh, that's all right," she said, a little ungraciously. "I do it because I enjoy it. We'll go to the Louvre tomorrow if you like, and then I'll take you to Durand-Ruel's."

"You're really awfully good to me."

"You don't think me such a beast as the most of them do."

"I don't," he smiled.

"They think they'll drive me away from the studio; but they won't; I shall stay there just exactly as long as it suits me. All that this morning, it was Lucy Otter's doing, I know it was. She always has hated me. She thought after that I'd take myself off. I daresay she'd like me to go. She's afraid I know too much about her."

Miss Price told him a long, involved story, which made out that Mrs. Otter, a humdrum and respectable little person, had scabrous intrigues. Then she talked of Ruth Chalice, the girl whom Foinet had praised that morning.

"She's been with every one of the fellows at the studio. She's nothing better than a street-walker. And she's dirty. She hasn't had a bath for a month. I know it for a fact."

Philip listened uncomfortably. He had heard already that various rumours were in circulation about Miss Chalice; but it was ridiculous to suppose that Mrs. Otter, living with her mother, was anything but rigidly virtuous. The woman walking by his side with her malignant lying positively horrified him.

"I don't care what they say. I shall go on just the same. I know I've got it in me. I feel I'm an artist. I'd sooner kill myself than give it up. Oh, I shan't be the first they've all laughed at in the schools and then he's turned out the only genius of the lot. Art's the only thing I care for, I'm willing to give my whole life to it. It's only a question of sticking to it and pegging away."

She found discreditable motives for everyone who would not take her at her own estimate of herself. She detested Clutton. She told Philip that his friend had no talent really; it was just flashy and superficial; he couldn't compose a figure to save his life. And Lawson:

"Little beast, with his red hair and his freckles. He's so afraid of Foinet that he won't let him see his work. After all, I don't funk it, do I? I don't care what Foinet says to me, I know I'm a real artist."

They reached the street in which she lived, and with a sigh of relief Philip left her.

Chapter 44

But notwithstanding when Miss Price on the following Sunday offered to take him to the Louvre Philip accepted. She showed him *Mona Lisa*. He looked at it with a slight feeling of disappointment, but he had read till he knew by heart the jewelled words with which Walter Pater has added beauty to the most famous picture in the world; and these now he repeated to Miss Price.

"That's all literature," she said, a little contemptuously. "You must get away from that."

She showed him the Rembrandts, and she said many appropriate things about them. She stood in front of the *Disciples at Emmaus*.

"When you feel the beauty of that," she said, "you'll know something about painting."

She showed him the *Odalisque* and *La Source* of Ingres. Fanny Price was a peremptory guide, she would not let him look at the things he wished, and attempted to force his admiration for all she admired. She was desperately in earnest with her study of art, and when Philip, passing in the Long Gallery a window that looked out

317

on the Tuileries, gay, sunny, and urbane, like a picture by Raffaëlli, exclaimed:

"I say, how jolly! Do let's stop here a minute," she said, indifferently. "Yes, it's all right. But we've come here to look at pictures."

The autumn air, blithe and vivacious, elated Philip; and when towards midday they stood in the great courtyard of the Louvre, he felt inclined to cry like Flanagan: To hell with art.

"I say, do let's go to one of those restaurants in the Boul' Mich' and have a snack together, shall we?" he suggested.

Miss Price gave him a suspicious look.

"I've got my lunch waiting for me at home," she answered.

"That doesn't matter. You can eat it tomorrow. Do let me stand you a lunch."

"I don't know why you want to."

"It would give me pleasure," he replied, smiling.

They crossed the river, and at the corner of the Boulevard St. Michel there was a restaurant.

"Let's go in there."

"No, I won't go there, it looks too expensive."

She walked on firmly, and Philip was obliged to follow. A few steps brought them to a smaller restaurant, where a dozen people were already lunching on the pavement under an awning; on the window was announced in large white letters: *Déjeuner 1.25, vin compris*.

"We couldn't have anything cheaper than this, and it looks quite all right."

They sat down at a vacant table and waited for the omelette

which was the first article on the bill of fare. Philip gazed with delight upon the passers-by. His heart went out to them. He was tired but very happy.

"I say, look at that man in the blouse. Isn't he ripping!"

He glanced at Miss Price, and to his astonishment saw that she was looking down at her plate, regardless of the passing spectacle, and two heavy tears were rolling down her cheeks.

"What on earth's the matter?" he exclaimed.

"If you say anything to me I shall get up and go at once," she answered.

He was entirely puzzled, but fortunately at that moment the omelette came. He divided it in half and they began to eat. Philip did his best to talk of indifferent things, and it seemed as though Miss Price were making an effort on her side to be agreeable; but the luncheon was not altogether a success. Philip was squeamish, and the way in which Miss Price ate took his appetite away. She ate noisily, greedily, a little like a wild beast in a menagerie, and after she had finished each course rubbed the plate with pieces of bread till it was white and shining, as if she did not wish to lose a single drop of gravy. They had Camembert cheese, and it disgusted Philip to see that she ate rind and all of the portion that was given her. She could not have eaten more ravenously if she were starving.

Miss Price was unaccountable, and having parted from her on one day with friendliness he could never tell whether on the next she would not be sulky and uncivil; but he learned a good deal from her: though she could not draw well herself, she knew all that could be taught, and her constant suggestions helped his progress. Mrs. Otter was useful to him too, and sometimes Miss Chalice criticized his work; he learned from the glib loquacity of Lawson and from the example of Clutton. But Fanny Price hated him to take suggestions from anyone but herself, and when he asked her help after someone else had been talking to him she would refuse with brutal rudeness. The other fellows, Lawson, Clutton, Flanagan, chaffed him about her.

"You be careful, my lad," they said, "she's in love with you."

"Oh, what nonsense," he laughed.

The thought that Miss Price could be in love with anyone was preposterous. It made him shudder when he thought of her uncomeliness, the bedraggled hair and the dirty hands, the brown dress she always wore, stained and ragged at the hem: he supposed she was hard up, they were all hard up, but she might at least be clean; and it was surely possible with a needle and thread to make her skirt tidy.

Philip began to sort his impressions of the people he was thrown in contact with. He was not so ingenuous as in those days which now seemed so long ago at Heidelberg, and, beginning to take a more deliberate interest in humanity, he was inclined to examine and to criticize. He found it difficult to know Clutton any better after seeing him every day for three months than on the first day of their acquaintance. The general impression at the studio was that he was able; it was supposed that he would do great things, and he shared the general opinion; but what exactly he was going to do neither he nor anybody else quite knew. He had worked at several studios before Amitrano's, at Julian's, the Beaux-Arts, and MacPherson's, and was remaining longer at Amitrano's than anywhere because he found himself more left alone. He was not fond of showing his work, and unlike most of the young men who were studying art neither sought nor gave advice. It was said that in the little studio in the Rue Campagne Première, which served him for workroom and bedroom, he had wonderful pictures which would make his reputation if only he could be induced to exhibit them. He could not afford a model but painted still life, and Lawson constantly talked of a plate of apples which he declared was a masterpiece. He was fastidious, and, aiming at something he did not quite fully grasp, was constantly dissatisfied with his work as a whole: perhaps a part would please him, the forearm or the leg and foot of a figure, a glass or a cup in a still-life; and he would cut this out and keep it, destroying the rest of the canvas; so that when people invited themselves to see his work he could truthfully answer that he had not a single picture to show. In Brittany he had come across a painter whom nobody else had heard of, a queer fellow who had been a stockbroker and taken up painting at middle age, and he was greatly influenced by his work. He was turning his back on the impressionists and working out for himself painfully an individual way not only of painting but of seeing. Philip felt in him something strangely original.

At Gravier's where they ate, and in the evening at the Versailles or at the Closerie des Lilas, Clutton was inclined to taciturnity. He sat quietly, with a sardonic expression on his gaunt face, and spoke only when the opportunity occurred to throw in a witticism. He liked a butt and was most cheerful when someone was there on whom he could exercise his sarcasm. He seldom talked of anything but painting, and then only with the one or two persons whom he thought worth while. Philip wondered whether there was in him really anything: his reticence, the haggard look of him, the pungent humour, seemed to suggest personality, but might be no more than an effective mask which covered nothing.

With Lawson on the other hand, Philip soon grew intimate. He had a variety of interests which made him an agreeable companion. He read more than most of the students, and though his income was small, loved to buy books. He lent them willingly; and Philip became acquainted with Flaubert and Balzac, with Verlaine, Heredia, and Villiers de L'Isle-Adam. They went to plays together and sometimes to the gallery of the Opéra Comique. There was the Odéon quite near them, and Philip soon shared his friend's passion for the tragedians of Louis XIV and the sonorous Alexandrine. In the Rue Taitbout were the Concerts Rouge, where for seventy-five centimes they could hear excellent music and get into the bargain something which it was quite possible to drink: the seats were uncomfortable, the place was crowded, the air thick with caporal horrible to breathe, but in their young enthusiasm they were indifferent. Sometimes they went to the Bal Bullier. On these occasions Flanagan accompanied them. His excitability and his roisterous enthusiasm made them laugh. He was an excellent dancer, and before they had been ten minutes in the room he was prancing round with some little shop-girl whose acquaintance he had just made.

The desire of all of them was to have a mistress. It was part of the paraphernalia of the art student in Paris. It gave consideration in the eyes of one's fellows. It was something to boast about. But the difficulty was that they had scarcely enough money to keep themselves, and though they argued that Frenchwomen were so clever it cost no more to keep two than one, they found it difficult to meet young women who were willing to take that view of the circumstances. They had to content themselves for the most part with envying and abusing the ladies who received protection from painters of more settled respectability than their own. It was extraordinary how difficult these things were in Paris. Lawson would become acquainted with some young thing and make an appointment; for twenty-four hours he would be all in a flutter and describe the charmer at length to everyone he met; but she never by any chance turned up at the time fixed. He would come to Gravier's very late, ill-tempered, and exclaim:

"Confound it, another rabbit! I don't know why it is they don't like me. I suppose it's because I don't speak French well, or my red hair. It's too sickening to have spent over a year in Paris without getting hold of anyone."

"You don't go the right way to work," said Flanagan.

He had a long and enviable list of triumphs to narrate, and though they took leave not to believe all he said, evidence forced them to acknowledge that he did not altogether lie. But he sought no permanent arrangement. He only had two years in Paris: he had persuaded his people to let him come and study art instead of going to college; but at the end of that period he was to return to Seattle and go into his father's business. He had made up his mind to get as much fun as possible into the time, and demanded variety rather than duration in his love affairs.

"I don't know how you get hold of them," said Lawson furiously.

"There's no difficulty about that, sonny," answered Flanagan.

"You just go right in. The difficulty is to get rid of them. That's where you want tact."

Philip was too much occupied with his work, the books he was reading, the plays he saw, the conversation he listened to, to trouble himself with the desire for female society. He thought there would be plenty of time for that when he could speak French more glibly.

It was more than a year now since he had seen Miss Wilkinson, and during his first weeks in Paris he had been too busy to answer a letter she had written to him just before he left Blackstable. When another came, knowing it would be full of reproaches and not being just then in the mood for them, he put it aside, intending to open it later; but he forgot and did not run across it till a month afterwards, when he was turning out a drawer to find some socks that had no holes in them. He looked at the unopened letter with dismay. He was afraid that Miss Wilkinson had suffered a good deal, and it made him feel a brute; but she had probably got over the suffering by now, at all events the worst of it. It suggested itself to him that women were often very emphatic in their expressions. These did not mean so much as when men used them. He had quite made up his mind that nothing would induce him ever to see her again. He had not written for so long that it seemed hardly worth while to write now. He made up his mind not to read the letter.

"I daresay she won't write again," he said to himself. "She can't help seeing the thing's over. After all, she was old enough to be my mother; she ought to have known better."

For an hour or two he felt a little uncomfortable. His attitude was obviously the right one, but he could not help a feeling of dissatisfaction with the whole business. Miss Wilkinson, however, did not write again; nor did she, as he absurdly feared, suddenly appear in Paris to make him ridiculous before his friends. In a little while he clean forgot her.

Meanwhile he definitely forsook his old gods. The amazement with which at first he had looked upon the works of the impressionists, changed to admiration; and presently he found himself talking as emphatically as the rest on the merits of Manet, Monet, and Degas. He bought a photograph of a drawing by Ingres of the *Odalisque* and a photograph of the *Olympia*. They were pinned side by side over his washing-stand so that he could contemplate their beauty while he shaved. He knew now quite positively that there had been no painting of landscape before Monet; and he felt a real thrill when he stood in front of Rembrandt's *Disciples at Emmaus* or Velasquez's *Lady with the Flea-bitten Nose*. That was not her real name, but by that she was distinguished at Gravier's to emphasize the picture's beauty notwithstanding the somewhat revolting peculiarity of the sitter's appearance. With Ruskin, Burne-Jones, and Watts, he had put aside his bowler hat and the neat blue tie with white spots which he had worn on coming to Paris; and now disported himself in a soft, broad-brimmed hat, a flowing black cravat, and a cape of romantic cut. He walked along the Boulevard du Montparnasse as though he had known it all his life, and by virtuous perseverance he had learnt to drink absinthe without distaste. He was letting his hair grow, and it was only because Nature is unkind and has no regard for the immortal longings of youth that he did not attempt a beard.

Chapter 45

Philip soon realized that the spirit which informed his friends was Cronshaw's. It was from him that Lawson got his paradoxes; and even Clutton, who strained after individuality, expressed himself in the terms he had insensibly acquired from the older man. It was his ideas that they bandied about at table, and on his authority they formed their judgments. They made up for the respect with which unconsciously they treated him by laughing at his foibles and lamenting his vices.

"Of course, poor old Cronshaw will never do any good," they said. "He's quite hopeless."

They prided themselves on being alone in appreciating his genius; and though, with the contempt of youth for the follies of middle age, they patronized him among themselves, they did not fail to look upon it as a feather in their caps if he had chosen a time when only one was there to be particularly wonderful. Cronshaw never came to Gravier's. For the last four years he had lived in squalid conditions with a woman whom only Lawson had once seen, in a tiny apartment on the sixth floor of one of the most dilapidated houses on the Quai des Grands Augustins: Lawson described with gusto the filth, the untidiness, the litter.

"And the stink nearly blew your head off."

"Not at dinner, Lawson," expostulated one of the others.

But he would not deny himself the pleasure of giving picturesque details of the odours which met his nostril. With a fierce delight in his own realism he described the woman who had opened the door for him. She was dark, small, and fat, quite young, with black hair that seemed always on the point of coming down. She wore a slatternly blouse and no corsets. With her red cheeks, large sensual mouth, and shining, lewd eyes, she reminded you of the *Bohémienne* in the Louvre by Franz Hals. She had a flaunting vulgarity which amused and yet horrified. A scrubby, unwashed baby was playing on the floor. It was known that the slut deceived Cronshaw with the most worthless ragamuffins of the Quarter, and it was a mystery to the ingenuous youths who absorbed his wisdom over a café table that Cronshaw with his keen intellect and his passion for beauty could ally himself to such a creature. But he seemed to revel in the coarseness of her language and would often report some phrase which reeked of the gutter. He referred to her ironically as *la fille de mon concierge*. Cronshaw was very poor. He earned a bare subsistence by writing on the exhibitions of pictures for one or two English papers, and he did a certain amount of translating. He had been on the staff of an English paper in Paris, but had been dismissed for drunkenness; he still, however, did odd jobs for it, describing sales at the Hôtel Drouot or the revues at music halls. The life of Paris had got into his bones, and he would not change it, notwithstanding its squalor, drudgery, and hardship, for any other in the world. He remained there all through the year, even in summer when everyone he knew was away, and felt himself only at ease within a mile of the Boulevard St. Michel. But the curious thing was that he had never learnt to speak French passably, and he kept, in his shabby clothes bought at *La Belle Jardinière,* an ineradicably English appearance.

He was a man who would have made a success of life a century and a half ago when conversation was a passport to good company and inebriety no bar.

"I ought to have lived in the eighteen hundreds," he said himself. "What I want is a patron. I should have published my poems by subscription and dedicated them to a nobleman. I long to compose rhymed couplets upon the poodle of a countess. My soul yearns for the love of chambermaids and the conversation of bishops."

He quoted the romantic Rolla:

Je suis venu trop tard dans un monde trop vieux.

He liked new faces, and he took a fancy to Philip, who seemed to achieve the difficult feat of talking just enough to suggest conversation and not too much to prevent monologue. Philip was captivated. He did not realize that little that Cronshaw said was new. His personality in conversation had a curious power. He had a beautiful and a sonorous voice, and a manner of putting things which was irresistible to youth. All he said seemed to excite thought, and often on the way home Lawson and Philip would walk to and from one another's hotels, discussing some point which a chance word of Cronshaw had suggested. It was disconcerting to Philip, who had a youthful eagerness for results, that Cronshaw's poetry hardly came up to expectation. It had never been published in a volume, but most of it had appeared in periodicals; and after a good deal of persuasion Cronshaw brought down a bundle of pages torn out of *The Yellow Book*, *The Saturday Review*, and other journals, on each of which was a poem. Philip was taken aback to find that most of them reminded him either of Henley or of Swinburne. It needed the splendour of Cronshaw's delivery to make them personal. He expressed his disappointment to Lawson, who carelessly repeated his words; and next time Philip went to the Closerie des Lilas the poet turned to him with his sleek smile:

"I hear you don't think much of my verses."

Philip was embarrassed.

"I don't know about that," he answered. "I enjoyed reading them very much."

"Do not attempt to spare my feelings," returned Cronshaw, with a wave of his fat hand. "I do not attach any exaggerated importance to my poetical works. Life is there to be lived rather than to be written about. My aim is to search out the manifold experience that it offers, wringing from each moment what of emotion it presents. I look upon my writing as a graceful accomplishment which does not absorb but rather adds pleasure to existence. And as for posterity—damn posterity."

Philip smiled, for it leaped to one's eyes that the artist in life had produced no more than a wretched daub. Cronshaw looked at him meditatively and filled his glass. He sent the waiter for a packet of cigarettes.

"You are amused because I talk in this fashion and you know that I am poor and live in an attic with a vulgar trollop who deceives me with hairdressers and *garçons de café*; I translate wretched books for the British public, and write articles upon contemptible pictures which deserve not even to be abused. But pray tell me what is the meaning of life?"

"I say, that's rather a difficult question. Won't you give the answer yourself?"

"No, because it's worthless unless you yourself discover it. But what do you suppose you are in the world for?"

Philip had never asked himself, and he thought for a moment before replying:

"Oh, I don't know: I suppose to do one's duty, and make the best possible use of one's faculties, and avoid hurting other people."

"In short, to do unto others as you would they should do unto you?"

"I suppose so."

"Christianity."

"No, it isn't," said Philip indignantly. "It has nothing to do with Christianity. It's just abstract morality."

"But there's no such thing as abstract morality."

"In that case, supposing under the influence of liquor you left your purse behind when you leave here and I picked it up, why do you imagine that I should return it to you? It's not the fear of the police."

"It's the dread of Hell if you sin and the hope of Heaven if you are virtuous."

"But I believe in neither."

"That may be. Neither did Kant when he devised the Categorical Imperative. You have thrown aside a creed, but you have preserved the ethic which was based upon it. To all intents you are a Christian still, and if there is a God in Heaven you will undoubtedly receive your reward. The Almighty can hardly be such a fool as the churches make out. If you keep His laws I don't think He can care a packet of pins whether you believe in Him or not."

"But if I left my purse behind you would certainly return it to me," said Philip.

"Not from motives of abstract morality, but only from fear of the police."

"It's a thousand to one that the police would never find out."

"My ancestors have lived in a civilized state so long that the fear of the police has eaten into my bones. The daughter of my *concierge* would not hesitate for a moment. You answer that she belongs to the criminal classes; not at all, she is merely devoid of vulgar prejudice."

"But then that does away with honour and virtue and goodness and decency and everything," said Philip.

"Have you ever committed a sin?"

"I don't know, I suppose so," answered Philip.

"You speak with the lips of a dissenting minister. I have never committed a sin."

Cronshaw in his shabby great-coat, with the collar turned up, and his hat well down on his head, with his red fat face and his little gleaming eyes, looked extraordinarily comic; but Philip was too much in earnest to laugh.

"Have you never done anything you regret?"

"How can I regret when what I did was inevitable?" asked Cronshaw in return.

"But that's fatalism."

"The illusion which man has that his will is free is so deeply rooted that I am ready to accept it. I act as though I were a free agent. But when an action is performed it is clear that all the forces of the universe from all eternity conspired to cause it, and nothing I could do could have prevented it. It was inevitable. If it was good I can claim no merit; if it was bad I can accept no censure."

"My brain reels," said Philip.

"Have some whiskey," returned Cronshaw, passing over the bottle. "There's nothing like it for clearing the head. You must expect to be thick-witted if you insist upon drinking beer."

Philip shook his head, and Cronshaw proceeded:

"You're not a bad fellow, but you won't drink. Sobriety disturbs conversation. But when I speak of good and bad..." Philip saw he was taking up the thread of his discourse, "I speak conventionally. I attach no meaning to those words. I refuse to make a hierarchy of human actions and ascribe worthiness to some and ill-repute to others. The terms vice and virtue have no signification for me. I do not confer praise or blame: I accept. I am the measure of all things. I am the centre of the world."

"But there are one or two other people in the world,"

objected Philip.

"I speak only for myself. I know them only as they limit my activities. Round each of them too the world turns, and each one for himself is the centre of the universe. My right over them extends only as far as my power. What I can do is the only limit of what I may do. Because we are gregarious we live in society, and society holds together by means of force, force of arms (that is the policeman) and force of public opinion (that is Mrs. Grundy). You have society on one hand and the individual on the other: each is an organism striving for self-preservation. It is might against might. I stand alone, bound to accept society and not unwilling, since in return for the taxes I pay it protects me, a weakling, against the tyranny of another stronger than I am; but I submit to its laws because I must; I do not acknowledge their justice; I do not know justice, I only know power. And when I have paid for the policeman who protects me and, if I live in a country where conscription is in force, served in the army which guards my house and land from the invader, I am quits with society: for the rest I counter its might with my wiliness. It makes laws for its self-preservation, and if I break them it imprisons or kills me: it has the might to do so and therefore the right. If I break the laws I will accept the vengeance of the state, but I will not regard it as punishment nor shall I feel myself convicted of wrong-doing. Society tempts me to its service by honours and riches and the good opinion of my fellows; but I am indifferent to their good opinion, I despise honours and I can do very well without riches."

"But if everyone thought like you things would go to pieces

at once."

"I have nothing to do with others, I am only concerned with myself. I take advantage of the fact that the majority of mankind are led by certain rewards to do things which directly or indirectly tend to my convenience."

"It seems to me an awfully selfish way of looking at things," said Philip.

"But are you under the impression that men ever do anything except for selfish reasons?"

"Yes."

"It is impossible that they should. You will find as you grow older that the first thing needful to make the world a tolerable place to live in is to recognize the inevitable selfishness of humanity. You demand unselfishness from others, which is a preposterous claim that they should sacrifice their desires to yours. Why should they? When you are reconciled to the fact that each is for himself in the world you will ask less from your fellows. They will not disappoint you, and you will look upon them more charitably. Men seek but one thing in life—their pleasure."

"No, no, no!" cried Philip.

Cronshaw chuckled.

"You rear like a frightened colt, because I use a word to which your Christianity ascribes a deprecatory meaning. You have a hierarchy of values; pleasure is at the bottom of the ladder, and you speak with a little thrill of self-satisfaction of duty, charity, and truthfulness. You think pleasure is only of the senses; the wretched slaves who manufactured your morality despised a satisfaction which they had small means of enjoying. You would not be so frightened if I had spoken of happiness instead of pleasure: it sounds less shocking, and your mind wanders from the sty of Epicurus to his garden. But I will speak of pleasure, for I see that men aim at that, and I do not know that they aim at happiness. It is pleasure that lurks in the practice of every one of your virtues. Man performs actions because they are good for him, and when they are good for other people as well they are thought virtuous: if he finds pleasure in giving alms he is charitable; if he finds pleasure in helping others he is benevolent; if he finds pleasure in working for society he is public-spirited; but it is for your private pleasure that you give twopence to a beggar as much as it is for my private pleasure that I drink another whiskey and soda. I, less of a humbug than you, neither applaud myself for my pleasure nor demand your admiration."

"But have you never known people do things they didn't want to instead of things they did?"

"No. You put your question foolishly. What you mean is that people accept an immediate pain rather than an immediate pleasure. The objection is as foolish as your manner of putting it. It is clear that men accept an immediate pain rather than an immediate pleasure, but only because they expect a greater pleasure in the future. Often the pleasure is illusory, but their error in calculation is no refutation of the rule. You are puzzled because you cannot get over the idea that pleasures are only of the senses; but, child, a man who dies for his country dies because he likes it as surely as a man eats pickled cabbage because he likes it. It is a law of creation. If it were possible for men to prefer pain to pleasure the human race would have long since become extinct."

"But if all that is true," cried Philip, "what is the use of anything? If you take away duty and goodness and beauty, why are we brought into the world?"

"Here comes the gorgeous East to suggest an answer," smiled Cronshaw.

He pointed to two persons who at that moment opened the door of the café, and, with a blast of cold air, entered. They were Levantines, itinerant vendors of cheap rugs, and each bore on his arm a bundle. It was Sunday evening, and the café was very full. They passed among the tables, and in that atmosphere heavy and discoloured with tobacco smoke, rank with humanity, they seemed to bring an air of mystery. They were clad in European, shabby clothes, their thin great-coats were threadbare, but each wore a tarboosh. Their faces were grey with cold. One was of middle age, with a black beard, but the other was a youth of eighteen, with a face deeply scarred by smallpox and with one eye only. They passed by Cronshaw and Philip.

"Allah is great, and Mahomet is his prophet," said Cronshaw impressively.

The elder advanced with a cringing smile, like a mongrel used to blows. With a sidelong glance at the door and a quick surreptitious movement he showed a pornographic picture.

"Are you Masr-ed-Deen, the merchant of Alexandria, or is it from far Bagdad that you bring your goods, O, my uncle; and yonder one-eyed youth, do I see in him one of the three kings of whom Scheherazade told stories to her lord?"

The pedlar's smile grew more ingratiating, though he understood no word of what Cronshaw said, and like a conjurer he produced a sandal-wood box.

"Nay, show us the priceless web of Eastern looms," quoth Cronshaw. "For I would point a moral and adorn a tale."

The Levantine unfolded a tablecloth, red and yellow, vulgar, hideous and grotesque.

"Thirty-five francs," he said.

"O, my uncle, this cloth knew not the weavers of Samarkand, and those colours were never made in the vasts of Bokhara."

"Twenty-five francs," smiled the pedlar obsequiously.

"Ultima Thule was the place of its manufacture, even Birmingham, the place of my birth."

"Fifteen francs," cringed the bearded man.

"Get thee gone, fellow," said Cronshaw. "May wild asses defile the grave of thy maternal grandmother."

Imperturbably, but smiling no more, the Levantine passed with his wares to another table. Cronshaw turned to Philip.

"Have you ever been to the Cluny, the museum? There you will see Persian carpets of the most exquisite hue and of a pattern the beautiful intricacy of which delights and amazes the eye. In them you will see the mystery and the sensual beauty of the East, the roses of Hafiz and the wine-cup of Omar; but presently you will see more. You were asking just now what was the meaning of life. Go and look at those Persian carpets, and one of these days the answer will come to you."

"You are cryptic," said Philip.

"I am drunk," answered Cronshaw.

Chapter 46

Philip did not find living in Paris as cheap as he had been led to believe and by February had spent most of the money with which he started. He was too proud to appeal to his guardian, nor did he wish Aunt Louisa to know that his circumstances were straitened, since he was certain she would make an effort to send him something from her own pocket, and he knew how little she could afford to. In three months he would attain his majority and come into possession of his small fortune. He tided over the interval by selling the few trinkets which he had inherited from his father.

At about this time Lawson suggested that they should take a small studio which was vacant in one of the streets that led out of the Boulevard Raspail. It was very cheap. It had a room attached, which they could use as a bedroom; and since Philip was at the school every morning Lawson could have the undisturbed use of the studio then; Lawson, after wandering from school to school, had come to the conclusion that he could work best alone, and proposed to get a model in three or four days a week. At first

Philip hesitated on account of the expense, but they reckoned it out; and it seemed (they were so anxious to have a studio of their own that they calculated pragmatically) that the cost would not be much greater than that of living in a hotel. Though the rent and the cleaning by the *concierge* would come to a little more, they would save on the *petit déjeuner*, which they could make themselves. A year or two earlier Philip would have refused to share a room with anyone, since he was so sensitive about his deformed foot, but his morbid way of looking at it was growing less marked: in Paris it did not seem to matter so much, and though he never by any chance forgot it himself, he ceased to feel that other people were constantly noticing it.

They moved in, bought a couple of beds, a washing-stand, a few chairs, and felt for the first time the thrill of possession. They were so excited that the first night they went to bed in what they could call a home they lay awake talking till three in the morning; and next day found lighting the fire and making their own coffee, which they had in pyjamas, such a jolly business that Philip did not get to Amitrano's till nearly eleven. He was in excellent spirits. He nodded to Fanny Price.

"How are you getting on?" he asked cheerily.

"What does that matter to you?" she asked in reply.

Philip could not help laughing.

"Don't jump down my throat. I was only trying to make myself polite."

"I don't want your politeness."

"D'you think it's worth while quarrelling with me too?" asked Philip mildly. "There are so few people you're on speaking terms with, as it is."

"That's my business, isn't it?"

"Quite."

He began to work, vaguely wondering why Fanny Price made herself so disagreeable. He had come to the conclusion that he thoroughly disliked her. Everyone did. People were only civil to her at all from fear of the malice of her tongue; for to their faces and behind their backs she said abominable things. But Philip was feeling so happy that he did not want even Miss Price to bear ill-feeling towards him. He used the artifice which had often before succeeded in banishing her ill-humour.

"I say, I wish you'd come and look at my drawing. I've got in an awful mess."

"Thank you very much, but I've got something better to do with my time."

Philip stared at her in surprise, for the one thing she could be counted upon to do with alacrity was to give advice. She went on quickly in a low voice, savage with fury:

"Now that Lawson's gone you think you'll put up with me. Thank you very much. Go and find somebody else to help you. I don't want anybody else's leavings."

Lawson had the pedagogic instinct; whenever he found anything out he was eager to impart it; and because he taught with delight he taught with profit. Philip, without thinking anything about it, had got into the habit of sitting by his side; it never occurred to him that Fanny Price was consumed with jealousy, and watched his acceptance of someone else's tuition with ever-increasing anger.

"You were very glad to put up with me when you knew nobody here," she said bitterly, "and as soon as you made friends with other people you threw me aside, like an old glove" —she repeated the stale metaphor with satisfaction— "like an old glove. All right, I don't care, but I'm not going to be made a fool of another time."

There was a suspicion of truth in what she said, and it made Philip angry enough to answer what first came into his head.

"Hang it all, I only asked your advice because I saw it pleased you."

She gave a gasp and threw him a sudden look of anguish. Then two tears rolled down her cheeks. She looked frowsy and grotesque. Philip, not knowing what on earth this new attitude implied, went back to his work. He was uneasy and conscience-stricken; but he would not go to her and say he was sorry if he had caused her pain, because he was afraid she would take the opportunity to snub him. For two or three weeks she did not speak to him, and after Philip had got over the discomfort of being cut by her, he was somewhat relieved to be free from so difficult a friendship. He had been a little disconcerted by the air of proprietorship she assumed over him. She was an extraordinary woman. She came every day to the studio at eight o'clock, and was ready to start working when the model was in position; she worked steadily, talking to no one, struggling hour after hour with difficulties she could not overcome, and remained till the clock struck twelve. Her work was hopeless. There was not in it the smallest approach even to the mediocre achievement at which most of the young persons were able after some months to arrive.

She wore every day the same ugly brown dress, with the mud of the last wet day still caked on the hem and with the raggedness, which Philip had noticed the first time he saw her, still unmended.

But one day she came up to him, and with a scarlet face asked whether she might speak to him afterwards.

"Of course, as much as you like," smiled Philip. "I'll wait behind at twelve."

He went to her when the day's work was over.

"Will you walk a little bit with me?" she said, looking away from him with embarrassment.

"Certainly."

They walked for two or three minutes in silence.

"D'you remember what you said to me the other day?" she asked then on a sudden.

"Oh, I say, don't let's quarrel," said Philip. "It really isn't worth while."

She gave a quick, painful inspiration.

"I don't want to quarrel with you. You're the only friend I had in Paris. I thought you rather liked me. I felt there was something between us. I was drawn towards you—you know what I mean, your club-foot."

Philip reddened and instinctively tried to walk without a limp. He did not like anyone to mention the deformity. He knew what Fanny Price meant. She was ugly and uncouth, and because he was deformed there was between them a certain sympathy. He was very angry with her, but he forced himself not to speak.

"You said you only asked my advice to please me. Don't you think my work's any good?"

"I've only seen your drawing at Amitrano's. It's awfully hard to judge from that."

"I was wondering if you'd come and look at my other work. I've never asked anyone else to look at it. I should like to show it to you."

"It's awfully kind of you. I'd like to see it very much."

"I live quite near here," she said apologetically. "It'll only take you ten minutes."

"Oh, that's all right," he said.

They were walking along the boulevard, and she turned down a side street, then led him into another, poorer still, with cheap shops on the ground floor, and at last stopped. They climbed flight after flight of stairs. She unlocked a door, and they went into a tiny attic with a sloping roof and a small window. This was closed and the room had a musty smell. Though it was very cold there was no fire and no sign that there had been one. The bed was unmade. A chair, a chest of drawers which served also as a washstand, and a cheap easel, were all the furniture. The place would have been squalid enough in any case, but the litter, the untidiness, made the impression revolting. On the chimney-piece, scattered over with paints and brushes, were a cup, a dirty plate, and a teapot.

"If you'll stand over there I'll put them on the chair so that you can see them better."

She showed him twenty small canvases, about eighteen by twelve. She placed them on the chair, one after the other, watching his face; he nodded as he looked at each one.

"You do like them, don't you?" she said anxiously, after a bit.

"I just want to look at them all first," he answered. "I'll talk afterwards."

He was collecting himself. He was panic-stricken. He did not know what to say. It was not only that they were ill-drawn, or that the colour was put on amateurishly by someone who had no eye for it; but there was no attempt at getting the values, and the perspective was grotesque. It looked like the work of a child of five, but a child would have had some naïveté and might at least have made an attempt to put down what he saw; but here was the work of a vulgar mind chock-full of recollections of vulgar pictures. Philip remembered that she had talked enthusiastically about Monet and the Impressionists, but here were only the worst traditions of the Royal Academy.

"There," she said at last, "that's the lot."

Philip was no more truthful than anybody else, but he had a great difficulty in telling a thundering, deliberate lie, and he blushed furiously when he answered:

"I think they're most awfully good."

A faint colour came into her unhealthy cheeks, and she smiled a little.

"You needn't say so if you don't think so, you know. I want the truth."

"But I do think so."

"Haven't you got any criticism to offer? There must be some you don't like as well as others."

Philip looked round helplessly. He saw a landscape, the typical picturesque "bit" of the amateur, an old bridge, a creeper-clad cottage, and a leafy bank.

"Of course, I don't pretend to know anything about it," he said. "But I wasn't quite sure about the values of that."

She flushed darkly and taking up the picture quickly turned its back to him.

"I don't know why you should have chosen that one to sneer at. It's the best thing I've ever done. I'm sure my values are all right. That's a thing you can't teach anyone, you either understand values or you don't."

"I think they're all most awfully good," repeated Philip.

She looked at them with an air of self-satisfaction.

"I don't think they're anything to be ashamed of."

Philip looked at his watch.

"I say, it's getting late. Won't you let me give you a little lunch?"

"I've got my lunch waiting for me here."

Philip saw no sign of it, but supposed perhaps the *concierge* would bring it up when he was gone. He was in a hurry to get away. The mustiness of the room made his head ache.

Chapter 47

In March there was all the excitement of sending in to the Salon. Clutton, characteristically, had nothing ready, and he was very scornful of the two heads that Lawson sent; they were obviously the work of a student, straightforward portraits of models, but they had a certain force; Clutton, aiming at perfection, had no patience with efforts which betrayed hesitancy, and with a shrug of the shoulders told Lawson it was an impertinence to exhibit stuff which should never have been allowed out of his studio; he was not less contemptuous when the two heads were accepted. Flanagan tried his luck too, but his picture was refused. Mrs. Otter sent a blameless *Portrait de ma Mère*, accomplished and second-rate; and was hung in a very good place.

Hayward, whom Philip had not seen since he left Heidelberg, arrived in Paris to spend a few days in time to come to the party which Lawson and Philip were giving in their studio to celebrate the hanging of Lawson's pictures. Philip had been eager to see Hayward again, but when at last they met, he experienced some disappointment. Hayward had altered a little in appearance: his fine hair was thinner, and with the rapid wilting of the very fair, he was becoming wizened and colourless; his blue eyes were paler than they had been, and there was a muzziness about his features. On the other hand, in mind he did not seem to have changed at all, and the culture which had impressed Philip at eighteen aroused somewhat the contempt of Philip at twenty-one. He had altered a good deal himself, and regarding with scorn all his old opinions of art, life, and letters, had no patience with anyone who still held them. He was scarcely conscious of the fact that he wanted to show off before Hayward, but when he took him round the galleries he poured out to him all the revolutionary opinions which himself had so recently adopted. He took him to Manet's *Olympia* and said dramatically:

"I would give all the old masters except Velasquez, Rembrandt, and Vermeer for that one picture."

"Who was Vermeer?" asked Hayward.

"Oh, my dear fellow, don't you know Vermeer? You're not civilized. You mustn't live a moment longer without making his acquaintance. He's the one old master who painted like a modern."

He dragged Hayward out of the Luxembourg and hurried him off to the Louvre.

"But aren't there any more pictures here?" asked Hayward, with the tourist's passion for thoroughness.

"Nothing of the least consequence. You can come and look at them by yourself with your Baedeker."

When they arrived at the Louvre Philip led his friend down the Long Gallery.

"I should like to see *La Gioconda*," said Hayward.

"Oh, my dear fellow, it's only literature," answered Philip.

At last, in a small room, Philip stopped before *The Lacemaker* of Vermeer van Delft.

"There, that's the best picture in the Louvre. It's exactly like a Manet."

With an expressive, eloquent thumb Philip expatiated on the charming work. He used the jargon of the studios with overpowering effect.

"I don't know that I see anything so wonderful as all that in it," said Hayward.

"Of course it's a painter's picture," said Philip. "I can quite believe the layman would see nothing much in it."

"The what?" said Hayward.

"The layman."

Like most people who cultivate an interest in the arts, Hayward was extremely anxious to be right. He was dogmatic with those who did not venture to assert themselves, but with the self-assertive he was very modest. He was impressed by Philip's assurance, and accepted meekly Philip's implied suggestion that the painter's arrogant claim to be the sole possible judge of painting has anything but its impertinence to recommend it.

A day or two later Philip and Lawson gave their party. Cronshaw, making an exception in their favour, agreed to eat their food; and Miss Chalice offered to come and cook for them. She took no interest in her own sex and declined the suggestion that other girls should be asked for her sake. Clutton, Flanagan, Potter, and two others made up the party. Furniture was scarce, so the model stand was used as a table, and the guests were to sit on portmanteaux if they liked, and if they didn't on the floor. The feast consisted of a *pot-au-feu*, which Miss Chalice had made, of a leg of mutton roasted round the corner and brought round hot and savoury (Miss Chalice had cooked the potatoes, and the studio was redolent of the carrots she had fried; fried carrots were her specialty); and this was to be followed by *poires flambées*, pears with burning brandy, which Cronshaw had volunteered to make. The meal was to finish with an enormous *fromage de Brie*, which stood near the window and added fragrant odours to all the others which filled the studio. Cronshaw sat in the place of honour on a Gladstone bag, with his legs curled under him like a Turkish bashaw, beaming good-naturedly on the young people who surrounded him. From force of habit, though the small studio with the stove lit was very hot, he kept on his great-coat, with the collar turned up, and his bowler hat: he looked with satisfaction on the four large *fiaschi* of Chianti which stood in front of him in a row, two on each side of a bottle of whiskey; he said it reminded him of a slim fair Circassian guarded by four corpulent eunuchs. Hayward in order to put the rest of them at their ease had clothed himself in a tweed suit and a Trinity Hall tie. He looked grotesquely British. The others were elaborately polite to him, and during the soup they talked of the weather and the political situation. There was a pause while they waited for the leg of mutton, and Miss Chalice lit a cigarette.

"Rampunzel, Rampunzel, let down your hair," she said suddenly.

With an elegant gesture she untied a ribbon so that her

tresses fell over her shoulders. She shook her head.

"I always feel more comfortable with my hair down."

With her large brown eyes, thin, ascetic face, her pale skin, and broad forehead, she might have stepped out of a picture by Burne-Jones. She had long, beautiful hands, with fingers deeply stained by nicotine. She wore sweeping draperies, mauve and green. There was about her the romantic air of High Street, Kensington. She was wantonly aesthetic; but she was an excellent creature, kind and good-natured; and her affectations were but skin-deep. There was a knock at the door, and they all gave a shout of exultation. Miss Chalice rose and opened. She took the leg of mutton and held it high above her, as though it were the head of John the Baptist on a platter; and, the cigarette still in her mouth, advanced with solemn, hieratic steps.

"Hail, daughter of Herodias," cried Cronshaw.

The mutton was eaten with gusto, and it did one good to see what a hearty appetite the pale-faced lady had. Clutton and Potter sat on each side of her, and everyone knew that neither had found her unduly coy. She grew tired of most people in six weeks, but she knew exactly how to treat afterwards the gentlemen who had laid their young hearts at her feet. She bore them no ill-will, though having loved them she had ceased to do so, and treated them with friendliness but without familiarity. Now and then she looked at Lawson with melancholy eyes. The *poires flambées* were a great success, partly because of the brandy and partly because Miss Chalice insisted that they should be eaten with the cheese.

"I don't know whether it's perfectly delicious or whether I'm just going to vomit," she said, after she had thoroughly tried the mixture.

Coffee and cognac followed with sufficient speed to prevent any untoward consequence, and they settled down to smoke in comfort. Ruth Chalice, who could do nothing that was not deliberately artistic, arranged herself in a graceful attitude by Cronshaw and just rested her exquisite head on his shoulder. She looked into the dark abyss of time with brooding eyes, and now and then with a long meditative glance at Lawson she sighed deeply.

Then came the summer, and restlessness seized these young people. The blue skies lured them to the sea, and the pleasant breeze sighing through the leaves of the plane-trees on the boulevard drew them towards the country. Everyone made plans for leaving Paris; they discussed what was the most suitable size for the canvases they meant to take; they laid in stores of panels for sketching; they argued about the merits of various places in Brittany. Flanagan and Potter went to Concarneau; Mrs. Otter and her mother, with a natural instinct for the obvious, went to Pont-Aven; Philip and Lawson made up their minds to go to the forest of Fontainebleau, and Miss Chalice knew of a very good hotel at Moret where there was lots of stuff to paint; it was near Paris, and neither Philip nor Lawson was indifferent to the railway fare. Ruth Chalice would be there, and Lawson had an idea for a portrait of her in the open air. Just then the Salon was full of portraits of people in gardens, in sunlight, with blinking eyes and green reflections of sunlit leaves on their faces. They asked Clutton to go with them, but he preferred spending the summer by himself.

He had just discovered Cézanne, and was eager to go to Provence; he wanted heavy skies from which the hot blue seemed to drip like beads of sweat, and broad white dusty roads, and pale roofs out of which the sun had burnt the colour, and olive trees grey with heat.

The day before they were to start, after the morning class, Philip, putting his things together, spoke to Fanny Price.

"I'm off tomorrow," he said cheerfully.

"Off where?" she said quickly. "You're not going away?" Her face fell.

"I'm going away for the summer. Aren't you?"

"No, I'm staying in Paris. I thought you were going to stay too. I was looking forward...."

She stopped and shrugged her shoulders.

"But won't it be frightfully hot here? It's awfully bad for you."

"Much you care if it's bad for me. Where are you going?"

"Moret."

"Chalice is going there. You're not going with her?"

"Lawson and I are going. And she's going there too. I don't know that we're actually going together."

She gave a low guttural sound, and her large face grew dark and red.

"How filthy! I thought you were a decent fellow. You were about the only one here. She's been with Clutton and Potter and Flanagan, even with old Foinet—that's why he takes so much trouble about her—and now two of you, you and Lawson. It makes me sick."

"Oh, what nonsense! She's a very decent sort. One treats her just as if she were a man."

"Oh, don't speak to me, don't speak to me."

"But what can it matter to you?" asked Philip. "It's really no business of yours where I spend my summer."

"I was looking forward to it so much," she gasped, speaking it seemed almost to herself. "I didn't think you had the money to go away, and there wouldn't have been anyone else here, and we could have worked together, and we'd have gone to see things." Then her thoughts flung back to Ruth Chalice. "The filthy beast," she cried. "She isn't fit to speak to."

Philip looked at her with a sinking heart. He was not a man to think girls were in love with him; he was too conscious of his deformity, and he felt awkward and clumsy with women; but he did not know what else this outburst could mean. Fanny Price, in the dirty brown dress, with her hair falling over her face, sloppy, untidy, stood before him; and tears of anger rolled down her cheeks. She was repellent. Philip glanced at the door, instinctively hoping that someone would come in and put an end to the scene.

"I'm awfully sorry," he said.

"You're just the same as all of them. You take all you can get, and you don't even say thank you. I've taught you everything you know. No one else would take any trouble with you. Has Foinet ever bothered about you? And I can tell you this—you can work here for a thousand years and you'll never do any good. You haven't got any talent. You haven't got any originality. And it's not only me—they all say it. You'll never be a painter as long as you live."

"That is no business of yours either, is it?" said Philip, flushing.

"Oh, you think it's only my temper. Ask Clutton, ask Lawson, ask Chalice. Never, never, never. You haven't got it in you."

Philip shrugged his shoulders and walked out. She shouted after him.

"Never, never, never."

Moret was in those days an old-fashioned town of one street at the edge of the Forest of Fontainebleau, and the Écu d'Or was a hotel which still had about it the decrepit air of the *Ancien Régime*. It faced the winding river, the Loing; and Miss Chalice had a room with a little terrace overlooking it, with a charming view of the old bridge and its fortified gateway. They sat here in the evenings after dinner, drinking coffee, smoking, and discussing art. There ran into the river, a little way off, a narrow canal bordered by poplars, and along the banks of this after their day's work they often wandered. They spent all day painting. Like most of their generation they were obsessed by the fear of the picturesque, and they turned their backs on the obvious beauty of the town to seek subjects which were devoid of a prettiness they despised. Sisley and Monet had painted the canal with its poplars, and they felt a desire to try their hands at what was so typical of France; but they were frightened of its formal beauty, and set themselves deliberately to avoid it. Miss Chalice, who had a clever dexterity which impressed Lawson notwithstanding his contempt for feminine art, started a picture in which she tried to circumvent the commonplace by leaving out the tops of the trees; and Lawson had the brilliant idea of putting in his foreground a large blue advertisement of *chocolat Menier* in order to emphasize his abhorrence of the chocolate box.

Philip began now to paint in oils. He experienced a thrill of delight when first he used that grateful medium. He went out with Lawson in the morning with his little box and sat by him painting a panel; it gave him so much satisfaction that he did not realize he was doing no more than copy; he was so much under his friend's influence that he saw only with his eyes. Lawson painted very low in tone, and they both saw the emerald of the grass like dark velvet, while the brilliance of the sky turned in their hands to a brooding ultramarine. Through July they had one fine day after another; it was very hot; and the heat, searing Philip's heart, filled him with languor; he could not work; his mind was eager with a thousand thoughts. Often he spent the mornings by the side of the canal in the shade of the poplars, reading a few lines and then dreaming for half an hour. Sometimes he hired a rickety bicycle and rode along the dusty road that led to the forest, and then lay down in a clearing. His head was full of romantic fancies. The ladies of Watteau, gay and insouciant, seemed to wander with their cavaliers among the great trees, whispering to one another careless, charming things, and yet somehow oppressed by a nameless fear.

They were alone in the hotel but for a fat Frenchwoman of middle age, a Rabelaisian figure with a broad, obscene laugh. She spent the day by the river patiently fishing for fish she never caught, and Philip sometimes went down and talked to her. He found out that she had belonged to a profession whose most notorious member for our generation was Mrs. Warren, and having made a competence she now lived the quiet life of the *bourgeoise*. She told Philip lewd stories.

"You must go to Seville," she said—she spoke a little broken English. "The most beautiful women in the world."

She leered and nodded her head. Her triple chin, her large belly, shook with inward laughter.

It grew so hot that it was almost impossible to sleep at night. The heat seemed to linger under the trees as though it were a material thing. They did not wish to leave the starlit night, and the three of them would sit on the terrace of Ruth Chalice's room, silent, hour after hour, too tired to talk any more, but in voluptuous enjoyment of the stillness. They listened to the murmur of the river. The church clock struck one and two and sometimes three before they could drag themselves to bed. Suddenly Philip became aware that Ruth Chalice and Lawson were lovers. He divined it in the way the girl looked at the young painter, and in his air of possession; and as Philip sat with them he felt a kind of effluence surrounding them, as though the air were heavy with something strange. The revelation was a shock. He had looked upon Miss Chalice as a very good fellow and he liked to talk to her, but it had never seemed to him possible to enter into a closer relationship. One Sunday they had all gone with a tea-basket into the forest, and when they came to a glade which was suitably sylvan, Miss Chalice, because it was idyllic, insisted on taking off her shoes and stockings. It would have been very charming only her feet were rather large and she had on both a large corn on the third toe. Philip felt it made her proceeding a little ridiculous. But now he looked upon her quite differently; there was something softly feminine in her large eyes and her olive skin; he felt himself a fool not to have seen that she was attractive. He thought he detected in her a touch of contempt for him, because he had not had the sense to see that she was there, in his way, and in Lawson a suspicion of superiority. He was envious of Lawson, and he was jealous, not of the individual concerned, but of his love. He wished that he was standing in his shoes and feeling with his heart. He was troubled, and the fear seized him that love would pass him by. He wanted a passion to seize him, he wanted to be swept off his feet and borne powerless in a mighty rush he cared not whither. Miss Chalice and Lawson seemed to him now somehow different, and the constant companionship with them made him restless. He was dissatisfied with himself. Life was not giving him what he wanted, and he had an uneasy feeling that he was losing his time.

The stout Frenchwoman soon guessed what the relations were between the couple, and talked of the matter to Philip with the utmost frankness.

"And you," she said, with the tolerant smile of one who had fattened on the lust of her fellows, "have you got a *petite amie*?"

"No," said Philip, blushing.

"And why not? *C'est de votre âge.*"

He shrugged his shoulders. He had a volume of Verlaine in his hands, and he wandered off. He tried to read, but his passion was too strong. He thought of the stray amours to which he had been introduced by Flanagan, the sly visits to houses in a *cul-de-*

sac, with the drawing-room in Utrecht velvet, and the mercenary graces of painted women. He shuddered. He threw himself on the grass, stretching his limbs like a young animal freshly awaked from sleep; and the rippling water, the poplars gently tremulous in the faint breeze, the blue sky, were almost more than he could bear. He was in love with love. In his fancy he felt the kiss of warm lips on his, and around his neck the touch of soft hands. He imagined himself in the arms of Ruth Chalice, he thought of her dark eyes and the wonderful texture of her skin; he was mad to have let such a wonderful adventure slip through his fingers. And if Lawson had done it why should not he? But this was only when he did not see her, when he lay awake at night or dreamed idly by the side of the canal; when he saw her he felt suddenly quite different; he had no desire to take her in his arms, and he could not imagine himself kissing her. It was very curious. Away from her he thought her beautiful, remembering only her magnificent eyes and the creamy pallor of her face; but when he was with her he saw only that she was flat-chested and that her teeth were slightly decayed; he could not forget the corns on her toes. He could not understand himself. Would he always love only in absence and be prevented from enjoying anything when he had the chance by that deformity of vision which seemed to exaggerate the revolting?

He was not sorry when a change in the weather, announcing the definite end of the long summer, drove them all back to Paris.

Chapter 48

When Philip returned to Amitrano's he found that Fanny Price was no longer working there. She had given up the key of her locker. He asked Mrs. Otter whether she knew what had become of her; and Mrs. Otter, with a shrug of the shoulders, answered that she had probably gone back to England. Philip was relieved. He was profoundly bored by her ill-temper. Moreover, she insisted on advising him about his work, looked upon it as a slight when he did not follow her precepts, and would not understand that he felt himself no longer the duffer he had been at first. Soon he forgot all about her. He was working in oils now and he was full of enthusiasm. He hoped to have something done of sufficient importance to send to the following year's Salon. Lawson was painting a portrait of Miss Chalice. She was very paintable, and all the young men who had fallen victims to her charm had made portraits of her. A natural indolence, joined with a passion for picturesque attitude, made her an excellent sitter; and she had enough technical knowledge to offer useful criticisms. Since her passion for art was chiefly a passion to live the life of artists, she was quite content to neglect her own work. She liked the warmth of the studio, and the opportunity to smoke innumerable cigarettes; and she spoke in a low, pleasant voice of the love of art and the art of love. She made no clear distinction between the two.

Lawson was painting with infinite labour, working till he could hardly stand for days and then scraping out all he had done. He would have exhausted the patience of anyone but Ruth Chalice. At last he got into a hopeless muddle.

"The only thing is to take a new canvas and start fresh," he said. "I know exactly what I want now, and it won't take me long."

Philip was present at the time, and Miss Chalice said to him:

"Why don't you paint me too? You'll be able to learn a lot by watching Mr. Lawson."

It was one of Miss Chalice's delicacies that she always addressed her lovers by their surnames.

"I should like it awfully if Lawson wouldn't mind."

"I don't care a damn," said Lawson.

It was the first time that Philip set about a portrait, and he began with trepidation but also with pride. He sat by Lawson and painted as he saw him paint. He profited by the example and by the advice which both Lawson and Miss Chalice freely gave him. At last Lawson finished and invited Clutton in to criticize. Clutton had only just come back to Paris. From Provence he had drifted down to Spain, eager to see Velasquez at Madrid, and thence he had gone to Toledo. He stayed there three months, and he was returned with a name new to the young men: he had wonderful things to say of a painter called El Greco, who it appeared could only be studied in Toledo.

"Oh, yes, I know about him," said Lawson, "he's the old master whose distinction it is that he painted as badly as the moderns."

Clutton, more taciturn than ever, did not answer, but he looked at Lawson with a sardonic air.

"Are you going to show us the stuff you've brought back from Spain?" asked Philip.

"I didn't paint in Spain, I was too busy."

"What did you do then?"

"I thought things out. I believe I'm through with the impressionists; I've got an idea they'll seem very thin and superficial in a few years. I want to make a clean sweep of everything I've learnt and start fresh. When I came back I destroyed everything I'd painted. I've got nothing in my studio now but an easel, my paints, and some clean canvases."

"What are you going to do?"

"I don't know yet. I've only got an inkling of what I want."

He spoke slowly, in a curious manner, as though he were straining to hear something which was only just audible. There seemed to be a mysterious force in him which he himself did not understand, but which was struggling obscurely to find an outlet. His strength impressed you. Lawson dreaded the criticism he asked for and had discounted the blame he thought he might get by affecting a contempt for any opinion of Clutton's; but Philip knew there was nothing which would give him more pleasure than Clutton's praise. Clutton looked at the portrait for some time in silence, then glanced at Philip's picture, which was standing on an easel.

"What's that?" he asked.

"Oh, I had a shot at a portrait too."

"The sedulous ape," he murmured.

He turned away again to Lawson's canvas. Philip reddened but did not speak.

"Well, what d'you think of it?" asked Lawson at length.

"The modelling's jolly good," said Clutton. "And I think it's very well drawn."

"D'you think the values are all right?"

"Quite."

Lawson smiled with delight. He shook himself in his clothes like a wet dog.

"I say, I'm jolly glad you like it."

"I don't. I don't think it's of the smallest importance."

Lawson's face fell, and he stared at Clutton with astonishment: he had no notion what he meant, Clutton had no gift of expression in words, and he spoke as though it were an effort. What he had to say was confused, halting, and verbose; but Philip knew the words which served as the text of his rambling discourse. Clutton, who never read, had heard them first from Cronshaw; and though they had made small impression, they had remained in his memory; and lately, emerging on a sudden, had acquired the character of a revelation: a good painter had two chief objects to paint, namely, man and the intention of his soul. The impressionists had been occupied with other problems, they had painted man admirably, but they had troubled themselves as little as the English portrait painters of the eighteenth century with the intention of his soul.

"But when you try to get that you become literary," said

Lawson, interrupting. "Let me paint the man like Manet, and the intention of his soul can go to the devil."

"That would be all very well if you could beat Manet at his own game, but you can't get anywhere near him. You can't feed yourself on the day before yesterday; it's ground which has been swept dry. You must go back. It's when I saw the Grecos that I felt one could get something more out of portraits than we knew before."

"It's just going back to Ruskin," cried Lawson.

"No—you see, he went for morality: I don't care a damn for morality: teaching doesn't come in, ethics and all that, but passion and emotion. The greatest portrait painters have painted both, man and the intention of his soul; Rembrandt and El Greco; it's only the second-raters who've only painted man. A lily of the valley would be lovely even if it didn't smell, but it's more lovely because it has perfume. That picture" —he pointed to Lawson's portrait— "Well, the drawing's all right and so's the modelling all right, but just conventional; it ought to be drawn and modelled so that you know the girl's a lousy slut. Correctness is all very well: El Greco made his people eight feet high because he wanted to express something he couldn't get any other way."

"Damn El Greco," said Lawson, "what's the good of jawing about a man when we haven't a chance of seeing any of his work?"

Clutton shrugged his shoulders, smoked a cigarette in silence, and went away. Philip and Lawson looked at one another.

"There's something in what he says," said Philip.

Lawson stared ill-temperedly at his picture.

"How the devil is one to get the intention of the soul except by painting exactly what one sees?"

About this time Philip made a new friend. On Monday morning models assembled at the school in order that one might be chosen for the week, and one day a young man was taken who was plainly not a model by profession. Philip's attention was attracted by the manner in which he held himself: when he got on to the stand he stood firmly on both feet, square, with clenched hands, and with his head defiantly thrown forward; the attitude emphasized his fine figure; there was no fat on him, and his muscles stood out as though they were of iron. His head, close-cropped, was well-shaped, and he wore a short beard; he had large, dark eyes and heavy eyebrows. He held the pose hour after hour without appearance of fatigue. There was in his mien a mixture of shame and of determination. His air of passionate energy excited Philip's romantic imagination, and when, the sitting ended, he saw him in his clothes, it seemed to him that he wore them as though he were a king in rags. He was uncommunicative, but in a day or two Mrs. Otter told Philip that the model was a Spaniard and that he had never sat before.

"I suppose he was starving," said Philip.

"Have you noticed his clothes? They're quite neat and decent, aren't they?"

It chanced that Potter, one of the Americans who worked at Amitrano's, was going to Italy for a couple of months, and offered his studio to Philip. Philip was pleased. He was growing a little impatient of Lawson's peremptory advice and wanted to be by himself. At the end of the week he went up to the model and on the pretence that his drawing was not finished asked whether he would come and sit to him one day.

"I'm not a model," the Spaniard answered. "I have other things to do next week."

"Come and have luncheon with me now, and we'll talk about it," said Philip, and as the other hesitated, he added with a smile: "It won't hurt you to lunch with me."

With a shrug of the shoulders the model consented, and they went off to a *crémerie*. The Spaniard spoke broken French, fluent but difficult to follow, and Philip managed to get on well enough with him. He found out that he was a writer. He had come to Paris to write novels and kept himself meanwhile by all the expedients possible to a penniless man; he gave lessons, he did any translations he could get hold of, chiefly business documents, and at last had been driven to make money by his fine figure. Sitting was well paid, and what he had earned during the last week was enough to keep him for two more; he told Philip, amazed, that he could live easily on two francs a day; but it filled him with shame that he was obliged to show his body for money, and he looked upon sitting as a degradation which only hunger could excuse. Philip explained that he did not want him to sit for the figure, but only for the head; he wished to do a portrait of him which he might send to the next Salon.

"But why should you want to paint me?" asked the Spaniard.

Philip answered that the head interested him, he thought he could do a good portrait.

"I can't afford the time. I grudge every minute that I have to rob from my writing."

"But it would only be in the afternoon. I work at the school in the morning. After all, it's better to sit to me than to do translations of legal documents."

There were legends in the Latin Quarter of a time when students of different countries lived together intimately, but this was long since passed, and now the various nations were almost as much separated as in an Oriental city. At Julian's and at the Beaux-Arts a French student was looked upon with disfavour by his fellow countrymen when he consorted with foreigners, and it was difficult for an Englishman to know more than quite superficially any native inhabitants of the city in which he dwelt. Indeed, many of the students after living in Paris for five years knew no more French than served them in shops and lived as English a life as though they were working in South Kensington.

Philip, with his passion for the romantic, welcomed the opportunity to get in touch with a Spaniard; he used all his persuasiveness to overcome the man's reluctance.

"I'll tell you what I'll do," said the Spaniard at last. "I'll sit to you, but not for money, for my own pleasure."

Philip expostulated, but the other was firm, and at length they arranged that he should come on the following Monday at one o'clock. He gave Philip a card on which was printed his name: Miguel Ajuria.

Miguel sat regularly, and though he refused to accept payment he borrowed fifty francs from Philip every now and then: it was a little more expensive than if Philip had paid for the sittings in the usual way; but gave the Spaniard a satisfactory feeling that he was not earning his living in a degrading manner.

His nationality made Philip regard him as a representative of romance, and he asked him about Seville and Granada, Velasquez and Calderón. But Miguel had no patience with the grandeur of his country. For him, as for so many of his compatriots, France was the only country for a man of intelligence and Paris the centre of the world.

"Spain is dead," he cried. "It has no writers, it has no art, it has nothing."

Little by little, with the exuberant rhetoric of his race, he revealed his ambitions. He was writing a novel which he hoped would make his name. He was under the influence of Zola, and he had set his scene in Paris. He told Philip the story at length. To Philip it seemed crude and stupid; the naïve obscenity—*c'est la vie, mon cher, c'est la vie*, he cried—the naïve obscenity served only to emphasize the conventionality of the anecdote. He had written for two years, amid incredible hardships, denying himself all the pleasures of life which had attracted him to Paris, fighting with starvation for art's sake, determined that nothing should hinder his great achievement. The effort was heroic.

"But why don't you write about Spain?" cried Philip. "It would be so much more interesting. You know the life."

"But Paris is the only place worth writing about. Paris is life."

One day he brought part of the manuscript, and in his bad French, translating excitedly as he went along so that Philip could scarcely understand, he read passages. It was lamentable. Philip, puzzled, looked at the picture he was painting: the mind behind that broad brow was trivial; and the flashing, passionate eyes saw nothing in life but the obvious. Philip was not satisfied with his portrait, and at the end of a sitting he nearly always scraped out what he had done. It was all very well to aim at the intention of the soul: who could tell what that was when people seemed a mass of contradictions? He liked Miguel, and it distressed him to realize that his magnificent struggle was futile: he had everything to make a good writer but talent. Philip looked at his own work. How could you tell whether there was anything in it or whether you were wasting your time? It was clear that the will to achieve could not help you and confidence in yourself meant nothing. Philip thought of Fanny Price; she had a vehement belief in her talent; her strength of will was extraordinary.

"If I thought I wasn't going to be really good, I'd rather give up painting," said Philip. "I don't see any use in being a second-rate painter."

Then one morning when he was going out, the *concierge* called out to him that there was a letter. Nobody wrote to him but his Aunt Louisa and sometimes Hayward, and this was a handwriting he did not know. The letter was as follows:

> *Please come at once when you get this. I couldn't put up with it any more. Please come yourself. I can't bear the thought that anyone else should touch me. I want you to have everything.*
>
> *F. Price.*
>
> *I have not had anything to eat for three days.*

Philip felt on a sudden sick with fear. He hurried to the house in which she lived. He was astonished that she was in Paris at all. He had not seen her for months and imagined she had long since returned to England. When he arrived he asked the *concierge* whether she was in.

"Yes, I've not seen her go out for two days."

Philip ran upstairs and knocked at the door. There was no reply. He called her name. The door was locked, and on bending down he found the key was in the lock.

"Oh, my God, I hope she hasn't done something awful," he cried aloud.

He ran down and told the porter that she was certainly in the room. He had had a letter from her and feared a terrible accident. He suggested breaking open the door. The porter, who had been sullen and disinclined to listen, became alarmed; he could not take the responsibility of breaking into the room; they must go for the *commissaire de police*. They walked together to the *bureau*, and then they fetched a locksmith. Philip found that Miss Price had not paid the last quarter's rent: on New Year's Day she had not given the *concierge* the present which old-established custom led him to regard as a right. The four of them went upstairs, and they knocked again at the door. There was no reply. The locksmith set to work, and at last they entered the room. Philip gave a cry and instinctively covered his eyes with his hands. The wretched woman was hanging with a rope round her neck, which she had tied to a hook in the ceiling fixed by some previous tenant to hold up the curtains of the bed. She had moved her own little bed out of the way and had stood on a chair, which had been kicked away. It was lying on its side on the floor. They cut her down. The body was quite cold.

Chapter 49

The story which Philip made out in one way and another was terrible. One of the grievances of the women-students was that Fanny Price would never share their gay meals in restaurants, and the reason was obvious: she had been oppressed by dire poverty. He remembered the luncheon they had eaten together when first he came to Paris and the ghoulish appetite which had disgusted him: he realized now that she ate in that manner because she was ravenous. The *concierge* told him what her food had consisted of. A bottle of milk was left for her every day and she brought in her own loaf of bread; she ate half the loaf and drank half the milk at midday when she came back from the school, and consumed the rest in the evening. It was the same day after day. Philip thought with anguish of what she must have endured. She had never given anyone to understand that she was poorer than the rest, but it was clear that her money had been coming to an end, and at last she could not afford to come any more to the studio. The little room was almost bare of furniture, and there were no other clothes than the shabby brown dress she had always worn. Philip searched among her things for the address of some friend with whom he could communicate. He found a piece of paper on which his own name was written a score of times. It gave him a peculiar shock. He supposed it was true that she had loved him; he thought of the emaciated body, in the brown dress, hanging from the nail in the ceiling; and he shuddered. But if she had cared for him, why did she not let him help her? He would so gladly have done all he could. He felt remorseful because he had refused to see that she looked upon him with any particular feeling, and now these words in her letter were infinitely pathetic: *I can't bear the thought that anyone else should touch me.* She had died of starvation.

Philip found at length a letter signed: *your loving brother, Albert.* It was two or three weeks old, dated from some road in Surbiton, and refused a loan of five pounds. The writer had his wife and family to think of, he didn't feel justified in lending money, and his advice was that Fanny should come back to London and try to get a situation. Philip telegraphed to Albert Price, and in a little while an answer came:

> *Deeply distressed. Very awkward to leave my business.*
> *Is presence essential? Price.*

Philip wired a succinct affirmative, and next morning a stranger presented himself at the studio.

"My name's Price," he said, when Philip opened the door.

He was a commonish man in black with a band round his bowler hat; he had something of Fanny's clumsy look; he wore a stubbly moustache, and had a Cockney accent. Philip asked him to come in. He cast sidelong glances round the studio while Philip gave him details of the accident and told him what he had done.

"I needn't see her, need I?" asked Albert Price. "My nerves aren't very strong, and it takes very little to upset me."

He began to talk freely. He was a rubber-merchant, and he had a wife and three children. Fanny was a governess, and he couldn't make out why she hadn't stuck to that instead of coming to Paris.

"Me and Mrs. Price told her Paris was no place for a girl. And there's no money in art—never 'as been."

It was plain enough that he had not been on friendly terms with his sister, and he resented her suicide as a last injury that she had done him. He did not like the idea that she had been forced to it by poverty; that seemed to reflect on the family. The idea struck him that possibly there was a more respectable reason for her act.

"I suppose she 'adn't any trouble with a man, 'ad she? You know what I mean, Paris and all that. She might 'ave done it so as not to disgrace herself."

Philip felt himself reddening and cursed his weakness. Price's keen little eyes seemed to suspect him of an intrigue.

"I believe your sister to have been perfectly virtuous," he answered acidly. "She killed herself because she was starving."

"Well, it's very 'ard on her family, Mr. Carey. She only 'ad to write to me. I wouldn't have let my sister want."

Philip had found the brother's address only by reading the letter in which he refused a loan; but he shrugged his shoulders: there was no use in recrimination. He hated the little man and wanted to have done with him as soon as possible. Albert Price also wished to get through the necessary business quickly so that he could get back to London. They went to the tiny room in which poor Fanny had lived. Albert Price looked at the pictures and the furniture.

"I don't pretend to know much about art," he said. "I suppose these pictures would fetch something, would they?"

"Nothing," said Philip.

"The furniture's not worth ten shillings."

Albert Price knew no French and Philip had to do everything. It seemed that it was an interminable process to get the poor body safely hidden away under ground: papers had to be obtained in one place and signed in another; officials had to be seen. For three days Philip was occupied from morning till night. At last he and Albert Price followed the hearse to the cemetery at Montparnasse.

"I want to do the thing decent," said Albert Price, "but there's no use wasting money."

The short ceremony was infinitely dreadful in the cold grey morning. Half a dozen people who had worked with Fanny Price at the studio came to the funeral, Mrs. Otter because she was *massière* and thought it her duty, Ruth Chalice because she had a kind heart, Lawson, Clutton, and Flanagan. They had all disliked her during her life. Philip, looking across the cemetery crowded on all sides with monuments, some poor and simple, others vulgar, pretentious, and ugly, shuddered. It was horribly sordid. When they came out Albert Price asked Philip to lunch with him. Philip loathed him now and he was tired; he had not been sleeping well, for he dreamed constantly of Fanny Price in the torn brown dress, hanging from the nail in the ceiling; but he could not think of an excuse.

"You take me somewhere where we can get a regular slap-up lunch. All this is the very worst thing for my nerves."

"Lavenue's is about the best place round here," answered Philip.

Albert Price settled himself on a velvet seat with a sigh of relief. He ordered a substantial luncheon and a bottle of wine.

"Well, I'm glad that's over," he said.

He threw out a few artful questions, and Philip discovered that he was eager to hear about the painter's life in Paris. He represented it to himself as deplorable, but he was anxious for details of the orgies which his fancy suggested to him. With sly winks and discreet sniggering he conveyed that he knew very well that there was a great deal more than Philip confessed. He was a man of the world, and he knew a thing or two. He asked Philip whether he had ever been to any of those places in Montmartre which are celebrated from Temple Bar to the Royal Exchange. He would like to say he had been to the Moulin Rouge. The luncheon was very good and the wine excellent. Albert Price expanded as the processes of digestion went satisfactorily forwards.

"Let's 'ave a little brandy," he said when the coffee was brought, "and blow the expense."

He rubbed his hands.

"You know, I've got 'alf a mind to stay over tonight and go back tomorrow. What d'you say to spending the evening together?"

"If you mean you want me to take you round Montmartre tonight, I'll see you damned," said Philip.

"I suppose it wouldn't be quite the thing."

The answer was made so seriously that Philip was tickled.

"Besides it would be rotten for your nerves," he said gravely.

Albert Price concluded that he had better go back to London by the four o'clock train, and presently he took leave of Philip.

"Well, good-bye, old man," he said. "I tell you what, I'll try and come over to Paris again one of these days and I'll look you up. And then we won't 'alf go on the razzle."

Philip was too restless to work that afternoon, so he jumped on a bus and crossed the river to see whether there were any pictures on view at Durand-Ruel's. After that he strolled along the boulevard. It was cold and wind-swept. People hurried by wrapped up in their coats, shrunk together in an effort to keep out of the cold, and their faces were pinched and careworn. It was icy underground in the cemetery at Montparnasse among all those white tombstones. Philip felt lonely in the world and strangely homesick. He wanted company. At that hour Cronshaw would be working, and Clutton never welcomed visitors; Lawson was painting another portrait of Ruth Chalice and would not care to be disturbed. He made up his mind to go and see Flanagan. He found him painting, but delighted to throw up his work and talk. The studio was comfortable, for the American had more money than most of them, and warm; Flanagan set about making tea. Philip looked at the two heads that he was sending to the Salon.

"It's awful cheek my sending anything," said Flanagan, "but I don't care, I'm going to send. D'you think they're rotten?"

"Not so rotten as I should have expected," said Philip.

They showed in fact an astounding cleverness. The difficulties had been avoided with skill, and there was a dash about the way in which the paint was put on which was surprising and even attractive. Flanagan, without knowledge or technique, painted with the loose brush of a man who has spent a lifetime in the practice of the art.

"If one were forbidden to look at any picture for more than thirty seconds you'd be a great master, Flanagan," smiled Philip.

These young people were not in the habit of spoiling one another with excessive flattery.

"We haven't got time in America to spend more than thirty seconds in looking at any picture," laughed the other.

Flanagan, though he was the most scatter-brained person in the world, had a tenderness of heart which was unexpected and charming. Whenever anyone was ill he installed himself as sick nurse. His gaiety was better than any medicine. Like many of his countrymen he had not the English dread of sentimentality which keeps so tight a hold on emotion; and, finding nothing absurd in the show of feeling, could offer an exuberant sympathy which was often grateful to his friends in distress. He saw that Philip was depressed by what he had gone through and with unaffected kindliness set himself boisterously to cheer him up. He exaggerated the Americanisms which he knew always made the Englishmen laugh and poured out a breathless stream of conversation, whimsical, high-spirited, and jolly. In due course they went out to dinner and afterwards to the Gaîté Montparnasse, which was Flanagan's favourite place of amusement. By the end of the evening he was in his most extravagant humour. He had drunk a good deal, but any inebriety from which he suffered was due much more to his own vivacity than to alcohol. He proposed that they should go to the Bal Bullier, and Philip, feeling too tired to go to bed, willingly enough consented. They sat down at a table on the platform at the side, raised a little from the level of the floor so that they could watch the dancing, and drank a *bock*. Presently Flanagan saw a friend and with a wild shout leaped over the barrier on to the space where they were dancing. Philip watched the people. Bullier was not the resort of fashion. It was Thursday night and the place was crowded. There were a number of students of the various faculties, but most of the men were clerks or assistants in shops; they wore their everyday clothes, ready-made tweeds or queer tailcoats, and their hats, for they had brought them in with them, and when they danced there was no place to put them but their heads. Some of the women looked like servant-girls, and some were painted hussies, but for the most part they were shop-girls. They were poorly dressed in cheap imitation of the fashions on the other side of the river. The hussies were got up to resemble the music hall artiste or the dancer who enjoyed notoriety at the moment; their eyes were heavy with black and their cheeks impudently scarlet. The hall was lit by great white lights, low down, which emphasized the shadows on the faces; all the lines seemed to harden under it, and the colours were most crude. It was a sordid scene. Philip leaned over the rail, staring down, and he ceased to hear the music. They danced furiously. They danced round the room, slowly, talking very little, with all their attention given to the dance. The room was hot, and their faces shone with sweat. It seemed to Philip that they had thrown off the guard which people wear on their expression, the homage to convention, and he saw them now as they really were. In that moment of abandon they were strangely animal: some were foxy and some were wolflike; and others had the long, foolish face of sheep. Their skins were sallow from the unhealthy life they led and the poor food they ate. Their features were blunted by mean interests, and their little eyes were shifty and cunning. There was nothing of nobility in their bearing, and you felt that for all of them life was a long succession of petty concerns and sordid thoughts. The air was heavy with the musty smell of humanity. But they danced furiously as though impelled by some strange power within them, and it seemed to Philip that they were driven forward by a rage for enjoyment. They were seeking desperately to escape from a world of horror. The desire for pleasure which Cronshaw said was the only motive of human action urged them blindly on, and the very vehemence of the desire seemed to rob it of all pleasure. They were hurried on by a great wind, helplessly, they knew not why and they knew not whither. Fate seemed to tower above them, and they danced as though everlasting darkness were beneath their feet. Their silence was vaguely alarming. It was as if life terrified them and robbed them of power of speech so that the shriek which was in their hearts died at their throats. Their eyes were haggard and grim; and notwithstanding the beastly lust that disfigured them, and the meanness of their faces, and the cruelty, notwithstanding the stupidity which was worst of all, the anguish of those fixed eyes made all that crowd terrible and pathetic. Philip loathed them, and yet his heart ached with the infinite pity which filled him.

He took his coat from the cloak-room and went out into the bitter coldness of the night.

Chapter 50

Philip could not get the unhappy event out of his head. What troubled him most was the uselessness of Fanny's effort. No one could have worked harder than she, nor with more sincerity; she believed in herself with all her heart; but it was plain that self-confidence meant very little, all his friends had it, Miguel Ajuria among the rest; and Philip was shocked by the contrast between the Spaniard's heroic endeavour and the triviality of the thing he attempted. The unhappiness of Philip's life at school had called up in him the power of self-analysis; and this vice, as subtle as drug-taking, had taken possession of him so that he had now a peculiar keenness in the dissection of his feelings. He could not help seeing that art affected him differently from others. A fine picture gave Lawson an immediate thrill. His appreciation was instinctive. Even Flanagan felt certain things which Philip was obliged to think out. His own appreciation was intellectual. He could not help thinking that if he had in him the artistic temperament (he hated the phrase, but could discover no other) he would feel beauty in the emotional, unreasoning way in which they did. He began to wonder whether he had anything more than a superficial cleverness of the hand which enabled him to copy objects with accuracy. That was nothing. He had learned to despise technical dexterity. The important thing was to feel in terms of paint. Lawson painted in a certain way because it was his nature to, and through the imitativeness of a student sensitive to every influence, there pierced individuality. Philip looked at his own portrait of Ruth Chalice, and now that three months had passed he realized that it was no more than a servile copy of Lawson. He felt himself barren. He painted with the brain, and he could not help knowing that the only painting worth anything was done with the heart.

He had very little money, barely sixteen hundred pounds, and it would be necessary for him to practise the severest economy. He could not count on earning anything for ten years. The history of painting was full of artists who had earned nothing at all. He must resign himself to penury; and it was worth while if he produced work which was immortal; but he had a terrible fear that he would never be more than second-rate. Was it worth while for that to give up one's youth, and the gaiety of life, and the manifold chances of being? He knew the existence of foreign painters in Paris enough to see that the lives they led were narrowly provincial. He knew some who had dragged along for twenty years in the pursuit of a fame which always escaped them till they sunk into sordidness and alcoholism. Fanny's suicide had aroused memories, and Philip heard ghastly stories of the way in which one person or another had escaped from despair. He remembered the scornful advice which the master had given poor

Fanny: it would have been well for her if she had taken it and given up an attempt which was hopeless.

Philip finished his portrait of Miguel Ajuria and made up his mind to send it to the Salon. Flanagan was sending two pictures, and he thought he could paint as well as Flanagan. He had worked so hard on the portrait that he could not help feeling it must have merit. It was true that when he looked at it he felt that there was something wrong, though he could not tell what; but when he was away from it his spirits went up and he was not dissatisfied. He sent it to the Salon and it was refused. He did not mind much, since he had done all he could to persuade himself that there was little chance that it would be taken, till Flanagan a few days later rushed in to tell Lawson and Philip that one of his pictures was accepted. With a blank face Philip offered his congratulations, and Flanagan was so busy congratulating himself that he did not catch the note of irony which Philip could not prevent from coming into his voice. Lawson, quicker-witted, observed it and looked at Philip curiously. His own picture was all right, he knew that a day or two before, and he was vaguely resentful of Philip's attitude. But he was surprised at the sudden question which Philip put to him as soon as the American was gone.

"If you were in my place would you chuck the whole thing?"

"What *do* you mean?"

"I wonder if it's worth while being a second-rate painter. You see, in other things, if you're a doctor or if you're in business, it doesn't matter so much if you're mediocre. You make a living and you get along. But what is the good of turning out second-rate pictures?"

Lawson was fond of Philip and, as soon as he thought he was seriously distressed by the refusal of his picture, he set himself to console him. It was notorious that the Salon had refused pictures which were afterwards famous; it was the first time Philip had sent, and he must expect a rebuff; Flanagan's success was explicable, his picture was showy and superficial: it was just the sort of thing a languid jury would see merit in. Philip grew impatient; it was humiliating that Lawson should think him capable of being seriously disturbed by so trivial a calamity and would not realize that his dejection was due to a deep-seated distrust of his powers.

Of late Clutton had withdrawn himself somewhat from the group who took their meals at Gravier's, and lived very much by himself. Flanagan said he was in love with a girl, but Clutton's austere countenance did not suggest passion; and Philip thought it more probable that he separated himself from his friends so that he might grow clear with the new ideas which were in him. But that evening, when the others had left the restaurant to go to a play and Philip was sitting alone, Clutton came in and ordered dinner. They began to talk, and finding Clutton more loquacious and less sardonic than usual, Philip determined to take advantage of his good humour.

"I say, I wish you'd come and look at my picture," he said. "I'd like to know what you think of it."

"No, I won't do that."

"Why not?" asked Philip, reddening.

The request was one which they all made of one another, and no one ever thought of refusing. Clutton shrugged his shoulders.

"People ask you for criticism, but they only want praise. Besides, what's the good of criticism? What does it matter if your picture is good or bad?"

"It matters to me."

"No. The only reason that one paints is that one can't help it. It's a function like any of the other functions of the body, only comparatively few people have got it. One paints for oneself: otherwise one would commit suicide. Just think of it, you spend God knows how long trying to get something on to canvas, putting the sweat of your soul into it, and what is the result? Ten to one it will be refused at the Salon; if it's accepted, people glance at it for ten seconds as they pass; if you're lucky some ignorant fool will buy it and put it on his walls and look at it as little as he looks at his dining-room table. Criticism has nothing to do with the artist. It judges objectively, but the objective doesn't concern the artist."

Clutton put his hands over his eyes so that he might concentrate his mind on what he wanted to say.

"The artist gets a peculiar sensation from something he sees, and is impelled to express it and, he doesn't know why, he can only express his feeling by lines and colours. It's like a musician; he'll read a line or two, and a certain combination of notes presents itself to him: he doesn't know why such and such words call forth in him such and such notes; they just do. And I'll tell you another reason why criticism is meaningless: a great painter forces the world to see nature as he sees it; but in the next generation another painter sees the world in another way, and then the public judges him not by himself but by his predecessor. So the Barbizon people taught our fathers to look at trees in a certain manner, and when Monet came along and painted differently, people said: But trees aren't like that. It never struck them that trees are exactly how a painter chooses to see them. We paint from within outwards—if we force our vision on the world it calls us great painters; if we don't it ignores us; but *we* are the same. We don't attach any meaning to greatness or to smallness. What happens to our work afterwards is unimportant; we have got all we could out of it while we were doing it."

There was a pause while Clutton with voracious appetite devoured the food that was set before him. Philip, smoking a cheap cigar, observed him closely. The ruggedness of the head, which looked as though it were carved from a stone refractory to the sculptor's chisel, the rough mane of dark hair, the great nose, and the massive bones of the jaw, suggested a man of strength; and yet Philip wondered whether perhaps the mask concealed a strange weakness. Clutton's refusal to show his work might be sheer vanity: he could not bear the thought of anyone's criticism, and he would not expose himself to the chance of a refusal from the Salon; he wanted to be received as a master and would not risk comparisons with other work which might force him to diminish his own opinion of himself. During the eighteen months Philip had known him Clutton had grown more harsh and bitter; though he would not come out into the open and compete with his fellows, he was indignant with the facile success of those who did. He had no patience with Lawson, and the pair were no longer on the intimate terms upon which they had been when Philip first knew them.

"Lawson's all right," he said contemptuously, "he'll go back to England, become a fashionable portrait painter, earn ten thousand a year and be an A. R. A. before he's forty. Portraits done by hand for the nobility and gentry!"

Philip, too, looked into the future, and he saw Clutton in twenty years, bitter, lonely, savage, and unknown; still in Paris, for the life there had got into his bones, ruling a small *cénacle* with a savage tongue, at war with himself and the world, producing little in his increasing passion for a perfection he could not reach; and perhaps sinking at last into drunkenness. Of late Philip had been captivated by an idea that since one had only one life it was important to make a success of it, but he did not count success by the acquiring of money or the achieving of fame; he did not quite know yet what he meant by it, perhaps variety of experience and the making the most of his abilities. It was plain anyway that the life which Clutton seemed destined to was failure. Its only justification would be the painting of imperishable masterpieces. He recollected Cronshaw's whimsical metaphor of the Persian carpet; he had thought of it often; but Cronshaw with his faun-like humour had refused to make his meaning clear: he repeated that it had none unless one discovered it for oneself. It was this desire to make a success of life which was at the bottom of Philip's uncertainty about continuing his artistic career. But Clutton began to talk again.

"D'you remember my telling you about that chap I met in Brittany? I saw him the other day here. He's just off to Tahiti. He was broke to the world. He was a *brasseur d'affaires*, a stockbroker

I suppose you call it in English; and he had a wife and family, and he was earning a large income. He chucked it all to become a painter. He just went off and settled down in Brittany and began to paint. He hadn't got any money and did the next best thing to starving."

"And what about his wife and family?" asked Philip.

"Oh, he dropped them. He left them to starve on their own account."

"It sounds a pretty low-down thing to do."

"Oh, my dear fellow, if you want to be a gentleman you must give up being an artist. They've got nothing to do with one another. You hear of men painting pot-boilers to keep an aged mother—well, it shows they're excellent sons, but it's no excuse for bad work. They're only tradesmen. An artist would let his mother go to the workhouse. There's a writer I know over here who told me that his wife died in childbirth. He was in love with her and he was mad with grief, but as he sat at the bedside watching her die he found himself making mental notes of how she looked and what she said and the things he was feeling. Gentlemanly, wasn't it?"

"But is your friend a good painter?" asked Philip.

"No, not yet, he paints just like Pissarro. He hasn't found himself, but he's got a sense of colour and a sense of decoration. But that isn't the question. It's the feeling, and that he's got. He's behaved like a perfect cad to his wife and children, he's always behaving like a perfect cad; the way he treats the people who've helped him—and sometimes he's been saved from starvation merely by the kindness of his friends—is simply beastly. He just happens to be a great artist."

Philip pondered over the man who was willing to sacrifice everything, comfort, home, money, love, honour, duty, for the sake of getting on to canvas with paint the emotion which the world gave him. It was magnificent, and yet his courage failed him.

Thinking of Cronshaw recalled to him the fact that he had not seen him for a week, and so, when Clutton left him, he wandered along to the café in which he was certain to find the writer. During the first few months of his stay in Paris Philip had accepted as gospel all that Cronshaw said, but Philip had a practical outlook and he grew impatient with the theories which resulted in no action. Cronshaw's slim bundle of poetry did not seem a substantial result for a life which was sordid. Philip could not wrench out of his nature the instincts of the middle-class from which he came; and the penury, the hack work which Cronshaw did to keep body and soul together, the monotony of existence between the slovenly attic and the café table, jarred with his respectability. Cronshaw was astute enough to know that the young man disapproved of him, and he attacked his philistinism with an irony which was sometimes playful but often very keen.

"You're a tradesman," he told Philip, "you want to invest life in consols so that it shall bring you in a safe three per cent. I'm a spendthrift, I run through my capital. I shall spend my last penny with my last heartbeat."

The metaphor irritated Philip, because it assumed for the speaker a romantic attitude and cast a slur upon the position which Philip instinctively felt had more to say for it than he could think of at the moment.

But this evening Philip, undecided, wanted to talk about himself. Fortunately it was late already and Cronshaw's pile of saucers on the table, each indicating a drink, suggested that he was prepared to take an independent view of things in general.

"I wonder if you'd give me some advice," said Philip suddenly.

"You won't take it, will you?"

Philip shrugged his shoulders impatiently.

"I don't believe I shall ever do much good as a painter. I don't see any use in being second-rate. I'm thinking of chucking it."

"Why shouldn't you?"

Philip hesitated for an instant.

"I suppose I like the life."

A change came over Cronshaw's placid, round face. The corners of the mouth were suddenly depressed, the eyes sunk dully in their orbits; he seemed to become strangely bowed and old.

"This?" he cried, looking round the café in which they sat. His voice really trembled a little.

"If you can get out of it, do while there's time."

Philip stared at him with astonishment, but the sight of emotion always made him feel shy, and he dropped his eyes. He knew that he was looking upon the tragedy of failure. There was silence. Philip thought that Cronshaw was looking upon his own life; and perhaps he considered his youth with its bright hopes and the disappointments which wore out the radiancy; the wretched monotony of pleasure, and the black future. Philip's eyes rested on the little pile of saucers, and he knew that Cronshaw's were on them too.

Chapter 51

Two months passed.

It seemed to Philip, brooding over these matters, that in the true painters, writers, musicians, there was a power which drove them to such complete absorption in their work as to make it inevitable for them to subordinate life to art. Succumbing to an influence they never realized, they were merely dupes of the instinct that possessed them, and life slipped through their fingers unlived. But he had a feeling that life was to be lived rather than portrayed, and he wanted to search out the various experiences of it and wring from each moment all the emotion that it offered. He made up his mind at length to take a certain step and abide by the result, and, having made up his mind, he determined to take the step at once. Luckily enough the next morning was one of Foinet's days, and he resolved to ask him point-blank whether it was worth his while to go on with the study of art. He had never forgotten the master's brutal advice to Fanny Price. It had been sound. Philip could never get Fanny entirely out of his head. The studio seemed strange without her, and now and then the gesture of one of the women working there or the tone of a voice would give him a sudden start, reminding him of her; her presence was more noticable now she was dead than it had ever been during her life; and he often dreamed of her at night, waking with a cry of terror. It was horrible to think of all the suffering she must have endured.

Philip knew that on the days Foinet came to the studio he lunched at a little restaurant in the Rue d'Odessa, and he hurried his own meal so that he could go and wait outside till the painter came out. Philip walked up and down the crowded street and at last saw Monsieur Foinet walking, with bent head, towards him; Philip was very nervous, but he forced himself to go up to him.

"*Pardon, monsieur*, I should like to speak to you for one moment."

Foinet gave him a rapid glance, recognized him, but did not smile a greeting.

"Speak," he said.

"I've been working here nearly two years now under you. I wanted to ask you to tell me frankly if you think it worth while for me to continue."

Philip's voice was trembling a little. Foinet walked on without looking up. Philip, watching his face, saw no trace of expression upon it.

"I don't understand."

"I'm very poor. If I have no talent I would sooner do something else."

"Don't you know if you have talent?"

"All my friends know they have talent, but I am aware some

of them are mistaken."

Foinet's bitter mouth outlined the shadow of a smile, and he asked:

"Do you live near here?"

Philip told him where his studio was. Foinet turned round.

"Let us go there? You shall show me your work."

"Now?" cried Philip.

"Why not?"

Philip had nothing to say. He walked silently by the master's side. He felt horribly sick. It had never struck him that Foinet would wish to see his things there and then; he meant, so that he might have time to prepare himself, to ask him if he would mind coming at some future date or whether he might bring them to Foinet's studio. He was trembling with anxiety. In his heart he hoped that Foinet would look at his picture, and that rare smile would come into his face, and he would shake Philip's hand and say: "*Pas mal*. Go on, my lad. You have talent, real talent." Philip's heart swelled at the thought. It was such a relief, such a joy! Now he could go on with courage; and what did hardship matter, privation, and disappointment, if he arrived at last? He had worked very hard, it would be too cruel if all that industry were futile. And then with a start he remembered that he had heard Fanny Price say just that. They arrived at the house, and Philip was seized with fear. If he had dared he would have asked Foinet to go away. He did not want to know the truth. They went in and the *concierge* handed him a letter as they passed. He glanced at the envelope and recognized his uncle's handwriting. Foinet followed him up the stairs. Philip could think of nothing to say; Foinet was mute, and the silence got on his nerves. The professor sat down; and Philip without a word placed before him the picture which the Salon had rejected; Foinet nodded but did not speak; then Philip showed him the two portraits he had made of Ruth Chalice, two or three landscapes which he had painted at Moret, and a number of sketches.

"That's all," he said presently, with a nervous laugh.

Monsieur Foinet rolled himself a cigarette and lit it.

"You have very little private means?" he asked at last.

"Very little," answered Philip, with a sudden feeling of cold at his heart. "Not enough to live on."

"There is nothing so degrading as the constant anxiety about one's means of livelihood. I have nothing but contempt for the people who despise money. They are hypocrites or fools. Money is like a sixth sense without which you cannot make a complete use of the other five. Without an adequate income half the possibilities of life are shut off. The only thing to be careful about is that you do not pay more than a shilling for the shilling you earn. You will hear people say that poverty is the best spur to the artist. They have never felt the iron of it in their flesh. They do not know how mean it makes you. It exposes you to endless humiliation, it cuts your wings, it eats into your soul like a cancer. It is not wealth one asks for, but just enough to preserve one's dignity, to work unhampered, to be generous, frank, and independent. I pity with all my heart the artist, whether he writes or paints, who is entirely dependent for subsistence upon his art."

Philip quietly put away the various things which he had shown.

"I'm afraid that sounds as if you didn't think I had much chance."

Monsieur Foinet slightly shrugged his shoulders.

"You have a certain manual dexterity. With hard work and perseverance there is no reason why you should not become a careful, not incompetent painter. You would find hundreds who painted worse than you, hundreds who painted as well. I see no talent in anything you have shown me. I see industry and intelligence. You will never be anything but mediocre."

Philip obliged himself to answer quite steadily.

"I'm very grateful to you for having taken so much trouble. I can't thank you enough."

Monsieur Foinet got up and made as if to go, but he changed his mind and, stopping, put his hand on Philip's shoulder.

"But if you were to ask my advice, I should say: take your courage in both hands and try your luck at something else. It sounds very hard, but let me tell you this: I would give all I have in the world if someone had given me that advice when I was your age and I had taken it."

Philip looked up at him with surprise. The master forced his lips into a smile, but his eyes remained grave and sad.

"It is cruel to discover one's mediocrity only when it is too late. It does not improve the temper."

He gave a little laugh as he said the last words and quickly walked out of the room.

Philip mechanically took up the letter from his uncle. The sight of his handwriting made him anxious, for it was his aunt who always wrote to him. She had been ill for the last three months, and he had offered to go over to England and see her; but she, fearing it would interfere with his work, had refused. She did not want him to put himself to inconvenience; she said she would wait till August and then she hoped he would come and stay at the vicarage for two or three weeks. If by any chance she grew worse she would let him know, since she did not wish to die without seeing him again. If his uncle wrote to him it must be because she was too ill to hold a pen. Philip opened the letter. It ran as follows:

My dear Philip,

I regret to inform you that your dear Aunt departed this life early this morning. She died very suddenly, but quite peacefully. The change for the worse was so rapid that we had no time to send for you. She was fully prepared for the end and entered into rest with the complete assurance of a blessed resurrection and with resignation to the divine will of our blessed Lord Jesus Christ. Your Aunt would have liked you to be present at the funeral so I trust you will come as soon as you can. There is naturally a great deal of work thrown upon my shoulders and I am very much upset. I trust that you will be able to do everything for me.

Your affectionate uncle,
William Carey.

Chapter 52

Next day Philip arrived at Blackstable. Since the death of his mother he had never lost anyone closely connected with him; his aunt's death shocked him and filled him also with a curious fear; he felt for the first time his own mortality. He could not realize what life would be for his uncle without the constant companionship of the woman who had loved and tended him for forty years. He expected to find him broken down with hopeless grief. He dreaded the first meeting; he knew that he could say nothing which would be of use. He rehearsed to himself a number of apposite speeches.

He entered the vicarage by the side door and went into the dining-room. Uncle William was reading the paper.

"Your train was late," he said, looking up.

Philip was prepared to give way to his emotion, but the matter-of-fact reception startled him. His uncle, subdued but calm, handed him the paper.

"There's a very nice little paragraph about her in *The Blackstable Times*," he said.

Philip read it mechanically.

"Would you like to come up and see her?"

Philip nodded and together they walked upstairs. Aunt Louisa was lying in the middle of the large bed, with flowers all round her.

"Would you like to say a short prayer?" said the Vicar.

He sank on his knees, and because it was expected of him Philip followed his example. He looked at the little shrivelled face. He was only conscious of one emotion: what a wasted life! In a minute Mr. Carey gave a cough, and stood up. He pointed to a wreath at the foot of the bed.

"That's from the Squire," he said. He spoke in a low voice as though he were in church, but one felt that, as a clergyman, he found himself quite at home. "I expect tea is ready."

They went down again to the dining-room. The drawn blinds gave a lugubrious aspect. The Vicar sat at the end of the table at which his wife had always sat and poured out the tea with ceremony. Philip could not help feeling that neither of them should have been able to eat anything, but when he saw that his uncle's appetite was unimpaired he fell to with his usual heartiness. They did not speak for a while. Philip set himself to eat an excellent cake with the air of grief which he felt was decent.

"Things have changed a great deal since I was a curate," said the Vicar presently. "In my young days the mourners used always to be given a pair of black gloves and a piece of black silk for their hats. Poor Louisa used to make the silk into dresses. She always said that twelve funerals gave her a new dress."

Then he told Philip who had sent wreaths; there were

twenty-four of them already; when Mrs. Rawlingson, wife of the Vicar at Ferne, had died she had had thirty-two; but probably a good many more would come the next day; the funeral would start at eleven o'clock from the vicarage, and they should beat Mrs. Rawlingson easily. Louisa never liked Mrs. Rawlingson.

"I shall take the funeral myself. I promised Louisa I would never let anyone else bury her."

Philip looked at his uncle with disapproval when he took a second piece of cake. Under the circumstances he could not help thinking it greedy.

"Mary Ann certainly makes capital cakes. I'm afraid no one else will make such good ones."

"She's not going?" cried Philip, with astonishment.

Mary Ann had been at the vicarage ever since he could remember. She never forgot his birthday, but made a point always of sending him a trifle, absurd but touching. He had a real affection for her.

"Yes," answered Mr. Carey. "I didn't think it would do to have a single woman in the house."

"But, good heavens, she must be over forty."

"Yes, I think she is. But she's been rather troublesome lately, she's been inclined to take too much on herself, and I thought this was a very good opportunity to give her notice."

"It's certainly one which isn't likely to recur," said Philip.

He took out a cigarette, but his uncle prevented him from lighting it.

"Not till after the funeral, Philip," he said gently.

"All right," said Philip.

"It wouldn't be respectful to smoke in the house so long as your poor Aunt Louisa is upstairs."

Josiah Graves, churchwarden and manager of the bank, came back to dinner at the vicarage after the funeral. The blinds had been drawn up, and Philip, against his will, felt a curious sensation of relief. The body in the house had made him uncomfortable: in life the poor woman had been all that was kind and gentle; and yet, when she lay upstairs in her bedroom, cold and stark, it seemed as though she cast upon the survivors a baleful influence. The thought horrified Philip.

He found himself alone for a minute or two in the dining-room with the churchwarden.

"I hope you'll be able to stay with your uncle a while," he said. "I don't think he ought to be left alone just yet."

"I haven't made any plans," answered Philip. "If he wants me I shall be very pleased to stay."

By way of cheering the bereaved husband the churchwarden during dinner talked of a recent fire at Blackstable which had partly destroyed the Wesleyan chapel.

"I hear they weren't insured," he said, with a little smile.

"That won't make any difference," said the Vicar. "They'll get as much money as they want to rebuild. Chapel people are always ready to give money."

"I see that Holden sent a wreath."

Holden was the dissenting minister, and though for Christ's sake, who died for both of them, Mr. Carey nodded to him in the street, he did not speak to him.

"I think it was very pushing," he remarked. "There were forty-one wreaths. Yours was beautiful. Philip and I admired it very much."

"Don't mention it," said the banker.

He had noticed with satisfaction that it was larger than anyone else's. It had looked very well. They began to discuss the people who attended the funeral. Shops had been closed for it, and the churchwarden took out of his pocket the notice which had been printed: *Owing to the funeral of Mrs. Carey this establishment will not be opened till one o'clock.*

"It was my idea," he said.

"I think it was very nice of them to close," said the Vicar. "Poor Louisa would have appreciated that."

Philip ate his dinner. Mary Ann had treated the day as Sunday, and they had roast chicken and a gooseberry tart.

"I suppose you haven't thought about a tombstone yet?" said the churchwarden.

"Yes, I have. I thought of a plain stone cross. Louisa was always against ostentation."

"I don't think one can do much better than a cross. If you're thinking of a text, what do you say to: *With Christ, which is far better?*"

The Vicar pursed his lips. It was just like Bismarck to try and settle everything himself. He did not like that text; it seemed to cast an aspersion on himself.

"I don't think I should put that. I much prefer: *The Lord has given and the Lord has taken away.*"

"Oh, do you? That always seems to me a little indifferent."

The Vicar answered with some acidity, and Mr. Graves

replied in a tone which the widower thought too authoritative for the occasion. Things were going rather far if he could not choose his own text for his own wife's tombstone. There was a pause, and then the conversation drifted to parish matters. Philip went into the garden to smoke his pipe. He sat on a bench, and suddenly began to laugh hysterically.

A few days later his uncle expressed the hope that he would spend the next few weeks at Blackstable.

"Yes, that will suit me very well," said Philip.

"I suppose it'll do if you go back to Paris in September."

Philip did not reply. He had thought much of what Foinet said to him, but he was still so undecided that he did not wish to speak of the future. There would be something fine in giving up art because he was convinced that he could not excel; but unfortunately it would seem so only to himself: to others it would be an admission of defeat, and he did not want to confess that he was beaten. He was an obstinate fellow, and the suspicion that his talent did not lie in one direction made him inclined to force circumstances and aim notwithstanding precisely in that direction. He could not bear that his friends should laugh at him. This might have prevented him from ever taking the definite step of abandoning the study of painting, but the different environment made him on a sudden see things differently. Like many another he discovered that crossing the Channel makes things which had seemed important singularly futile. The life which had been so charming that he could not bear to leave it now seemed inept; he was seized with a distaste for the cafés, the restaurants with their ill-cooked food, the shabby way in which they all lived. He did not care any more what his friends thought about him: Cronshaw with his rhetoric, Mrs. Otter with her respectability, Ruth Chalice with her affectations. Lawson and Clutton with their quarrels; he felt a revulsion from them all. He wrote to Lawson and asked him to send over all his belongings. A week later they arrived. When he unpacked his canvases he found himself able to examine his work without emotion. He noticed the fact with interest. His uncle was anxious to see his pictures. Though he had so greatly disapproved of Philip's desire to go to Paris, he accepted the situation now with equanimity. He was interested in the life of students and constantly put Philip questions about it. He was in fact a little proud of him because he was a painter, and when people were present made attempts to draw him out. He looked eagerly at the studies of models which Philip showed him. Philip set before him his portrait of Miguel Ajuria.

"Why did you paint him?" asked Mr. Carey.

"Oh, I wanted a model, and his head interested me."

"As you haven't got anything to do here I wonder you don't paint me."

"It would bore you to sit."

"I think I should like it."

"We must see about it."

Philip was amused at his uncle's vanity. It was clear that he was dying to have his portrait painted. To get something for nothing was a chance not to be missed. For two or three days he threw out little hints. He reproached Philip for laziness, asked him when he was going to start work, and finally began telling everyone he met that Philip was going to paint him. At last there came a rainy day, and after breakfast Mr. Carey said to Philip:

"Now, what d'you say to starting on my portrait this morning?" Philip put down the book he was reading and leaned back in his chair.

"I've given up painting," he said.

"Why?" asked his uncle in astonishment.

"I don't think there's much object in being a second-rate painter, and I came to the conclusion that I should never be anything else."

"You surprise me. Before you went to Paris you were quite certain that you were a genius."

"I was mistaken," said Philip.

"I should have thought now you'd taken up a profession you'd have the pride to stick to it. It seems to me that what you lack is perseverance."

Philip was a little annoyed that his uncle did not even see how truly heroic his determination was.

" 'A rolling stone gathers no moss,' " proceeded the clergyman. Philip hated that proverb above all, and it seemed to him perfectly meaningless. His uncle had repeated it often during the arguments which had preceded his departure from business. Apparently it recalled that occasion to his guardian.

"You're no longer a boy, you know; you must begin to think of settling down. First you insist on becoming a chartered accountant, and then you get tired of that and you want to become a painter. And now, if you please, you change your mind again. It points to…"

He hesitated for a moment to consider what defects of character exactly it indicated, and Philip finished the sentence.

"Irresolution, incompetence, want of foresight, and lack of deter-mination."

The Vicar looked up at his nephew quickly to see whether he was laughing at him. Philip's face was serious, but there was a twinkle in his eyes which irritated him. Philip should really be getting more serious. He felt it right to give him a rap over the knuckles.

"Your money matters have nothing to do with me now. You're your own master; but I think you should remember that your money won't last for ever, and the unlucky deformity you have doesn't exactly make it easier for you to earn your living."

Philip knew by now that whenever anyone was angry with him his first thought was to say something about his club-foot. His estimate of the human race was determined by the fact that scarcely anyone failed to resist the temptation. But he had trained himself not to show any sign that the reminder wounded him. He had even acquired control over the blushing which in his boyhood had been one of his torments.

"As you justly remark," he answered, "my money matters have nothing to do with you and I am my own master."

"At all events you will do me the justice to acknowledge that I was justified in my opposition when you made up your mind to become an art student."

"I don't know so much about that. I daresay one profits more by the mistakes one makes off one's own bat than by doing the right thing on somebody else's advice. I've had my fling, and I don't mind settling down now."

"What at?"

Philip was not prepared for the question, since in fact he had not made up his mind. He had thought of a dozen callings.

"The most suitable thing you could do is to enter your father's profession and become a doctor."

"Oddly enough, that is precisely what I intend."

He had thought of doctoring among other things, chiefly because it was an occupation which seemed to give a good deal of personal freedom, and his experience of life in an office had made him determine never to have anything more to do with one; his answer to the Vicar slipped out almost unawares, because it was in the nature of a repartee. It amused him to make up his mind in that accidental way, and he resolved then and there to enter his father's old hospital in the autumn.

"Then your two years in Paris may be regarded as so much wasted time?"

"I don't know about that. I had a very jolly two years, and I learned one or two useful things."

"What?"

Philip reflected for an instant, and his answer was not devoid of a gentle desire to annoy.

"I learned to look at hands, which I'd never looked at before. And instead of just looking at houses and trees I learned to look at houses and trees against the sky. And I learned also that shadows are not black but coloured."

"I suppose you think you're very clever. I think your flippancy is quite inane."

Chapter 53

Taking the paper with him Mr. Carey retired to his study. Philip changed his chair for that in which his uncle had been sitting (it was the only comfortable one in the room), and looked out of the window at the pouring rain. Even in that sad weather there was something restful about the green fields that stretched to the horizon. There was an intimate charm in the landscape which he did not remember ever to have noticed before. Two years in France had opened his eyes to the beauty of his own countryside.

He thought with a smile of his uncle's remark. It was lucky that the turn of his mind tended to flippancy. He had begun to realize what a great loss he had sustained in the death of his father and mother. That was one of the differences in his life which prevented him from seeing things in the same way as other people. The love of parents for their children is the only emotion which is quite disinterested. Among strangers he had grown up as best he could, but he had seldom been used with patience or forbearance. He prided himself on his self-control. It had been whipped into him by the mockery of his fellows. Then they called him cynical and callous. He had acquired calmness of demeanour and under most circumstances an unruffled exterior, so that now he could not show his feelings. People told him he was unemotional; but he knew that he was at the mercy of his emotions: an accidental kindness touched him so much that sometimes he did not venture to speak in order not to betray the unsteadiness of his voice. He remembered the bitterness of his life at school, the humiliation which he had endured, the banter which had made him morbidly afraid of making himself ridiculous; and he remembered the loneliness he had felt since, faced with the world, the disillusion and the disappointment caused by the difference between what it promised to his active imagination and what it gave. But notwithstanding he was able to look at himself from the outside and smile with amusement.

"By Jove, if I weren't flippant, I should hang myself," he thought cheerfully.

His mind went back to the answer he had given his uncle when he asked him what he had learnt in Paris. He had learnt a good deal more than he told him. A conversation with Cronshaw had stuck in his memory, and one phrase he had used, a commonplace one enough, had set his brain working.

"My dear fellow," Cronshaw said, "there's no such thing as abstract morality."

When Philip ceased to believe in Christianity he felt that a great weight was taken from his shoulders; casting off the responsibility which weighed down every action, when every action was infinitely important for the welfare of his immortal soul, he experienced a vivid sense of liberty. But he knew now that this was an illusion. When he put away the religion in which he had been brought up, he had kept unimpaired the morality which was part and parcel of it. He made up his mind therefore to think things out for himself. He determined to be swayed by no prejudices. He swept away the virtues and the vices, the established laws of good and evil, with the idea of finding out the rules of life for himself. He did not know whether rules were necessary at all. That was one of the things he wanted to discover. Clearly much that seemed valid seemed so only because he had been taught it from his earliest youth. He had read a number of books, but they did not help him much, for they were based on the morality of Christianity; and even the writers who emphasized the fact that they did not believe in it were never satisfied till they had framed a system of ethics in accordance with that of the Sermon on the Mount. It seemed hardly worth while to read a long volume in order to learn that you ought to behave exactly like everybody else. Philip wanted to find out how he ought to behave, and he thought he could prevent himself from being influenced by the opinions that surrounded him. But meanwhile he had to go on living, and, until he formed a theory of conduct, he made himself a provisional rule.

"Follow your inclinations with due regard to the policeman round the corner."

He thought the best thing he had gained in Paris was a complete liberty of spirit, and he felt himself at last absolutely free. In a desultory way he had read a good deal of philosophy, and he looked forward with delight to the leisure of the next few months. He began to read at haphazard. He entered upon each system with a little thrill of excitement, expecting to find in each some guide by which he could rule his conduct; he felt himself like a traveller in unknown countries and as he pushed forward the enterprise fascinated him; he read emotionally, as other men read pure literature, and his heart leaped as he discovered in noble words what himself had obscurely felt. His mind was concrete and moved with difficulty in regions of the abstract; but, even when he could not follow the reasoning, it gave him a curious pleasure to follow the tortuosities of thoughts that threaded their nimble way on the edge of the incomprehensible. Sometimes great philosophers seemed to have nothing to say to him, but at others he recognized a mind with which he felt himself at home. He was like the explorer in Central Africa who comes suddenly upon wide uplands, with great trees in them and stretches of meadow, so that he might fancy himself in an English park. He delighted in the robust common sense of Thomas Hobbes; Spinoza filled him with awe, he had never before come in contact with a mind so noble, so unapproachable and austere; it reminded him of that statue by Rodin, *L'Âge d'Airain*, which he passionately admired; and then there was Hume: the scepticism of that charming philosopher touched a kindred note in Philip; and, revelling in the lucid style which seemed able to put complicated thought into simple words, musical and measured, he read as he might have read a novel, a smile of pleasure on his lips. But in none could he find exactly what he wanted. He had read somewhere that every man was born a Platonist, an Aristotelian, a Stoic, or an Epicurean; and the history of George Henry Lewes (besides telling you that philosophy was all moonshine) was there to show that the thought of each philosopher was inseparably connected with the man he was. When you knew that you could guess to a great extent the philosophy he wrote. It looked as though you did not act in a certain way because you thought in a certain way, but rather that you thought in a certain way because you were made in a certain way. Truth had nothing to do with it. There was no such thing as truth. Each man was his own philosopher, and the elaborate systems which the great men of the past had composed were only valid for the writers.

The thing then was to discover what one was and one's system of philosophy would devise itself. It seemed to Philip that there were three things to find out: man's relation to the world he lives in, man's relation with the men among whom he lives, and finally man's relation to himself. He made an elaborate plan of study.

The advantage of living abroad is that, coming in contact with the manners and customs of the people among whom you live, you observe them from the outside and see that they have not the necessity which those who practise them believe. You cannot fail to discover that the beliefs which to you are self-evident to the foreigner are absurd. The year in Germany, the long stay in Paris, had prepared Philip to receive the sceptical teaching which came to him now with such a feeling of relief. He saw that nothing was good and nothing was evil: things were merely adapted to an end. He read *The Origin of Species*. It seemed to offer an explanation of much that troubled him. He was like an explorer now who has reasoned that certain natural features must present themselves, and, beating up a broad river, finds here the tributary that he expected, there the fertile, populated plains, and further on the mountains. When some great discovery is made the world is surprised afterwards that it was not accepted at once, and even on those who acknowledge its truth the effect is unimportant. The first readers of *The Origin of Species* accepted it with their reason; but their emotions, which are the ground of conduct, were untouched. Philip was born a generation after this great book was published, and much that horrified its contemporaries had passed into the feeling of the time, so that he was able to accept it with a joyful heart. He was intensely moved by the grandeur of the struggle for life, and the ethical rule which it suggested seemed to fit in with his predispositions. He said to himself that might was right. Society stood on one side, an organism with its own laws of growth and self-preservation, while the individual stood on the other. The actions which were to the advantage of society it termed virtuous and those which were not it called vicious. Good and evil meant nothing more than that. Sin was a prejudice from which the free man should rid himself. Society had three arms in its contest with the individual, laws, public opinion, and conscience: the first two could be met by guile, guile is the only weapon of the weak against the strong: common opinion put the matter well when it stated that sin consisted in being found out; but conscience was the traitor within the gates; it fought in each heart the battle of society, and caused the individual to throw himself, a wanton sacrifice, to the prosperity of his enemy. For it was clear that the two were irreconcilable, the state and the individual conscious of himself. *That* uses the individual for its own ends, trampling upon him if he thwarts it, rewarding him with medals, pensions, honours, when he serves it faithfully; *This*, strong only in his independence, threads his way through the state, for convenience' sake, paying in money or service for certain benefits, but with no sense of obligation; and, indifferent to the rewards, asks only to be left alone. He is the independent traveller, who uses Cook's tickets because they save trouble, but looks with good-humoured contempt on the personally conducted parties. The free man can do no wrong. He does everything he likes— if he can. His power is the only measure of his morality. He recognizes the laws of the state and he can break them without sense of sin, but if he is punished he accepts the punishment without rancour. Society has the power.

But if for the individual there was no right and no wrong, then it seemed to Philip that conscience lost its power. It was with a cry of triumph that he seized the knave and flung him from his breast. But he was no nearer to the meaning of life than he had been before. Why the world was there and what men had come into existence for at all was as inexplicable as ever. Surely there must be some reason. He thought of Cronshaw's parable of the Persian Carpet. He offered it as a solution of the riddle, and mysteriously he stated that it was no answer at all unless you found it out for yourself.

"I wonder what the devil he meant," Philip smiled.

And so, on the last day of September, eager to put into practice all these new theories of life, Philip, with sixteen hundred pounds and his club-foot, set out for the second time to London to make his third start in life.

Chapter 54

The examination Philip had passed before he was articled to a chartered accountant was sufficient qualification for him to enter a medical school. He chose St. Luke's because his father had been a student there, and before the end of the summer session had gone up to London for a day in order to see the secretary. He got a list of rooms from him, and took lodgings in a dingy house which had the advantage of being within two minutes' walk of the hospital.

"You'll have to arrange about a part to dissect," the secretary told him. "You'd better start on a leg; they generally do; they seem to think it easier."

Philip found that his first lecture was in anatomy, at eleven, and about half past ten he limped across the road, and a little nervously made his way to the Medical School. Just inside the door a number of notices were pinned up, lists of lectures, football fixtures, and the like; and these he looked at idly, trying to seem at his ease. Young men and boys dribbled in and looked for letters in the rack, chatted with one another, and passed downstairs to the basement, in which was the students' reading-room. Philip saw several fellows with a desultory, timid look dawdling around, and surmised that, like himself, they were there for the first time. When he had exhausted the notices he saw a glass door which led into what was apparently a museum, and having still twenty minutes to spare he walked in. It was a collection of pathological specimens. Presently a boy of about eighteen came up to him.

"I say, are you first year?" he said.

"Yes," answered Philip.

"Where's the lecture room, d'you know? It's getting on for eleven."

"We'd better try to find it."

They walked out of the museum into a long, dark corridor, with the walls painted in two shades of red, and other youths walking along suggested the way to them. They came to a door marked Anatomy Theatre. Philip found that there were a good many people already there. The seats were arranged in tiers, and just as Philip entered an attendant came in, put a glass of water on the table in the well of the lecture-room, and then brought in a pelvis and two thigh-bones, right and left. More men entered and took their seats, and by eleven the theatre was fairly full. There were about sixty students. For the most part they were a good deal younger than Philip, smooth-faced boys of eighteen, but there were a few who were older than he: he noticed one tall man, with a fierce red moustache, who might have been thirty; another little fellow with black hair, only a year or two younger; and there was one man with spectacles and a beard which was quite grey.

The lecturer came in, Mr. Cameron, a handsome man with

white hair and clean-cut features. He called out the long list of names. Then he made a little speech. He spoke in a pleasant voice, with well-chosen words, and he seemed to take a discreet pleasure in their careful arrangement. He suggested one or two books which they might buy and advised the purchase of a skeleton. He spoke of anatomy with enthusiasm: it was essential to the study of Surgery; a knowledge of it added to the appreciation of art. Philip pricked up his ears. He heard later that Mr. Cameron lectured also to the students at the Royal Academy. He had lived many years in Japan, with a post at the University of Tokyo, and he flattered himself on his appreciation of the beautiful.

"You will have to learn many tedious things," he finished, with an indulgent smile, "which you will forget the moment you have passed your final examination, but in anatomy it is better to have learned and lost than never to have learned at all."

He took up the pelvis which was lying on the table and began to describe it. He spoke well and clearly.

At the end of the lecture the boy who had spoken to Philip in the pathological museum and sat next to him in the theatre suggested that they should go to the dissecting-room. Philip and he walked along the corridor again, and an attendant told them where it was. As soon as they entered Philip understood what the acrid smell was which he had noticed in the passage. He lit a pipe. The attendant gave a short laugh.

"You'll soon get used to the smell. I don't notice it myself."

He asked Philip's name and looked at a list on the board.

"You've got a leg—number four."

Philip saw that another name was bracketed with his own.

"What's the meaning of that?" he asked.

"We're very short of bodies just now. We've had to put two on each part."

The dissecting-room was a large apartment painted like the corridors, the upper part a rich salmon and the dado a dark terracotta. At regular intervals down the long sides of the room, at right angles with the wall, were iron slabs, grooved like meat-dishes; and on each lay a body. Most of them were men. They were very dark from the preservative in which they had been kept, and the skin had almost the look of leather. They were extremely emaciated. The attendant took Philip up to one of the slabs. A youth was standing by it.

"Is your name Carey?" he asked.

"Yes."

"Oh, then we've got this leg together. It's lucky it's a man, isn't it?"

"Why?" asked Philip.

"They generally always like a male better," said the attendant. "A female's liable to have a lot of fat about her."

Philip looked at the body. The arms and legs were so thin that there was no shape in them, and the ribs stood out so that the skin over them was tense. A man of about forty-five with a thin, grey beard, and on his skull scanty, colourless hair: the eyes were closed and the lower jaw sunken. Philip could not feel that this had ever been a man, and yet in the row of them there was something terrible and ghastly.

"I thought I'd start at two," said the young man who was dissecting with Philip.

"All right, I'll be here then."

He had bought the day before the case of instruments which was needful, and now he was given a locker. He looked at the boy who had accompanied him into the dissecting-room and saw that he was white.

"Make you feel rotten?" Philip asked him.

"I've never seen anyone dead before."

They walked along the corridor till they came to the entrance of the school. Philip remembered Fanny Price. She was the first dead person he had ever seen, and he remembered how strangely it affected him. There was an immeasurable distance between the quick and the dead; they did not seem to belong to the same species; and it was strange to think that but a little while before they had spoken and moved and eaten and laughed. There was something horrible about the dead, and you could imagine that they might cast an evil influence on the living.

"What d'you say to having something to eat?" said his new friend to Philip.

They went down into the basement, where there was a dark room fitted up as a restaurant, and here the students were able to get the same sort of fare as they might have at an aerated bread shop. While they ate (Philip had a scone and butter and a cup of chocolate), he discovered that his companion was called Dunsford. He was a fresh-complexioned lad, with pleasant blue eyes and curly, dark hair, large-limbed, slow of speech and movement. He had just come from Clifton.

"Are you taking the Conjoint?" he asked Philip.

"Yes, I want to get qualified as soon as I can."

"I'm taking it too, but I shall take the F. R. C. S. afterwards. I'm going in for surgery."

Most of the students took the curriculum of the Conjoint Board of the College of Surgeons and the College of Physicians; but the more ambitious or the more industrious added to this the longer studies which led to a degree from the University of London. When Philip went to St. Luke's changes had recently been made in the regulations, and the course took five years instead of four as it had done for those who registered before the autumn of 1892. Dunsford was well up in his plans and told Philip the usual course of events. The "first conjoint" examination consisted of Biology, Anatomy, and Chemistry; but it could be taken in sections, and most fellows took their biology three months after entering the school. This science had been recently added to the list of subjects upon which the student was obliged to inform himself, but the amount of knowledge required was very small.

When Philip went back to the dissecting-room, he was a few minutes late, since he had forgotten to buy the loose sleeves which they wore to protect their shirts, and he found a number of men already working. His partner had started on the minute and was busy dissecting out cutaneous nerves. Two others were engaged on the second leg, and more were occupied with the arms.

"You don't mind my having started?"

"That's all right, fire away," said Philip.

He took the book, open at a diagram of the dissected part, and looked at what they had to find.

"You're rather a dab at this," said Philip.

"Oh, I've done a good deal of dissecting before, animals, you know, for the Pre Sci."

There was a certain amount of conversation over the dissecting-table, partly about the work, partly about the prospects of the football season, the demonstrators, and the lectures. Philip felt himself a great deal older than the others. They were raw schoolboys. But age is a matter of knowledge rather than of years; and Newson, the active young man who was dissecting with him, was very much at home with his subject. He was perhaps not sorry to show off, and he explained very fully to Philip what he was about. Philip, notwithstanding his hidden stores of wisdom, listened meekly. Then Philip took up the scalpel and the tweezers and began working while the other looked on.

"Ripping to have him so thin," said Newson, wiping his hands. "The blighter can't have had anything to eat for a month."

"I wonder what he died of," murmured Philip.

"Oh, I don't know, any old thing, starvation chiefly, I suppose…. I say, look out, don't cut that artery."

"It's all very fine to say, 'don't cut that artery,' " remarked one of the men working on the opposite leg. "Silly old fool's got an artery in the wrong place."

"Arteries always are in the wrong place," said Newson. "The normal's the one thing you practically never get. That's why it's called the normal."

"Don't say things like that," said Philip, "or I shall cut myself."

"If you cut yourself," answered Newson, full of information, "wash it at once with antiseptic. It's the one thing you've got to be careful about. There was a chap here last year who gave himself only a prick, and he didn't bother about it, and he got septicaemia."

"Did he get all right?"

"Oh, no, he died in a week. I went and had a look at him in the P. M. room."

Philip's back ached by the time it was proper to have tea, and his luncheon had been so light that he was quite ready for it. His hands smelt of that peculiar odour which he had first noticed that morning in the corridor. He thought his muffin tasted of it too.

"Oh, you'll get used to that," said Newson. "When you don't have the good old dissecting-room stink about, you feel quite lonely."

"I'm not going to let it spoil my appetite," said Philip, as he followed up the muffin with a piece of cake.

Chapter 55

Philip's ideas of the life of medical students, like those of the public at large, were founded on the pictures which Charles Dickens drew in the middle of the nineteenth century. He soon discovered that Bob Sawyer, if he ever existed, was no longer at all like the medical student of the present.

It is a mixed lot which enters upon the medical profession, and naturally there are some who are lazy and reckless. They think it is an easy life, idle away a couple of years; and then, because their funds come to an end or because angry parents refuse any longer to support them, drift away from the hospital. Others find the examinations too hard for them; one failure after another robs them of their nerve; and, panic-stricken, they forget as soon as they come into the forbidding buildings of the Conjoint Board the knowledge which before they had so pat. They remain year after year, objects of good-humoured scorn to younger men: some of them crawl through the examination of the Apothecaries' Hall; others become non-qualified assistants, a precarious position in which they are at the mercy of their employer; their lot is poverty, drunkenness, and Heaven only knows their end. But for the most part medical students are industrious young men of the middle-class with a sufficient allowance to live in the respectable fashion they have been used to; many are the sons of doctors who have already something of the professional manner; their career is mapped out: as soon as they are qualified they propose to apply for a hospital appointment, after holding which (and perhaps a trip to the Far East as a ship's doctor), they will join their father and spend the rest of their days in a country practice. One or two are marked out as exceptionally brilliant; they will take the various prizes and scholarships which are open each year to the deserving, get one appointment after another at the hospital, go on the staff, take a consulting-room in Harley Street and, specializing in one subject or another, become prosperous, eminent, and titled.

The medical profession is the only one which a man may enter at any age with some chance of making a living. Among the men of Philip's year were three or four who were past their first youth: one had been in the Navy, from which according to report he had been dismissed for drunkenness; he was a man of thirty, with a red face, a brusque manner, and a loud voice. Another was a married man with two children, who had lost money through a defaulting solicitor; he had a bowed look as if the world were too much for him; he went about his work silently, and it was plain that he found it difficult at his age to commit facts to memory. His mind worked slowly. His effort at application was painful to see.

Philip made himself at home in his tiny rooms. He arranged his books and hung on the walls such pictures and sketches as he possessed. Above him, on the drawing-room floor, lived a fifth-year man called Griffiths; but Philip saw little of him, partly because he was occupied chiefly in the wards and partly because he had been to Oxford. Such of the students as had been to a university kept a good deal together: they used a variety of means natural to the young in order to impress upon the less fortunate a proper sense of their inferiority; the rest of the students found their Olympian serenity rather hard to bear. Griffiths was a tall fellow, with a quantity of curly red hair and blue eyes, a white skin, and a very red mouth; he was one of those fortunate people whom everybody liked, for he had high spirits and a constant gaiety. He strummed a little on the piano and sang comic songs with gusto; and evening after evening, while Philip was reading in his solitary room, he heard the shouts and the uproarious laughter of Griffiths's friends above him. He thought of those delightful evenings in Paris when they would sit in the studio, Lawson and he, Flanagan and Clutton, and talk of art and morals, the love-affairs of the present, and the fame of the future. He felt sick at heart. He found that it was easy to make a heroic gesture, but hard to abide by its results. The worst of it was that the work seemed to him very tedious. He had got out of the habit of being asked questions by demonstrators. His attention wandered at lectures. Anatomy was a dreary science, a mere matter of learning by heart an enormous number of facts; dissection bored him; he did not see the use of dissecting out laboriously nerves and arteries when with much less trouble you could see in the diagrams of a book or in the specimens of the pathological museum exactly where they were.

He made friends by chance, but not intimate friends, for he seemed to have nothing in particular to say to his companions. When he tried to interest himself in their concerns, he felt that they found him patronizing. He was not of those who can talk of what moves them without caring whether it bores or not the people they talk to. One man, hearing that he had studied art in Paris, and fancying himself on his taste, tried to discuss art with him; but Philip was impatient of views which did not agree with his own; and, finding quickly that the other's ideas were conventional, grew monosyllabic. Philip desired popularity but could bring himself to make no advances to others. A fear of rebuff prevented him from affability, and he concealed his shyness, which was still intense, under a frigid taciturnity. He was going through the same experience as he had done at school, but here the freedom of the medical students' life made it possible for him to live a good deal by himself.

It was through no effort of his that he became friendly with Dunsford, the fresh-complexioned, heavy lad whose acquaintance he had made at the beginning of the session. Dunsford attached himself to Philip merely because he was the first person he had known at St. Luke's. He had no friends in London, and on Saturday nights he and Philip got into the habit of going together to the pit of a music hall or the gallery of a theatre. He was stupid, but he was good-humoured and never took offence; he always said the obvious thing, but when Philip laughed at him merely smiled. He had a very sweet smile. Though Philip made him his butt, he liked him; he was amused by his candour and delighted with his agreeable nature: Dunsford had the charm which himself was acutely conscious of not possessing.

They often went to have tea at a shop in Parliament Street, because Dunsford admired one of the young women who waited. Philip did not find anything attractive in her. She was tall and thin, with narrow hips and the chest of a boy.

"No one would look at her in Paris," said Philip scornfully.

"She's got a ripping face," said Dunsford.

"What *does* the face matter?"

She had the small regular features, the blue eyes, and the broad low brow which the Victorian painters, Lord Leighton, Alma-Tadema, and a hundred others, induced the world they lived in to accept as a type of Greek beauty. She seemed to have a great deal of hair: it was arranged with peculiar elaboration and done over the forehead in what she called an Alexandra fringe. She was very anaemic. Her thin lips were pale, and her skin was delicate, of a faint green colour, without a touch of red even in the cheeks. She had very good teeth. She took great pains to prevent her work from spoiling her hands, and they were small, thin, and white. She went about her duties with a bored look.

Dunsford, very shy with women, had never succeeded in getting into conversation with her; and he urged Philip to help him.

"All I want is a lead," he said, "and then I can manage for myself."

Philip, to please him, made one or two remarks, but she answered with monosyllables. She had taken their measure. They were boys, and she surmised they were students. She had no use for them. Dunsford noticed that a man with sandy hair and a bristly moustache, who looked like a German, was favoured with her attention whenever he came into the shop; and then it was only by calling her two or three times that they could induce her to take their order. She used the clients whom she did not know with frigid insolence, and when she was talking to a friend was perfectly indifferent to the calls of the hurried. She had the art of treating women who desired refreshment with just that degree of impertinence which irritated them without affording them an opportunity of complaining to the management. One day Dunsford told him her name was Mildred. He had heard one of the other girls in the shop address her.

"What an odious name," said Philip.

"Why?" asked Dunsford. "I like it."

"It's so pretentious."

It chanced that on this day the German was not there, and, when she brought the tea, Philip, smiling, remarked:

"Your friend's not here today."

"I don't know what you mean," she said coldly.

"I was referring to the nobleman with the sandy moustache. Has he left you for another?"

"Some people would do better to mind their own business," she retorted.

She left them, and, since for a minute or two there was no one to attend to, sat down and looked at the evening paper which a customer had left behind him.

"You are a fool to put her back up," said Dunsford.

"I'm really quite indifferent to the attitude of her vertebrae," replied Philip.

But he was piqued. It irritated him that when he tried to be agreeable with a woman she should take offence. When he asked for the bill, he hazarded a remark which he meant to lead further.

"Are we no longer on speaking terms?" he smiled.

"I'm here to take orders and to wait on customers. I've got nothing to say to them, and I don't want them to say anything to me."

She put down the slip of paper on which she had marked the sum they had to pay, and walked back to the table at which she had been sitting. Philip flushed with anger.

"That's one in the eye for you, Carey," said Dunsford, when they got outside.

"Ill-mannered slut," said Philip. "I shan't go there again."

His influence with Dunsford was strong enough to get him to take their tea elsewhere, and Dunsford soon found another young woman to flirt with. But the snub which the waitress inflicted on him rankled. If she had treated him with civility he would have been perfectly indifferent to her; but it was obvious that she disliked him rather than otherwise, and his pride was wounded. He could not suppress a desire to be even with her. He was impatient with himself because he had so petty a feeling, but three or four days' firmness, during which he would not go to the shop, did not help him to surmount it; and he came to the conclusion that it would be least trouble to see her. Having done so he would certainly cease to think of her. Pretexting an appointment one afternoon, for he was not a little ashamed of his weakness, he left Dunsford and went straight to the shop which he had vowed never again to enter. He saw the waitress the moment he came in and sat down at one of her tables. He expected her to make some reference to the fact that he had not been there for a week, but when she came up for his order she said nothing. He had heard her say to other customers:

"You're quite a stranger."

She gave no sign that she had ever seen him before. In order to see whether she had really forgotten him, when she brought his tea, he asked:

"Have you seen my friend tonight?"

"No, he's not been in here for some days."

He wanted to use this as the beginning of a conversation, but he was strangely nervous and could think of nothing to say. She gave him no opportunity, but at once went away. He had no chance of saying anything till he asked for his bill.

"Filthy weather, isn't it?" he said.

It was mortifying that he had been forced to prepare such a phrase as that. He could not make out why she filled him with such embarrassment.

"It don't make much difference to me what the weather is, having to be in here all day."

There was an insolence in her tone that peculiarly irritated him. A sarcasm rose to his lips, but he forced himself to be silent.

"I wish to God she'd say something really cheeky," he raged to himself, "so that I could report her and get her sacked. It would serve her damned well right."

Chapter 56

He could not get her out of his mind. He laughed angrily at his own foolishness: it was absurd to care what an anaemic little waitress said to him; but he was strangely humiliated. Though no one knew of the humiliation but Dunsford, and he had certainly forgotten, Philip felt that he could have no peace till he had wiped it out. He thought over what he had better do. He made up his mind that he would go to the shop every day; it was obvious that he had made a disagreeable impression on her, but he thought he had the wits to eradicate it; he would take care not to say anything at which the most susceptible person could be offended. All this he did, but it had no effect. When he went in and said good evening she answered with the same words, but when once he omitted to say it in order to see whether she would say it first, she said nothing at all. He murmured in his heart an expression which though frequently applicable to members of the female sex is not often used of them in polite society; but with an unmoved face he ordered his tea. He made up his mind not to speak a word, and left the shop without his usual good night. He promised himself that he would not go any more, but the next day at tea-time he grew restless. He tried to think of other things, but he had no command over his thoughts. At last he said desperately:

"After all there's no reason why I shouldn't go if I want to."

The struggle with himself had taken a long time, and it was getting on for seven when he entered the shop.

"I thought you weren't coming," the girl said to him, when he sat down.

His heart leaped in his bosom and he felt himself reddening. "I was detained. I couldn't come before."

"Cutting up people, I suppose?"

"Not so bad as that."

"You are a stoodent, aren't you?"

"Yes."

But that seemed to satisfy her curiosity. She went away and, since at that late hour there was nobody else at her tables, she immersed herself in a novelette. This was before the time of the sixpenny reprints. There was a regular supply of inexpensive fiction written to order by poor hacks for the consumption of the illiterate. Philip was elated; she had addressed him of her own accord; he saw the time approaching when his turn would come and he would tell her exactly what he thought of her. It would be a great comfort to express the immensity of his contempt. He looked at her. It was true that her profile was beautiful; it was extraordinary how English girls of that class had so often a perfection of outline which took your breath away, but it was as cold as marble; and the faint green of her delicate skin gave an impression of unhealthiness. All the waitresses were dressed alike, in plain black dresses, with a white apron, cuffs, and a small cap. On a half sheet of paper that he had in his pocket Philip made a sketch of her as she sat leaning over her book (she outlined the words with her lips as she read), and left it on the table when he went away. It was an inspiration, for next day, when he came in, she smiled at him.

"I didn't know you could draw," she said.

"I was an art student in Paris for two years."

"I showed that drawing you left be'ind you last night to the manageress and she *was* struck by it. Was it meant to be me?"

"It was," said Philip.

When she went for his tea, one of the other girls came up to him.

"I saw that picture you done of Miss Rogers. It was the very image of her," she said.

That was the first time he had heard her name, and when he wanted his bill he called her by it.

"I see you know my name," she said, when she came.

"Your friend mentioned it when she said something to me about that drawing."

"She wants you to do one of her. Don't you do it. If you once begin you'll have to go on, and they'll all be wanting you to do them." Then without a pause, with peculiar inconsequence, she said: "Where's that young fellow that used to come with you? Has he gone away?"

"Fancy your remembering him," said Philip.

"He was a nice-looking young fellow."

Philip felt quite a peculiar sensation in his heart. He did

not know what it was. Dunsford had jolly curling hair, a fresh complexion, and a beautiful smile. Philip thought of these advantages with envy.

"Oh, he's in love," said he, with a little laugh.

Philip repeated every word of the conversation to himself as he limped home. She was quite friendly with him now. When opportunity arose he would offer to make a more finished sketch of her, he was sure she would like that; her face was interesting, the profile was lovely, and there was something curiously fascinating about the chlorotic colour. He tried to think what it was like; at first he thought of pea soup; but, driving away that idea angrily, he thought of the petals of a yellow rosebud when you tore it to pieces before it had burst. He had no ill-feeling towards her now.

"She's not a bad sort," he murmured.

It was silly of him to take offence at what she had said; it was doubtless his own fault; she had not meant to make herself disagreeable: he ought to be accustomed by now to making at first sight a bad impression on people. He was flattered at the success of his drawing; she looked upon him with more interest now that she was aware of this small talent. He was restless next day. He thought of going to lunch at the tea-shop, but he was certain there would be many people there then, and Mildred would not be able to talk to him. He had managed before this to get out of having tea with Dunsford, and, punctually at half past four (he had looked at his watch a dozen times), he went into the shop.

Mildred had her back turned to him. She was sitting down, talking to the German whom Philip had seen there every day till a fortnight ago and since then had not seen at all. She was laughing at what he said. Philip thought she had a common laugh, and it made him shudder. He called her, but she took no notice; he called her again; then, growing angry, for he was impatient, he rapped the table loudly with his stick. She approached sulkily.

"How d'you do?" he said.

"You seem to be in a great hurry."

She looked down at him with the insolent manner which he knew so well.

"I say, what's the matter with you?" he asked.

"If you'll kindly give your order I'll get what you want. I can't stand talking all night."

"Tea and toasted bun, please," Philip answered briefly.

He was furious with her. He had *The Star* with him and read it elaborately when she brought the tea.

"If you'll give me my bill now I needn't trouble you again," he said icily.

She wrote out the slip, placed it on the table, and went back to the German. Soon she was talking to him with animation. He was a man of middle height, with the round head of his nation and a sallow face; his moustache was large and bristling; he had on a tailcoat and grey trousers, and he wore a massive gold watch-chain. Philip thought the other girls looked from him to the pair at the table and exchanged significant glances. He felt certain they were laughing at him, and his blood boiled. He detested Mildred now with all his heart. He knew that the best thing he could do was to cease coming to the tea-shop, but he could not bear to think that he had been worsted in the affair, and he devised a plan to show her that he despised her. Next day he sat down at another table and ordered his tea from another waitress. Mildred's friend was there again and she was talking to him. She paid no attention to Philip, and so when he went out he chose a moment when she had to cross his path: as he passed he looked at her as though he had never seen her before. He repeated this for three or four days. He expected that presently she would take the opportunity to say something to him; he thought she would ask why he never came to one of her tables now, and he had prepared an answer charged with all the loathing he felt for her. He knew it was absurd to trouble, but he could not help himself. She had beaten him again. The German suddenly disappeared, but Philip still sat at other tables. She paid no attention to him. Suddenly he realized that what he did was a matter of complete indifference to her; he could go on in that way till doomsday, and it would have no effect.

"I've not finished yet," he said to himself.

The day after he sat down in his old seat, and when she came up said good evening as though he had not ignored her for a week. His face was placid, but he could not prevent the mad beating of his heart. At that time the musical comedy had lately leaped into public favour, and he was sure that Mildred would be delighted to go to one.

"I say," he said suddenly, "I wonder if you'd dine with me one night and come to *The Belle of New York*. I'll get a couple of stalls."

He added the last sentence in order to tempt her. He knew that when the girls went to the play it was either in the pit, or, if some man took them, seldom to more expensive seats than the upper circle. Mildred's pale face showed no change of expression.

"I don't mind," she said.

"When will you come?"

"I get off early on Thursdays."

They made arrangements. Mildred lived with an aunt at Herne Hill. The play began at eight, so they must dine at seven. She proposed that he should meet her in the second-class waiting-room at Victoria Station. She showed no pleasure, but accepted the invitation as though she conferred a favour. Philip was vaguely irritated.

Chapter 57

Philip arrived at Victoria Station nearly half an hour before the time which Mildred had appointed, and sat down in the second-class waiting-room. He waited and she did not come. He began to grow anxious, and walked into the station to watch the incoming suburban trains; the hour which she had fixed passed, and still there was no sign of her. Philip was impatient. He went into the other waiting-rooms and looked at the people sitting in them. Suddenly his heart gave a great thud.

"There you are. I thought you were never coming."

"I like that after keeping me waiting all this time. I had half a mind to go back home again."

"But you said you'd come to the second-class waiting-room."

"I didn't say any such thing. It isn't exactly likely I'd sit in the second-class room when I could sit in the first, is it?"

Though Philip was sure he had not made a mistake, he said nothing, and they got into a cab.

"Where are we dining?" she asked.

"I thought of the Adelphi Restaurant. Will that suit you?"

"I don't mind where we dine."

She spoke ungraciously. She was put out by being kept waiting and answered Philip's attempt at conversation with monosyllables. She wore a long cloak of some rough, dark material and a crochet shawl over her head. They reached the restaurant and sat down at a table. She looked round with satisfaction. The red shades to the candles on the tables, the gold of the decorations, the looking-glasses, lent the room a sumptuous air.

"I've never been here before."

She gave Philip a smile. She had taken off her cloak; and he saw that she wore a pale blue dress, cut square at the neck; and her hair was more elaborately arranged than ever. He had ordered champagne and when it came her eyes sparkled.

"You are going it," she said.

"Because I've ordered fizz?" he asked carelessly, as though he never drank anything else.

"I *was* surprised when you asked me to do a theatre with you."

Conversation did not go very easily, for she did not seem to have much to say; and Philip was nervously conscious that he was not amusing her. She listened carelessly to his remarks, with her eyes on other diners, and made no pretence that she was interested in him. He made one or two little jokes, but she took them quite seriously. The only sign of vivacity he got was when he spoke of the other girls in the shop; she could not bear the manageress and told him all her misdeeds at length.

"I can't stick her at any price and all the airs she gives herself. Sometimes I've got more than half a mind to tell her something she doesn't think I know about."

"What is that?" asked Philip.

"Well, I happen to know that she's not above going to Eastbourne with a man for the weekend now and again. One of the girls has a married sister who goes there with her husband, and she's seen her. She was staying at the same boarding-house, and she 'ad a wedding-ring on, and I know for one she's not married."

Philip filled her glass, hoping that champagne would make her more affable; he was anxious that his little jaunt should be a success. He noticed that she held her knife as though it were a penholder, and when she drank protruded her little finger. He started several topics of conversation, but he could get little out of her, and he remembered with irritation that he had seen her talking nineteen to the dozen and laughing with the German. They finished dinner and went to the play. Philip was a very cultured young man, and he looked upon musical comedy with scorn. He thought the jokes vulgar and the melodies obvious; it seemed to him that they did these things much better in France; but Mildred enjoyed herself thoroughly; she laughed till her sides ached, looking at Philip now and then when something tickled her to exchange a glance of pleasure; and she applauded rapturously.

"This is the seventh time I've been," she said, after the first act, "and I don't mind if I come seven times more."

She was much interested in the women who surrounded them in the stalls. She pointed out to Philip those who were painted and those who wore false hair.

"It is horrible, these West-end people," she said. "I don't

know how they can do it." She put her hand to her hair. "Mine's all my own, every bit of it."

She found no one to admire, and whenever she spoke of anyone it was to say something disagreeable. It made Philip uneasy. He supposed that next day she would tell the girls in the shop that he had taken her out and that he bored her to death. He disliked her, and yet, he knew not why, he wanted to be with her. On the way home he asked:

"I hope you've enjoyed yourself?"

"Rather."

"Will you come out with me again one evening?"

"I don't mind."

He could never get beyond such expressions as that. Her indifference maddened him.

"That sounds as if you didn't much care if you came or not."

"Oh, if you don't take me out some other fellow will. I need never want for men who'll take me to the theatre."

Philip was silent. They came to the station, and he went to the booking-office.

"I've got my season," she said.

"I thought I'd take you home as it's rather late, if you don't mind."

"Oh, I don't mind if it gives you any pleasure."

He took a single first for her and a return for himself.

"Well, you're not mean, I will say that for you," she said, when he opened the carriage door.

Philip did not know whether he was pleased or sorry when other people entered and it was impossible to speak. They got out at Herne Hill, and he accompanied her to the corner of the road in which she lived.

"I'll say good night to you here," she said, holding out her hand. "You'd better not come up to the door. I know what people are, and I don't want to have anybody talking."

She said good night and walked quickly away. He could see the white shawl in the darkness. He thought she might turn round, but she did not. Philip saw which house she went into, and in a moment he walked along to look at it. It was a trim, common little house of yellow brick, exactly like all the other little houses in the street. He stood outside for a few minutes, and presently the window on the top floor was darkened. Philip strolled slowly back to the station. The evening had been unsatisfactory. He felt irritated, restless, and miserable.

When he lay in bed he seemed still to see her sitting in the corner of the railway carriage, with the white crochet shawl over her head. He did not know how he was to get through the hours that must pass before his eyes rested on her again. He thought drowsily of her thin face, with its delicate features, and the greenish pallor of her skin. He was not happy with her, but he was unhappy away from her. He wanted to sit by her side and look at her, he wanted to touch her, he wanted… the thought came to him and he did not finish it, suddenly he grew wide awake… he wanted to kiss the thin, pale mouth with its narrow lips. The truth came to him at last. He was in love with her. It was incredible.

He had often thought of falling in love, and there was one scene which he had pictured to himself over and over again. He saw himself coming into a ballroom; his eyes fell on a little group of men and women talking; and one of the women turned round. Her eyes fell upon him, and he knew that the gasp in his throat was in her throat too. He stood quite still. She was tall and dark and beautiful, with eyes like the night; she was dressed in white, and in her black hair shone diamonds; they stared at one another, forgetting that people surrounded them. He went straight up to her, and she moved a little towards him. Both felt that the formality of introduction was out of place. He spoke to her.

"I've been looking for you all my life," he said.

"You've come at last," she murmured.

"Will you dance with me?"

She surrendered herself to his outstretched hands and they danced. (Philip always pretended that he was not lame.) She danced divinely.

"I've never danced with anyone who danced like you," she said.

She tore up her programme, and they danced together the whole evening.

"I'm so thankful that I waited for you," he said to her. "I knew that in the end I must meet you."

People in the ballroom stared. They did not care. They did not wish to hide their passion. At last they went into the garden. He flung a light cloak over her shoulders and put her in a waiting cab. They caught the midnight train to Paris; and they sped through the silent, star-lit night into the unknown.

He thought of this old fancy of his, and it seemed impossible that he should be in love with Mildred Rogers. Her name was grotesque. He did not think her pretty; he hated the thinness of her, only that evening he had noticed how the bones of her chest stood out in evening dress; he went over her features one by one; he did not like her mouth, and the unhealthiness of her colour vaguely repelled him. She was common. Her phrases, so bald and few, constantly repeated, showed the emptiness of her mind; he recalled her vulgar little laugh at the jokes of the musical comedy; and he remembered the little finger carefully extended when she held her glass to her mouth; her manners, like her conversation, were odiously genteel. He remembered her insolence; sometimes he had felt inclined to box her ears; and suddenly, he knew not why, perhaps it was the thought of hitting her or the recollection of her tiny, beautiful ears, he was seized by an uprush of emotion. He yearned for her. He thought of taking her in his arms, the thin, fragile body, and kissing her pale mouth; he wanted to pass his fingers down the slightly greenish cheeks. He wanted her.

He had thought of love as a rapture which seized one so that all the world seemed spring-like, he had looked forward to an ecstatic happiness; but this was not happiness; it was a hunger of the soul, it was a painful yearning, it was a bitter anguish, he had never known before. He tried to think when it had first come to him. He did not know. He only remembered that each time he had gone into the shop, after the first two or three times, it had been with a little feeling in the heart that was pain; and he remembered that when she spoke to him he felt curiously breathless. When she left him it was wretchedness, and when she came to him again it was despair.

He stretched himself in his bed as a dog stretches himself. He wondered how he was going to endure that ceaseless aching of his soul.

Chapter 58

Philip woke early next morning, and his first thought was of Mildred. It struck him that he might meet her at Victoria Station and walk with her to the shop. He shaved quickly, scrambled into his clothes, and took a bus to the station. He was there by twenty to eight and watched the incoming trains. Crowds poured out of them, clerks and shop-people at that early hour, and thronged up the platform: they hurried along, sometimes in pairs, here and there a group of girls, but more often alone. They were white, most of them, ugly in the early morning, and they had an abstracted look; the younger ones walked lightly, as though the cement of the platform were pleasant to tread, but the others went as though impelled by a machine: their faces were set in an anxious frown.

At last Philip saw Mildred, and he went up to her eagerly.

"Good morning," he said. "I thought I'd come and see how you were after last night."

She wore an old brown ulster and a sailor hat. It was very clear that she was not pleased to see him.

"Oh, I'm all right. I haven't got much time to waste."

"D'you mind if I walk down Victoria Street with you?"

"I'm none too early. I shall have to walk fast," she answered, looking down at Philip's club-foot.

He turned scarlet.

"I beg your pardon. I won't detain you."

"You can please yourself."

She went on, and he with a sinking heart made his way home to breakfast. He hated her. He knew he was a fool to bother about her; she was not the sort of woman who would ever care two straws for him, and she must look upon his deformity with distaste. He made up his mind that he would not go in to tea that afternoon, but, hating himself, he went. She nodded to him as he came in and smiled.

"I expect I was rather short with you this morning," she said. "You see, I didn't expect you, and it came like a surprise."

"Oh, it doesn't matter at all."

He felt that a great weight had suddenly been lifted from him. He was infinitely grateful for one word of kindness.

"Why don't you sit down?" he asked. "Nobody's wanting you just now."

"I don't mind if I do."

He looked at her, but could think of nothing to say; he racked his brains anxiously, seeking for a remark which should keep her by him; he wanted to tell her how much she meant to him; but he did not know how to make love now that he loved in earnest.

"Where's your friend with the fair moustache? I haven't seen him lately."

"Oh, he's gone back to Birmingham. He's in business there. He only comes up to London every now and again."

"Is he in love with you?"

"You'd better ask him," she said, with a laugh. "I don't know what it's got to do with you if he is."

A bitter answer leaped to his tongue, but he was learning self-restraint.

"I wonder why you say things like that," was all he permitted himself to say.

She looked at him with those indifferent eyes of hers.

"It looks as if you didn't set much store on me," he added.

"Why should I?"

"No reason at all."

He reached over for his paper.

"You are quick-tempered," she said, when she saw the gesture. "You do take offence easily."

He smiled and looked at her appealingly.

"Will you do something for me?" he asked.

"That depends what it is."

"Let me walk back to the station with you tonight."

"I don't mind."

He went out after tea and went back to his rooms, but at eight o'clock, when the shop closed, he was waiting outside.

"You are a caution," she said, when she came out. "I don't understand you."

"I shouldn't have thought it was very difficult," he answered bitterly.

"Did any of the girls see you waiting for me?"

"I don't know and I don't care."

"They all laugh at you, you know. They say you're spoony on me."

"Much you care," he muttered.

"Now then, quarrelsome."

At the station he took a ticket and said he was going to accompany her home.

"You don't seem to have much to do with your time," she said.

"I suppose I can waste it in my own way."

They seemed to be always on the verge of a quarrel. The fact was that he hated himself for loving her. She seemed to be constantly humiliating him, and for each snub that he endured he owed her a grudge. But she was in a friendly mood that evening, and talkative: she told him that her parents were dead; she gave him to understand that she did not have to earn her living, but worked for amusement.

"My aunt doesn't like my going to business. I can have the best of everything at home. I don't want you to think I work because I need to."

Philip knew that she was not speaking the truth. The gentility of her class made her use this pretence to avoid the stigma attached to earning her living.

"My family's very well-connected," she said.

Philip smiled faintly, and she noticed it.

"What are you laughing at?" she said quickly. "Don't you believe I'm telling you the truth?"

"Of course I do," he answered.

She looked at him suspiciously, but in a moment could not resist the temptation to impress him with the splendour of her early days.

"My father always kept a dog-cart, and we had three servants. We had a cook and a housemaid and an odd man. We used to grow beautiful roses. People used to stop at the gate and ask who the house belonged to, the roses were so beautiful. Of course it isn't very nice for me having to mix with them girls in the shop, it's not the class of person I've been used to, and sometimes I really think I'll give up business on that account. It's not the work I mind, don't think that; but it's the class of people I have to mix with."

They were sitting opposite one another in the train, and Philip, listening sympathetically to what she said, was quite happy. He was amused at her *naïveté* and slightly touched. There was a very faint colour in her cheeks. He was thinking that it would be delightful to kiss the tip of her chin.

"The moment you come into the shop I saw you was a gentleman in every sense of the word. Was your father a professional man?"

"He was a doctor."

"You can always tell a professional man. There's something about them, I don't know what it is, but I know at once."

They walked along from the station together.

"I say, I want you to come and see another play with me," he said.

"I don't mind," she said.

"You might go so far as to say you'd like to."

"Why?"

"It doesn't matter. Let's fix a day. Would Saturday night suit you?"

"Yes, that'll do."

They made further arrangements, and then found themselves at the corner of the road in which she lived. She gave him her hand, and he held it.

"I say, I do so awfully want to call you Mildred."

"You may if you like, I don't care."

"And you'll call me Philip, won't you?"

"I will if I can think of it. It seems more natural to call you Mr. Carey."

He drew her slightly towards him, but she leaned back.

"What are you doing?"

"Won't you kiss me good night?" he whispered.

"Impudence!" she said.

She snatched away her hand and hurried towards her house.

Philip bought tickets for Saturday night. It was not one of the days on which she got off early and therefore she would have no time to go home and change; but she meant to bring a frock up with her in the morning and hurry into her clothes at the shop. If the manageress was in a good temper she would let her go at seven. Philip had agreed to wait outside from a quarter past seven onwards. He looked forward to the occasion with painful eagerness, for in the cab on the way from the theatre to the station he thought she would let him kiss her. The vehicle gave every facility for a man to put his arm round a girl's waist (an advantage which the hansom had over the taxi of the present day), and the delight of that was worth the cost of the evening's entertainment.

But on Saturday afternoon when he went in to have tea, in order to confirm the arrangements, he met the man with the fair moustache coming out of the shop. He knew by now that he was called Miller. He was a naturalized German, who had anglicized his name, and he had lived many years in England. Philip had heard him speak, and, though his English was fluent and natural, it had not quite the intonation of the native. Philip knew that he was flirting with Mildred, and he was horribly jealous of him; but he took comfort in the coldness of her temperament, which otherwise distressed him; and, thinking her incapable of passion, he looked upon his rival as no better off than himself. But his heart sank now, for his first thought was that Miller's sudden appearance might interfere with the jaunt which he had so looked forward to. He entered, sick with apprehension. The waitress came up to him, took his order for tea, and presently brought it.

"I'm awfully sorry," she said, with an expression on her face of real distress. "I shan't be able to come tonight after all."

"Why?" said Philip.

"Don't look so stern about it," she laughed. "It's not my fault. My aunt was taken ill last night, and it's the girl's night out so I must go and sit with her. She can't be left alone, can she?"

"It doesn't matter. I'll see you home instead."

"But you've got the tickets. It would be a pity to waste them."

He took them out of his pocket and deliberately tore them

up.

"What are you doing that for?"

"You don't suppose I want to go and see a rotten musical comedy by myself, do you? I only took seats there for your sake."

"You can't see me home if that's what you mean?"

"You've made other arrangements."

"I don't know what you mean by that. You're just as selfish as all the rest of them. You only think of yourself. It's not my fault if my aunt's queer."

She quickly wrote out his bill and left him. Philip knew very little about women, or he would have been aware that one should accept their most transparent lies. He made up his mind that he would watch the shop and see for certain whether Mildred went out with the German. He had an unhappy passion for certainty. At seven he stationed himself on the opposite pavement. He looked about for Miller, but did not see him. In ten minutes she came out, she had on the cloak and shawl which she had worn when he took her to the Shaftesbury Theatre. It was obvious that she was not going home. She saw him before he had time to move away, started a little, and then came straight up to him.

"What are you doing here?" she said.

"Taking the air," he answered.

"You're spying on me, you dirty little cad. I thought you was a gentleman."

"Did you think a gentleman would be likely to take any interest in you?" he murmured.

There was a devil within him which forced him to make matters worse. He wanted to hurt her as much as she was hurting him.

"I suppose I can change my mind if I like. I'm not obliged to come out with you. I tell you I'm going home, and I won't be followed or spied upon."

"Have you seen Miller today?"

"That's no business of yours. In point of fact I haven't, so you're wrong again."

"I saw him this afternoon. He'd just come out of the shop when I went in."

"Well, what if he did? I can go out with him if I want to, can't I? I don't know what you've got to say to it."

"He's keeping you waiting, isn't he?"

"Well, I'd rather wait for him than have you wait for me. Put that in your pipe and smoke it. And now p'raps you'll go off home and mind your own business in future."

His mood changed suddenly from anger to despair, and his voice trembled when he spoke.

"I say, don't be beastly with me, Mildred. You know I'm awfully fond of you. I think I love you with all my heart. Won't you change your mind? I was looking forward to this evening so awfully. You see, he hasn't come, and he can't care twopence about you really. Won't you dine with me? I'll get some more tickets, and we'll go anywhere you like."

"I tell you I won't. It's no good you talking. I've made up my mind, and when I make up my mind I keep to it."

He looked at her for a moment. His heart was torn with anguish. People were hurrying past them on the pavement, and cabs and omnibuses rolled by noisily. He saw that Mildred's eyes were wandering. She was afraid of missing Miller in the crowd.

"I can't go on like this," groaned Philip. "It's too degrading. If I go now I go for good. Unless you'll come with me tonight you'll never see me again."

"You seem to think that'll be an awful thing for me. All I say is, good riddance to bad rubbish."

"Then, good-bye."

He nodded and limped away slowly, for he hoped with all his heart that she would call him back. At the next lamp post he stopped and looked over his shoulder. He thought she might beckon to him—he was willing to forget everything, he was ready for any humiliation—but she had turned away, and apparently had ceased to trouble about him. He realized that she was glad to be quit of him.

Chapter 59

Philip passed the evening wretchedly. He had told his landlady that he would not be in, so there was nothing for him to eat, and he had to go to Gatti's for dinner. Afterwards he went back to his rooms, but Griffiths on the floor above him was having a party, and the noisy merriment made his own misery more hard to bear. He went to a music hall, but it was Saturday night and there was standing-room only: after half an hour of boredom his legs grew tired and he went home. He tried to read, but he could not fix his attention; and yet it was necessary that he should work hard. His examination in biology was in little more than a fortnight, and, though it was easy, he had neglected his lectures of late and was conscious that he knew nothing. It was only a *viva*, however, and he felt sure that in a fortnight he could find out enough about the subject to scrape through. He had confidence in his intelligence. He threw aside his book and gave himself up to thinking deliberately of the matter which was in his mind all the time.

He reproached himself bitterly for his behaviour that

evening. Why had he given her the alternative that she must dine with him or else never see him again? Of course she refused. He should have allowed for her pride. He had burnt his ships behind him. It would not be so hard to bear if he thought that she was suffering now, but he knew her too well: she was perfectly indifferent to him. If he hadn't been a fool he would have pretended to believe her story; he ought to have had the strength to conceal his disappointment and the self-control to master his temper. He could not tell why he loved her. He had read of the idealization that takes place in love, but he saw her exactly as she was. She was not amusing or clever, her mind was common; she had a vulgar shrewdness which revolted him, she had no gentleness nor softness. As she would have put it herself, she was "on the make." What aroused her admiration was a clever trick played on an unsuspecting person; to "do" somebody always gave her satisfaction. Philip laughed savagely as he thought of her gentility and the refinement with which she ate her food; she could not bear a coarse word, so far as her limited vocabulary reached she had a passion for euphemisms, and she scented indecency everywhere; she never spoke of trousers but referred to them as nether garments; she thought it slightly indelicate to blow her nose and did it in a deprecating way. She was dreadfully anaemic and suffered from the dyspepsia which accompanies that ailing. Philip was repelled by her flat breast and narrow hips, and he hated the vulgar way in which she did her hair. He loathed and despised himself for loving her.

The fact remained that he was helpless. He felt just as he had felt sometimes in the hands of a bigger boy at school. He had struggled against the superior strength till his own strength was gone, and he was rendered quite powerless—he remembered the peculiar languor he had felt in his limbs, almost as though he were paralysed—so that he could not help himself at all. He might have been dead. He felt just that same weakness now. He loved the woman so that he knew he had never loved before. He did not mind her faults of person or of character, he thought he loved them too: at all events they meant nothing to him. It did not seem himself that was concerned; he felt that he had been seized by some strange force that moved him against his will, contrary to his interests; and because he had a passion for freedom he hated the chains which bound him. He laughed at himself when he thought how often he had longed to experience the overwhelming passion. He cursed himself because he had given way to it. He thought of the beginnings; nothing of all this would have happened if he had not gone into the shop with Dunsford. The whole thing was his own fault. Except for his ridiculous vanity he would never have troubled himself with the ill-mannered slut.

At all events the occurrences of that evening had finished the whole affair. Unless he was lost to all sense of shame he could not go back. He wanted passionately to get rid of the love that obsessed him; it was degrading and hateful. He must prevent himself from thinking of her. In a little while the anguish he suffered must grow less. His mind went back to the past. He wondered whether Emily Wilkinson and Fanny Price had endured on his account anything like the torment that he suffered now. He felt a pang of remorse.

"I didn't know then what it was like," he said to himself.

He slept very badly. The next day was Sunday, and he worked at his biology. He sat with the book in front of him, forming the words with his lips in order to fix his attention, but he could remember nothing. He found his thoughts going back to Mildred every minute, and he repeated to himself the exact words of the quarrel they had had. He had to force himself back to his book. He went out for a walk. The streets on the south side of the river were dingy enough on weekdays, but there was an energy, a coming and going, which gave them a sordid vivacity; but on Sundays, with no shops open, no carts in the roadway, silent and depressed, they were indescribably dreary. Philip thought that day would never end. But he was so tired that he slept heavily, and when Monday came he entered upon life with determination. Christmas was approaching, and a good many of the students had gone into the country for the short holiday between the two parts of the winter session; but Philip had refused his uncle's invitation to go down to Blackstable. He had given the approaching examination as his excuse, but in point of fact he had been unwilling to leave London and Mildred. He had neglected his work so much that now he had only a fortnight to learn what the curriculum allowed three months for. He set to work seriously. He found it easier each day not to think of Mildred. He congratulated himself on his force of character. The pain he suffered was no longer anguish, but a sort of soreness, like what one might be expected to feel if one had been thrown off a horse and, though no bones were broken, were bruised all over and shaken. Philip found that he was able to observe with curiosity the condition he had been in during the last few weeks. He analysed his feelings with interest. He was a little amused at himself. One thing that struck him was how little under those circumstances it mattered what one thought; the system of personal philosophy, which had given him great satisfaction to devise, had not served him. He was puzzled by this.

But sometimes in the street he would see a girl who looked so like Mildred that his heart seemed to stop beating. Then he could not help himself, he hurried on to catch her up, eager and anxious, only to find that it was a total stranger. Men came back from the country, and he went with Dunsford to have tea at an A. B. C. shop. The well-known uniform made him so miserable that he could not speak. The thought came to him that perhaps she had been transferred to another establishment of the firm for which she worked, and he might suddenly find himself face to face with her. The idea filled him with panic, so that he feared Dunsford would see that something was the matter with him: he could not think of anything to say; he pretended to listen to what Dunsford was talking about; the conversation maddened him; and it was all he could do to prevent himself from crying out to Dunsford for Heaven's sake to hold his tongue.

Then came the day of his examination. Philip, when his turn arrived, went forward to the examiner's table with the utmost confidence. He answered three or four questions. Then they showed him various specimens; he had been to very few lectures and, as soon as he was asked about things which he could not learn from books, he was floored. He did what he could to hide his ignorance, the examiner did not insist, and soon his ten minutes were over. He felt certain he had passed; but next day, when he went up to the examination buildings to see the result posted on the door, he was astounded not to find his number among those who had satisfied the examiners. In amazement he read the list three times. Dunsford was with him.

"I say, I'm awfully sorry you're ploughed," he said.

He had just inquired Philip's number. Philip turned and saw by his radiant face that Dunsford had passed.

"Oh, it doesn't matter a bit," said Philip. "I'm jolly glad you're all right. I shall go up again in July."

He was very anxious to pretend he did not mind, and on their way back along The Embankment insisted on talking of indifferent things. Dunsford good naturedly wanted to discuss the causes of Philip's failure, but Philip was obstinately casual. He was horribly mortified; and the fact that Dunsford, whom he looked upon as a very pleasant but quite stupid fellow, had passed made his own rebuff harder to bear. He had always been proud of his intelligence, and now he asked himself desperately whether he was not mistaken in the opinion he held of himself. In the three months of the winter session the students who had joined in October had already shaken down into groups, and it was clear which were brilliant, which were clever or industrious, and which were "rotters." Philip was conscious that his failure was a surprise to no one but himself. It was tea-time, and he knew that a lot of men would be having tea in the basement of the Medical School: those who had passed the examination would be exultant, those who disliked him would look at him with satisfaction, and the poor devils who had failed would sympathize with him in order to receive sympathy. His instinct was not to go near the hospital for a week, when the affair would be no more thought of, but, because he hated so much to go just then, he went: he wanted to inflict suffering upon himself. He forgot for the moment his maxim of life to follow his inclinations with due regard for the policeman round the corner; or, if he acted in accordance with it, there must have been some strange morbidity in his nature which made him take a grim pleasure in self-torture.

But later on, when he had endured the ordeal to which he forced himself, going out into the night after the noisy conversation in the smoking-room, he was seized with a feeling of utter loneliness. He seemed to himself absurd and futile. He had an urgent need of consolation, and the temptation to see Mildred was irresistible. He thought bitterly that there was small chance of consolation from her; but he wanted to see her even if he did not speak to her; after all, she was a waitress and would be obliged to serve him. She was the only person in the world he cared for. There was no use in hiding that fact from himself. Of course it would be humiliating to go back to the shop as though nothing had happened, but he had not much self-respect left. Though he would not confess it to himself, he had hoped each day that she would write to him; she knew that a letter addressed to the hospital would find him; but she had not written: it was evident that she cared nothing if she saw him again or not. And he kept on repeating to himself:

"I must see her. I must see her."

The desire was so great that he could not give the time necessary to walk, but jumped in a cab. He was too thrifty to use one when it could possibly be avoided. He stood outside the shop for a minute or two. The thought came to him that perhaps she had left, and in terror he walked in quickly. He saw her at once. He sat down and she came up to him.

"Cup of tea and a muffin, please," he ordered.

He could hardly speak. He was afraid for a moment that he was going to cry.

"I almost thought you was dead," she said.

She was smiling. Smiling! She seemed to have forgotten completely that last scene which Philip had repeated to himself a hundred times.

"I thought if you'd wanted to see me you'd write," he answered.

"I've got too much to do to think about writing letters."

It seemed impossible for her to say a gracious thing. Philip cursed the fate which chained him to such a woman. She went away to fetch his tea.

"Would you like me to sit down for a minute or two?" she said, when she brought it.

"Yes."

"Where have you been all this time?"

"I've been in London."

"I thought you'd gone away for the holidays. Why haven't you been in then?"

Philip looked at her with haggard, passionate eyes.

"Don't you remember that I said I'd never see you again?"

"What are you doing now then?"

She seemed anxious to make him drink up the cup of his humiliation; but he knew her well enough to know that she spoke at random; she hurt him frightfully, and never even tried to. He did not answer.

"It was a nasty trick you played on me, spying on me like that. I always thought you was a gentleman in every sense of the word."

"Don't be beastly to me, Mildred. I can't bear it."

"You are a funny feller. I can't make you out."

"It's very simple. I'm such a blasted fool as to love you with all my heart and soul, and I know that you don't care twopence for me."

"If you had been a gentleman I think you'd have come next day and begged my pardon."

She had no mercy. He looked at her neck and thought how he would like to jab it with the knife he had for his muffin. He knew enough anatomy to make pretty certain of getting the carotid artery. And at the same time he wanted to cover her pale, thin face with kisses.

"If I could only make you understand how frightfully I'm in love with you."

"You haven't begged my pardon yet."

He grew very white. She felt that she had done nothing wrong on that occasion. She wanted him now to humble himself. He was very proud. For one instant he felt inclined to tell her to go to hell, but he dared not. His passion made him abject. He was willing to submit to anything rather than not see her.

"I'm very sorry, Mildred. I beg your pardon."

He had to force the words out. It was a horrible effort.

"Now you've said that I don't mind telling you that I wish

I had come out with you that evening. I thought Miller was a gentleman, but I've discovered my mistake now. I soon sent him about his business."

Philip gave a little gasp.

"Mildred, won't you come out with me tonight? Let's go and dine somewhere."

"Oh, I can't. My aunt'll be expecting me home."

"I'll send her a wire. You can say you've been detained in the shop; she won't know any better. Oh, do come, for God's sake. I haven't seen you for so long, and I want to talk to you."

She looked down at her clothes.

"Never mind about that. We'll go somewhere where it doesn't matter how you're dressed. And we'll go to a music hall afterwards. Please say yes. It would give me so much pleasure."

She hesitated a moment; he looked at her with pitifully appealing eyes.

"Well, I don't mind if I do. I haven't been out anywhere since I don't know how long."

It was with the greatest difficulty he could prevent himself from seizing her hand there and then to cover it with kisses.

Chapter 60

They dined in Soho, Philip was tremulous with joy. It was not one of the more crowded of those cheap restaurants where the respectable and needy dine in the belief that it is bohemian and the assurance that it is economical. It was a humble establishment, kept by a good man from Rouen and his wife, that Philip had discovered by accident. He had been attracted by the Gallic look of the window, in which was generally an uncooked steak on one plate and on each side two dishes of raw vegetables. There was one seedy French waiter, who was to learn English in a house where he never heard anything but French; and the customers were a few ladies of easy virtue, a *ménage* or two, who had their own napkins reserved for them, and a few queer men who came in for hurried, scanty meals.

Here Mildred and Philip were able to get a table to themselves. Philip sent the waiter for a bottle of Burgundy from the neighbouring tavern, and they had a *potage aux herbes*, a steak from the window *aux pommes*, and an *omelette au kirsch*. There was really an air of romance in the meal and in the place. Mildred, at first a little reserved in her appreciation— "I never quite trust these foreign places, you never know what there is in these messed-up dishes" —was insensibly moved by it.

"I like this place, Philip," she said. "You feel you can put your elbows on the table, don't you?"

A tall fellow came in, with a mane of grey hair and a ragged thin beard. He wore a dilapidated cloak and a wide-awake hat. He nodded to Philip, who had met him there before.

"He looks like an anarchist," said Mildred.

"He is, one of the most dangerous in Europe. He's been in every prison on the Continent and has assassinated more persons than any gentleman unhung. He always goes about with a bomb in his pocket, and of course it makes conversation a little difficult because if you don't agree with him he lays it on the table in a marked manner."

She looked at the man with horror and surprise, and then glanced suspiciously at Philip. She saw that his eyes were laughing. She frowned a little.

"You're getting at me."

He gave a little shout of joy. He was so happy. But Mildred didn't like being laughed at.

"I don't see anything funny in telling lies."

"Don't be cross."

He took her hand, which was lying on the table, and pressed it gently.

"You are lovely, and I could kiss the ground you walk on," he said.

The greenish pallor of her skin intoxicated him, and her thin white lips had an extraordinary fascination. Her anaemia made her rather short of breath, and she held her mouth slightly open. It seemed to add somehow to the attractiveness of her face.

"You do like me a bit, don't you?" he asked.

"Well, if I didn't I suppose I shouldn't be here, should I? You're a gentleman in every sense of the word, I will say that for you."

They had finished their dinner and were drinking coffee. Philip, throwing economy to the winds, smoked a threepenny cigar.

"You can't imagine what a pleasure it is to me just to sit opposite and look at you. I've yearned for you. I was sick for a sight of you."

Mildred smiled a little and faintly flushed. She was not then suffering from the dyspepsia which generally attacked her immediately after a meal. She felt more kindly disposed to Philip than ever before, and the unaccustomed tenderness in her eyes filled him with joy. He knew instinctively that it was madness to give himself into her hands; his only chance was to treat her casually and never allow her to see the untamed passions that seethed in his breast; she would only take advantage of his weakness; but he could not be prudent now: he told her all the agony he had endured during the separation from her; he told her of his struggles with himself, how he had tried to get over his passion, thought he had succeeded, and how he found out that it was as strong as ever. He knew that he had never really wanted to get over it. He loved her so much that he did not mind suffering. He bared his heart to her. He showed her proudly all his weakness.

Nothing would have pleased him more than to sit on in the cosy, shabby restaurant, but he knew that Mildred wanted entertainment. She was restless and, wherever she was, wanted after a while to go somewhere else. He dared not bore her.

"I say, how about going to a music hall?" he said.

He thought rapidly that if she cared for him at all she would say she preferred to stay there.

"I was just thinking we ought to be going if we are going," she answered.

"Come on then."

Philip waited impatiently for the end of the performance. He had made up his mind exactly what to do, and when they got into the cab he passed his arm, as though almost by accident, round her waist. But he drew it back quickly with a little cry. He had pricked himself. She laughed.

"There, that comes of putting your arm where it's got no business to be," she said. "I always know when men try and put their arm round my waist. That pin always catches them."

"I'll be more careful."

He put his arm round again. She made no objection.

"I'm so comfortable," he sighed blissfully.

"So long as you're happy," she retorted.

They drove down St. James' Street into the Park, and Philip quickly kissed her. He was strangely afraid of her, and it required all his courage. She turned her lips to him without speaking. She neither seemed to mind nor to like it.

"If you only knew how long I've wanted to do that," he murmured.

He tried to kiss her again, but she turned her head away.

"Once is enough," she said.

On the chance of kissing her a second time he travelled down to Herne Hill with her, and at the end of the road in which she lived he asked her:

"Won't you give me another kiss?"

She looked at him indifferently and then glanced up the road to see that no one was in sight.

"I don't mind."

He seized her in his arms and kissed her passionately, but she pushed him away.

"Mind my hat, silly. You are clumsy," she said.

Chapter 61

He saw her then every day. He began going to lunch at the shop, but Mildred stopped him: she said it made the girls talk; so he had to content himself with tea; but he always waited about to walk with her to the station; and once or twice a week they dined together. He gave her little presents, a gold bangle, gloves, handkerchiefs, and the like. He was spending more than he could afford, but he could not help it: it was only when he gave her anything that she showed any affection. She knew the price of everything, and her gratitude was in exact proportion with the value of his gift. He did not care. He was too happy when she volunteered to kiss him to mind by what means he got her demonstrativeness. He discovered that she found Sundays at home tedious, so he went down to Herne Hill in the morning, met her at the end of the road, and went to church with her.

"I always like to go to church once," she said. "It looks well, doesn't it?"

Then she went back to dinner, he got a scrappy meal at a hotel, and in the afternoon they took a walk in Brockwell

Park. They had nothing much to say to one another, and Philip, desperately afraid she was bored (she was very easily bored), racked his brain for topics of conversation. He realized that these walks amused neither of them, but he could not bear to leave her, and did all he could to lengthen them till she became tired and out of temper. He knew that she did not care for him, and he tried to force a love which his reason told him was not in her nature: she was cold. He had no claim on her, but he could not help being exacting. Now that they were more intimate he found it less easy to control his temper; he was often irritable and could not help saying bitter things. Often they quarrelled, and she would not speak to him for a while; but this always reduced him to subjection, and he crawled before her. He was angry with himself for showing so little dignity. He grew furiously jealous if he saw her speaking to any other man in the shop, and when he was jealous he seemed to be beside himself. He would deliberately insult her, leave the shop, and spend afterwards a sleepless night tossing on his bed, by turns angry and remorseful. Next day he would go to the shop and appeal for forgiveness.

"Don't be angry with me," he said. "I'm so awfully fond of you that I can't help myself."

"One of these days you'll go too far," she answered.

He was anxious to come to her home in order that the greater intimacy should give him an advantage over the stray acquaintances she made during her working hours; but she would not let him.

"My aunt would think it so funny," she said.

He suspected that her refusal was due only to a disinclination to let him see her aunt. Mildred had represented her as the widow of a professional man (that was her formula of distinction), and was uneasily conscious that the good woman could hardly be called distinguished. Philip imagined that she was in point of fact the widow of a small tradesman. He knew that Mildred was a snob. But he found no means by which he could indicate to her that he did not mind how common the aunt was.

Their worst quarrel took place one evening at dinner when she told him that a man had asked her to go to a play with him. Philip turned pale, and his face grew hard and stern.

"You're not going?" he said.

"Why shouldn't I? He's a very nice gentlemanly fellow."

"I'll take you anywhere you like."

"But that isn't the same thing. I can't always go about with you. Besides he's asked me to fix my own day, and I'll just go one evening when I'm not going out with you. It won't make any difference to you."

"If you had any sense of decency, if you had any gratitude, you wouldn't dream of going."

"I don't know what you mean by gratitude. If you're referring to the things you've given me you can have them back. I don't want them."

Her voice had the shrewish tone it sometimes got.

"It's not very lively, always going about with you. It's always, 'do you love me? do you love me?' till I just get about sick of it."

(He knew it was madness to go on asking her that, but he could not help himself.

"Oh, I like you all right," she would answer.

"Is that all? I love you with all my heart."

"I'm not that sort, I'm not one to say much."

"If you knew how happy just one word would make me!"

"Well, what I always say is, people must take me as they find me, and if they don't like it they can lump it."

But sometimes she expressed herself more plainly still, and, when he asked the question, answered:

"Oh, don't go on at that again."

Then he became sulky and silent. He hated her.)

And now he said:

"Oh, well, if you feel like that about it I wonder you condescend to come out with me at all."

"It's not my seeking, you can be very sure of that, you just force me to."

His pride was bitterly hurt, and he answered madly:

"You think I'm just good enough to stand you dinners and theatres when there's no one else to do it, and when someone else turns up I can go to hell. Thank you, I'm about sick of being made a convenience."

"I'm not going to be talked to like that by anyone. I'll just show you how much I want your dirty dinner."

She got up, put on her jacket, and walked quickly out of the restaurant. Philip sat on. He determined he would not move, but ten minutes afterwards he jumped in a cab and followed her. He guessed that she would take a bus to Victoria, so that they would arrive about the same time. He saw her on the platform, escaped her notice, and went down to Herne Hill in the same train. He did not want to speak to her till she was on the way home and could not escape him.

As soon as she had turned out of the main street, brightly lit and noisy with traffic, he caught her up.

"Mildred," he called.

She walked on and would neither look at him nor answer. He repeated her name. Then she stopped and faced him.

"What d'you want? I saw you hanging about Victoria. Why don't you leave me alone?"

"I'm awfully sorry. Won't you make it up?"

"No, I'm sick of your temper and your jealousy. I don't care for you, I never have cared for you, and I never shall care for you. I don't want to have anything more to do with you."

She walked on quickly, and he had to hurry to keep up with her.

"You never make allowances for me," he said. "It's all very well to be jolly and amiable when you're indifferent to anyone. It's very hard when you're as much in love as I am. Have mercy on me. I don't mind that you don't care for me. After all you can't help it. I only want you to let me love you."

She walked on, refusing to speak, and Philip saw with agony that they had only a few hundred yards to go before they reached her house. He abased himself. He poured out an incoherent story of love and penitence.

"If you'll only forgive me this time I promise you you'll never have to complain of me in future. You can go out with whoever you choose. I'll be only too glad if you'll come with me when you've got nothing better to do."

She stopped again, for they had reached the corner at which

he always left her.

"Now you can take yourself off. I won't have you coming up to the door."

"I won't go till you say you'll forgive me."

"I'm sick and tired of the whole thing."

He hesitated a moment, for he had an instinct that he could say something that would move her. It made him feel almost sick to utter the words.

"It is cruel, I have so much to put up with. You don't know what it is to be a cripple. Of course you don't like me. I can't expect you to."

"Philip, I didn't mean that," she answered quickly, with a sudden break of pity in her voice. "You know it's not true."

He was beginning to act now, and his voice was husky and low.

"Oh, I've felt it," he said.

She took his hand and looked at him, and her own eyes were filled with tears.

"I promise you it never made any difference to me. I never thought about it after the first day or two."

He kept a gloomy, tragic silence. He wanted her to think he was overcome with emotion.

"You know I like you awfully, Philip. Only you are so trying sometimes. Let's make it up."

She put up her lips to his, and with a sigh of relief he kissed her.

"Now are you happy again?" she asked.

"Madly."

She bade him good night and hurried down the road. Next day he took her in a little watch with a brooch to pin on her dress. She had been hankering for it.

But three or four days later, when she brought him his tea, Mildred said to him:

"You remember what you promised the other night? You mean to keep that, don't you?"

"Yes."

He knew exactly what she meant and was prepared for her next words.

"Because I'm going out with that gentleman I told you about tonight."

"All right. I hope you'll enjoy yourself."

"You don't mind, do you?"

He had himself now under excellent control.

"I don't like it," he smiled, "but I'm not going to make myself more disagreeable than I can help."

She was excited over the outing and talked about it willingly. Philip wondered whether she did so in order to pain him or merely because she was callous. He was in the habit of condoning her cruelty by the thought of her stupidity. She had not the brains to see when she was wounding him.

"It's not much fun to be in love with a girl who has no imagination and no sense of humour," he thought, as he listened.

But the want of these things excused her. He felt that if he had not realized this he could never forgive her for the pain she caused him.

"He's got seats for the Tivoli," she said. "He gave me my

choice and I chose that. And we're going to dine at the Café Royal. He says it's the most expensive place in London."

"He's a gentleman in every sense of the word," thought Philip, but he clenched his teeth to prevent himself from uttering a syllable.

Philip went to the Tivoli and saw Mildred with her companion, a smooth-faced young man with sleek hair and the spruce look of a commercial traveller, sitting in the second row of the stalls. Mildred wore a black picture hat with ostrich feathers in it, which became her well. She was listening to her host with that quiet smile which Philip knew; she had no vivacity of expression, and it required broad farce to excite her laughter; but Philip could see that she was interested and amused. He thought to himself bitterly that her companion, flashy and jovial, exactly suited her. Her sluggish temperament made her appreciate noisy people. Philip had a passion for discussion, but no talent for small-talk. He admired the easy drollery of which some of his friends were masters, Lawson for instance, and his sense of inferiority made him shy and awkward. The things which interested him bored Mildred. She expected men to talk about football and racing, and he knew nothing of either. He did not know the catchwords which only need be said to excite a laugh.

Printed matter had always been a fetish to Philip, and now, in order to make himself more interesting, he read industriously *The Sporting Times*.

Chapter 62

Philip did not surrender himself willingly to the passion that consumed him. He knew that all things human are transitory and therefore that it must cease one day or another. He looked forward to that day with eager longing. Love was like a parasite in his heart, nourishing a hateful existence on his life's blood; it absorbed his existence so intensely that he could take pleasure in nothing else. He had been used to delight in the grace of St. James's Park, and often he sat and looked at the branches of a tree silhouetted against the sky, it was like a Japanese print; and he found a continual magic in the beautiful Thames with its barges and its wharves; the changing sky of London had filled his soul with pleasant fancies. But now beauty meant nothing to him. He was bored and restless when he was not with Mildred. Sometimes he thought he would console his sorrow by looking at pictures, but he walked through the National Gallery like a sightseer; and no picture called up in him a thrill of emotion. He wondered if he could ever care again for all the things he had loved. He had been devoted to reading, but now books were meaningless; and he spent his spare hours in the smoking-room of the hospital club, turning over innumerable periodicals. This love was a torment, and he resented bitterly the subjugation in which it held him; he was a prisoner and he longed for freedom.

Sometimes he awoke in the morning and felt nothing; his soul leaped, for he thought he was free; he loved no longer; but in a little while, as he grew wide awake, the pain settled in his heart, and he knew that he was not cured yet. Though he yearned for Mildred so madly he despised her. He thought to himself that there could be no greater torture in the world than at the same time to love and to contemn.

Philip, burrowing as was his habit into the state of his feelings, discussing with himself continually his condition, came to the conclusion that he could only cure himself of his degrading passion by making Mildred his mistress. It was sexual hunger that he suffered from, and if he could satisfy this he might free himself from the intolerable chains that bound him. He knew that Mildred did not care for him at all in that way. When he kissed her passionately she withdrew herself from him with instinctive distaste. She had no sensuality. Sometimes he had tried to make her jealous by talking of adventures in Paris, but they did not interest her; once or twice he had sat at other tables in the tea-shop and affected to flirt with the waitress who attended them, but she was entirely indifferent. He could see that it was no pretence on her part.

"You didn't mind my not sitting at one of your tables this afternoon?" he asked once, when he was walking to the station with her. "Yours seemed to be all full."

This was not a fact, but she did not contradict him. Even if his desertion meant nothing to her, he would have been grateful if she had pretended it did. A reproach would have been balm to his soul.

"I think it's silly of you to sit at the same table every day. You ought to give the other girls a turn now and again."

But the more he thought of it the more he was convinced that complete surrender on her part was his only way to freedom. He was like a knight of old, metamorphosed by magic spells, who sought the potions which should restore him to his fair and proper form. Philip had only one hope. Mildred greatly desired to go to Paris. To her, as to most English people, it was the centre of gaiety and fashion: she had heard of the Magasin du Louvre, where you could get the very latest thing for about half the price you had to pay in London; a friend of hers had passed her honeymoon in Paris and had spent all day at the Louvre; and she and her husband, my dear, they never went to bed till six in the morning all the time they were there; the Moulin Rouge and I don't know what all. Philip did not care that if she yielded to his desires it would only be the unwilling price she paid for the gratification of her wish. He did not care upon what terms he satisfied his passion. He had even had a mad, melodramatic idea to drug her. He had plied her with liquor in the hope of exciting her, but she had no taste for wine; and though she liked him to order champagne because it looked well, she never drank more than half a glass. She liked to leave untouched a large glass filled to the brim.

"It shows the waiters who you are," she said.

Philip chose an opportunity when she seemed more than usually friendly. He had an examination in anatomy at the end of March. Easter, which came a week later, would give Mildred three whole days' holiday.

"I say, why don't you come over to Paris then?" he suggested. "We'd have such a ripping time."

"How could you? It would cost no end of money."

Philip had thought of that. It would cost at least five-and-twenty-pounds. It was a large sum to him. He was willing to spend his last penny on her.

"What does that matter? Say you'll come, darling."

"What next, I should like to know. I can't see myself going away with a man that I wasn't married to. You oughtn't to suggest such a thing."

"What does it matter?"

He enlarged on the glories of the Rue de la Paix and the garish splendour of the Folies Bergères. He described the Louvre and the Bon Marché. He told her about the Cabaret du Néant, the Abbaye, and the various haunts to which foreigners go. He painted in glowing colours the side of Paris which he despised. He pressed her to come with him.

"You know, you say you love me, but if you really loved me you'd want to marry me. You've never asked me to marry you."

"You know I can't afford it. After all, I'm in my first year, I shan't earn a penny for six years."

"Oh, I'm not blaming you. I wouldn't marry you if you went down on your bended knees to me."

He had thought of marriage more than once, but it was a

step from which he shrank. In Paris he had come by the opinion that marriage was a ridiculous institution of the philistines. He knew also that a permanent tie would ruin him. He had middle-class instincts, and it seemed a dreadful thing to him to marry a waitress. A common wife would prevent him from getting a decent practice. Besides, he had only just enough money to last him till he was qualified; he could not keep a wife even if they arranged not to have children. He thought of Cronshaw bound to a vulgar slattern, and he shuddered with dismay. He foresaw what Mildred, with her genteel ideas and her mean mind, would become: it was impossible for him to marry her. But he decided only with his reason; he felt that he must have her whatever happened; and if he could not get her without marrying her he would do that; the future could look after itself. It might end in disaster; he did not care. When he got hold of an idea it obsessed him, he could think of nothing else, and he had a more than common power to persuade himself of the reasonableness of what he wished to do. He found himself overthrowing all the sensible arguments which had occurred to him against marriage. Each day he found that he was more passionately devoted to her; and his unsatisfied love became angry and resentful.

"By George, if I marry her I'll make her pay for all the suffering I've endured," he said to himself.

At last he could bear the agony no longer. After dinner one evening in the little restaurant in Soho, to which now they often went, he spoke to her.

"I say, did you mean it the other day that you wouldn't marry me if I asked you?"

"Yes, why not?"

"Because I can't live without you. I want you with me always. I've tried to get over it and I can't. I never shall now. I want you to marry me."

She had read too many novelettes not to know how to take such an offer.

"I'm sure I'm very grateful to you, Philip. I'm very much flattered at your proposal."

"Oh, don't talk rot. You will marry me, won't you?"

"D'you think we should be happy?"

"No. But what does that matter?"

The words were wrung out of him almost against his will. They surprised her.

"Well, you are a funny chap. Why d'you want to marry me then? The other day you said you couldn't afford it."

"I think I've got about fourteen hundred pounds left. Two can live just as cheaply as one. That'll keep us till I'm qualified and have got through with my hospital appointments, and then I can get an assistantship."

"It means you wouldn't be able to earn anything for six years. We should have about four pounds a week to live on till then, shouldn't we?"

"Not much more than three. There are all my fees to pay."

"And what would you get as an assistant?"

"Three pounds a week."

"D'you mean to say you have to work all that time and spend a small fortune just to earn three pounds a week at the end of it? I don't see that I should be any better off than I am now."

He was silent for a moment.

"D'you mean to say you won't marry me?" he asked hoarsely. "Does my great love mean nothing to you at all?"

"One has to think of oneself in those things, don't one? I shouldn't mind marrying, but I don't want to marry if I'm going to be no better off than what I am now. I don't see the use of it."

"If you cared for me you wouldn't think of all that."

"P'raps not."

He was silent. He drank a glass of wine in order to get rid of the choking in his throat.

"Look at that girl who's just going out," said Mildred. "She got them furs at the Bon Marché at Brixton. I saw them in the window last time I went down there."

Philip smiled grimly.

"What are you laughing at?" she asked. "It's true. And I said to my aunt at the time, I wouldn't buy anything that had been in the window like that, for everyone to know how much you paid for it."

"I can't understand you. You make me frightfully unhappy, and in the next breath you talk rot that has nothing to do with what we're speaking about."

"You are nasty to me," she answered, aggrieved. "I can't help noticing those furs, because I said to my aunt…"

"I don't care a damn what you said to your aunt," he interrupted impatiently.

"I wish you wouldn't use bad language when you speak to me, Philip. You know I don't like it."

Philip smiled a little, but his eyes were wild. He was silent for a while. He looked at her sullenly. He hated, despised and loved her.

"If I had an ounce of sense I'd never see you again," he said at last. "If you only knew how heartily I despise myself for loving you!"

"That's not a very nice thing to say to me," she replied sulkily.

"It isn't," he laughed. "Let's go to the Pavilion."

"That's what's so funny in you, you start laughing just when one doesn't expect you to. And if I make you that unhappy why d'you want to take me to the Pavilion? I'm quite ready to go home."

"Merely because I'm less unhappy with you than away from you."

"I should like to know what you really think of me."

He laughed outright.

"My dear, if you did you'd never speak to me again."